ALL MANKIND IS ONE

A Study of the Disputation
Between Bartolomé de Las Casas
and Juan Ginés de Sepúlveda
in 1550 on the Intellectual
and Religious Capacity of
the American Indians

Don Barthélemi de Las Casas, Évêque de Chiapa,
Protecteur des naturels de l'Amérique. From the
Paris, 1822, edition by J. A. Llorente,
Oeuvres de don Barthélemi de Las Casas.

ALL MANKIND
IS ONE ✍ *A Study*
of the Disputation Between
Bartolomé de Las Casas and
Juan Ginés de Sepúlveda in 1550 on
the Intellectual and Religious Capacity
of the American Indians

By

LEWIS HANKE

NORTHERN ILLINOIS UNIVERSITY PRESS • DeKalb

Excerpts throughout the text have been reprinted by permission of the publishers for the following:

Hanke, Lewis, *Aristotle and the American Indians.* Chicago: Henry Regnery Company, 1959 [British permission by the Bodley Head, Ltd., London];

Las Casas, Bartolomé de. *Tratado de Indias y el doctor Sepúlveda.* vol. 56. Caracas: Biblioteca de la Academia Nacional de la Historia, 1962;

Sepulveda, Juan Gines de. *Democrates segundo o de las justas causas de la guerra contra los indios.* ed. Ángel Losada. Madrid: Consejo Superior de Investigaciones Cientificas, Instituto Francisco de Vitoria, 1951.

We wish to thank the trustees of The Newberry Library for permission to use the following from the Edward E. Ayer collection:

Five Aztec Indian drawings and Mexican Calendar motif on half-title page, collected by Waldeck, Ayer Ms. 1271;

Don Barthélemi de Las Casas portrait from J. A. Llorente, *Oeuvres de don Barthélemi de Las Casas,* 1822;

Ornamental letters used on chapter openings from Las Casas, *Brevissima Relacion de la Destruycion de las Indias,* Seville, 1552.

We also wish to thank Johns Hopkins University Press for permission to reprint the four herbals shown in the Appendices, taken from *The Badianus Manuscript,* by Emily Emmart, copyright © 1940 by Johns Hopkins University Press.

Library of Congress Cataloging in Publication Data
Hanke, Lewis.
    All mankind is one.
    "Intended to serve as an introduction for
Dr. Stafford Poole's English translation of Bartolomé
de las Casas's treatise against Juan Ginés de
Sepúlveda's argument at Valladolid."
    Bibliography: p.
    1. Indians, Treatment of. 2. Casas, Bartolomé
de las, Bp. of Chiapa, 1474-1566. 3. Sepúlveda,
Juan Ginés de, 1490-1573. I. Casas, Bartolomé de las,
Bp. of Chiapa, 1474-1566. In defense of the Indians.
II. Title.
F1411.H32   301.45'19'7   73-15095
ISBN 0-87580-043-2

To the Memory of

Johannes Beckmann, S.M.B. (1901-1971)
Vicente Beltrán de Heredia, O.P. (1885-1973)
Benno M. Biermann, O.P. (1885-1970)
Frans Blom (1893-1963)
Gabriel Méndez Plancarte (1905-1949)

And to Honor the Work of

Marcel Bataillon (Paris)
Ángel Losada (Geneva)
Juan Pérez de Tudela (Madrid)
Antonine Zaninovič, O.P. (Dubrovnik)

Contributors All to Our Knowledge of the Life and Impact
of Bartolomé de Las Casas on His World, on Our World

Contents

Xochipilli, god of song, dance, and poetry. Aztec sculpture in stone, originating in Tlalmanalco, Mexico; now in the National Museum of Anthropology, Mexico City. (Photo by Manuel Álvarez Bravo)

Explanations and Acknowledgments

THIS study is intended to serve as an introduction for Dr. Stafford Poole's English translation of Bartolomé de Las Casas's treatise against Juan Ginés de Sepúlveda's argument at Valladolid in 1550 that the American Indians should be considered as the natural slaves of Spaniards. The debate between these two outstanding figures of sixteenth-century Spain was one of the most curious episodes in the history of the Western world. For the first time, and probably for the last, a colonizing nation organized a formal inquiry into the justice of the methods used to extend its empire. For the first time, too, in the modern world, we see an attempt to stigmatize an entire race as inferior, as born slaves according to the theory elaborated centuries before by Aristotle.

The analysis of Las Casas's treatise, *Defense Against the Persecutors and Slanderers of the Peoples of the New World Discovered Across the Seas,* forms the core of this study, but the controversies in Spain and America over the nature of the Indians up to 1550 are developed as background for the disputation at Valladolid, and some attention is given to the continuation of the dispute after Las Casas and Sepúlveda's battle in 1550. Why did this basic treatise for an understanding of the expansion of Europe have to wait more than four centuries for publication? The Marqués de Olivart tried in vain to make it available to the public during the later years of the nineteenth century, and the Fondo de Cultura Económica in Mexico was about to sponsor an edition when the austerities of World War II halted such plans, despite an eloquent plea by Agustín Millares Carlo.[1] Since those years even the great

---

1. Olivart (1908), p. viii; Millares Carlo (1950), pp. 33-51 on "Una obra inédita de Fray Bartolomé de Las Casas."

crescendo of interest in everything connected with the life and doctrines of Las Casas did not suffice to launch a version of the treatise
in any language.

Its very size was a problem, of course, but perhaps even more
significant an obstacle has been the fact that Las Casas published a
résumé in Spanish of his argument and that of his opponent, Juan
Ginés de Sepúlveda, in the famous collection of *Tratados* that appeared
in Seville in 1552, a year after their discussion ended in Valladolid.[2]
With this material in print, plus the introduction Antonio María Fabié
included in his work on Las Casas,[3] historians seemed to be satisfied
that they knew enough about the topic debated at Valladolid: Was it
lawful for the King of Spain to wage war on the Indians in America
before preaching the faith to them, in order to subject them to his rule,
so that afterward they might be more easily instructed in the faith?

After Ángel Losada brought out his excellent edition of the basic
treatise by Sepúlveda,[4] it became clear that the large Latin manuscript
embodying Las Casas's views—consulted only occasionally by such
scholars as Marcel Bataillon and André Saint-Lu—would eventually
have to be printed. Dr. William Hinnebusch, O.P., and his colleagues of
the House of Dominican Studies in Washington, D.C., made valiant
efforts in this direction, but the project languished until Dr. Stafford
Poole, C.M., accepted the responsibility for the transcription of the
Latin text and its translation into English. All those concerned with
the history of Spain in America owe a special debt to Dr. Poole for
his great labor in making this treatise accessible. It is most unfortunate that Manuel Giménez Fernández did not live to bring his deep
knowledge of law and his passionate concern for the history of the
struggle for justice in America to the story of the great confrontation
at Valladolid.

As for myself, the experience of again studying and meditating
upon the problems involved in the Spanish struggle for justice in the
conquest of America, of which I first began to become aware in 1930 in
Widener Library, has been a fruitful period. Though I have spent

2. "Aqui se contiene una disputa o controversia entre el obispo don fray Bartolomé
   de Las Casas o Casaus, obispo que fue de la Ciudad Real de Chiapa . . . y el doctor
   Ginés de Sepúlveda, coronista del Emperador." Las Casas (1966), I, 216-459.
3. Fabié (1879), II, 539-42.
4. Sepúlveda (1951).

much time in the ensuing years on Las Casas, research for the present study has uncovered new facts and fresh approaches to the complex reality of Spanish-Indian relationships that demonstrate how rich and almost inexhaustible for the historian is the conquest of America. But this is my last publication on Las Casas, as the time has come for me to turn to other projects long postponed. As Spaniards say when they have definitely completed their remarks on a subject: *He dicho.*

For more than 450 years abrasive arguments have been heard on the ideas and actions of Bartolomé de Las Casas during the Spanish conquest of America. The 400th anniversary of his death, in 1966, loosed a new avalanche of publications by and about this controversial Spanish Dominican, and the end is not in sight.

One explanation for the ever-growing bibliography might be that some of us who are attracted to examine the life of Las Casas are peculiarly contentious fellows who delight in controversy for its own sake; certainly many of us have individualistic approaches to the past, and no one *Lascasista* seems to approve wholly of the interpretations of his colleagues. In a certain subtle way, Las Casas brings out in many of us our deep-seated feelings on life and the meaning of history.[5] And *Lascasistas* sometimes change their minds. Don Ramón Menéndez Pidal delivered one of the most virulent attacks ever made on Las Casas, but not long before he died he asked that word be sent to inform "English Hispanists" that if he were to write his book again he would make it less polemical.[6] Presumably he felt no desire to so inform his Spanish-speaking friends, as they expect passionate debate on important

5. After writing this paper I chanced to re-read Charles Gibson's sophisticated remarks on this subject, which express the same thought in a more direct and meaningful way: "In Hispanic American studies conquest is a notorious and an enduring subject . . . . One's handling of conquest implies a series of judgments upon an entire Hispanic world, present as well as past. We who study Hispanic America feel obliged to define attitudes toward Freud. The resultant definitions can hardly be other than symptomatic, replete with synecdoche and self-betrayal." Gibson (1955), p. 1. See also the introduction to Gibson's volume on the Black Legend in the Borzoi Books on Latin America, Gibson (1971), pp. 3-27.

6. Letter from Rafael Lapesa to Alvaro J. Moreno, dated 27 December 1968: "En marzo de 1965, a los pocos días de haber sufrido Don Ramón Menéndez Pidal la trombosis que le impidió continuar su labor, me dió el encargo de hacer saber a los hispanistas ingleses que si volviera a escribir su libro sobre Fray Bartolomé de Las Casas lo haría menos polémico." *Boletín Bibliográfico Mexicano* (Mexico, Librería de Porrúa Hermanos) (January-February 1969), p. 3.

matters. Indeed, no subject in all Spanish history has been so bitterly and so continuously discussed by Spaniards as their conquest of the New World, and especially their treatment of the Indians and their interpretation of indigenous cultures.[7]

A reading of Las Casas's *opera* (even though some works have been lost, five large volumes are required to print only his works written in Spanish) might lead one to the conclusion that in reality he was always composing the same treatise.[8] Or rather to the realization that, apparently, he had one large file of ideas and material that he kept as an ever-increasing reservoir of facts and doctrines to draw on for the particular battle he was fighting. This explains how interrelated are all of his writings, how he could write endlessly on the same subject by giving special emphases to certain topics in the various treatises he worked out during his long and exceedingly laborious life. Henry R. Wagner once remarked that it is difficult to see how Las Casas could have written more about peaceful preaching than he had in the manuscript (incomplete but still quite large) of his first treatise, *The Only Method of Preaching the True Faith.*[9] But he could have done so, and probably did.

What distinguishes the *Defense* and justifies extended treatment of its origin and contents is its broad, ecumenical character. If we could save only one of Las Casas's numerous writings, this is the one that

7. Daniel Moreno points out that even the selection of material for an anthology on Indian culture may lead to polemics (*Historia Mexicana,* no. 53 [1964], pp. 150-52); he made this statement in reviewing Luis Nicolau D'Olwer's *Cronistas de las culturas precolombianas.* Mariano A. Montero emphasized the continuing nature of the dispute: "La etnología en México no es ni ciencia de gabinete ni gimnasia mental . . . está en la calle. Se topa uno con sus problemas al doblar una esquina o al descender de un camión." Montero (1943), p. 164.

8. Las Casas (1957). As one great authority has emphasized, Las Casas was not a monolithic figure; rather, he exhibited certain "constant aspects of his extraordinary personality" as well as a tendency to be influenced in his actions by the differing circumstances in which he found himself during his long and agitated life (Giménez Fernández [1958], pp. 703-4). Las Casas's basic thoughts on the nature of the Indians and on the proper way for Spaniards to treat them did not, however, alter substantially after he again took up the struggle in 1531. For illustrations of this, see Biermann (1969) and Las Casas (1964).

9. Wagner (1967), p. 265. Las Casas treated the same subject at various times and in various ways. For example, one of his favorite ideas was that Spaniards must make restitution to Indians for wrongs committed against them. On this subject, he remarked late in life: "Esto parecerá, placiendo a Dios, en nuestro tractado *De restitución,* en latín escrito, en el libro I y II *De unico vocationis modo omnium gentium ad veram*

would give the world the most universal view of the doctrine that undergirds all the battles he fought as Protector of the Indians. In these pages the reader sees that combination of legal theory, Christian principles, his special views on the Spanish Conquest, and—especially—his convictions on the capacity of the Indians that endow his words with their enduring vitality.

Many Spaniards, from the sixteenth century until today, have justified their conquest of America by their efforts to convert the Indians to Christianity. During these centuries ecclesiastics and laymen alike have given much thought to the reasons why the Indies were discovered, why the conversion of the natives was entrusted to Spain, and what consequences this missionary action had.[10] Dr. Poole's publication of the text of Las Casas's *Defense* makes one of the fundamental works on the theory and practice of this transcendental conversion effort during the expansion of Europe available to every reader of English.

This introduction to the *Defense*, begun in 1968 at the University of California (Irvine) and concluded in Amherst at the University of Massachusetts, would not have been possible without the assistance of Janice Aitken, Carmen Aranovich, Ernest J. Burrus, S. J., Donald Chipman, Juan Comas, James Cummins, Antonio de Egaña, S. J., J. H. Elliott, Antonio Gómez Robledo, Harold B. Johnson, Jr., José María F. Kazuhiro Kobayishi, Richard Konetzke, Archibald R. Lewis, Ángel Losada, John Lynch, Raymond Marcus, Louis Necker, Juan Pérez de Tudela Bueso, Stafford Poole, C. M., André Saint-Lu, William L. Sherman, Antonine Tibesar, O.F.M., and E. Daymond Turner, Jr. Lucretia

religionem y en suma, parece en nuestro *Confesionario* en romance, ya impreso, mayormente en el *Confesionario* nuestro grande, que no está impreso" (Las Casas [1951], III, 356). (Note that he had written *two* works titled *Confesionario,* one in Spanish, which had been printed, and a larger work in manuscript.) These ideas had some practical effect, as may be seen from the valuable work by Lohmann Villena (1966).

10. Borges (1956) shows how much thought was expended on these questions in the sixteenth century. It is surprising that during the course of his study Borges makes no reference to the problem Las Casas treated in the *Defense:* the need to preach Christianity by peaceful means. Even in his larger work on mission methods (1960) there is no reference to Sepúlveda's doctrine of force, though there is some consideration of Las Casas's *De Unico Modo Vocationis.* For a commentary on the many publications on the basic issues of Spanish actions in America, with copious bibliographical citations, see Zavala (1971).

Bishko was particularly helpful in spotting errors, fractured grammar, and unclear prose. Charles Julian Bishko once more helped me with his deep and detailed knowledge of the Iberian world. Pauline Collins and other members of the University of Massachusetts Library staff have been efficient and imaginative in responding to my many requests for help. To all of these old and new friends I offer my grateful thanks. All errors remaining are now my exclusive responsibility.

A special tribute is due Benjamin Keen, whose courage and care have made it possible for this work to be brought out on the eve of the 500th anniversary of the birth of Bartolomé de Las Casas.

LEWIS HANKE

ALL MANKIND IS ONE

A Study of the Disputation Between Bartolomé de Las Casas and Juan Ginés de Sepúlveda in 1550 on the Intellectual and Religious Capacity of the American Indians

I

The Nature of the American Indians
According to the Spaniards

The Controversy up to 1550

HE treatise that Bartolomé de Las Casas read in all its tremendous detail before the learned judges of the Royal Council convoked at Valladolid in 1550 was intimately and directly related to the bitter dispute that had raged in both Spain and the New World since 1492—what manner of beings were these American natives, and what was their capacity for the Christian religion and for European civilization? The very title of the work that Las Casas later wrote in final form and that he believed would demolish the arguments of his opponent, the Renaissance scholar Juan Ginés de Sepúlveda, indicates the main thrust of the Domin-

ican's treatise: *Defense Against the Persecutors and Slanderers of the Peoples of the New World Discovered Across the Seas.*

The first biographer of Christopher Columbus, the humanist Dominican Bishop Agostino Giustiniani, referred to the new-found lands as "almost another world" that had "been discovered and added to the Christian Church."[1] At the time he was publishing this biography as a part of the first Polyglot Bible (1516), opinion was beginning to divide in America on the nature of the Indians, and some Spaniards seemed to believe that the Indians were almost, but perhaps not quite, men and that their capacity for becoming Christians was slight or perhaps even nonexistent.

Columbus had founded a kind of "noble savage" school when he filled his diary of the first voyage with references to the gentle, beautiful, and friendly people on the island of Hispaniola who seemed eminently ready to accept the truths of Christianity.[2] Actual experience with the natives did not bear out these rosy predictions, however, and there were some Spaniards who held such a low opinion of the Indians in the two decades after 1492 that a Dominican, Antonio de Montesinos, preached a famous sermon on the island of Hispaniola in 1511 in which he dramatically urged the Christianization of the Indians and inquired: "Are these Indians not men? Do they not have rational souls?"[3] Montesinos evidently astounded and shocked the colonists; never before, apparently, had the indoctrination of non-Christians who were living in Christian kingdoms been considered the duty of all Spaniards. Thus developed the first significant and public clash in America between the zeal for the propagation of the gospel and the greed for gold and silver among Spaniards, who for centuries had been accustomed to an economy based to some extent on war booty wrested from the Moors.

Encomenderos, who were assigned Indians for their own profit, were expected to provide for the Indians' religious instruction, but this was a New World development, as the *encomienda* grants in medieval Spain included no such requirement.[4] Why was it not natural for the *conquistadores,* inquired Richard Konetzke a few years ago, to look upon the newly found lands principally as a boundless field for the spirit of conquest engendered during the medieval *Reconquista* and to continue overseas "their habitual courtship of wealth at spearpoint"? He also maintained that it is a "mistake and an anachronism to suppose that the Christianization of the infidels was a moving factor in the antecedent history of the discovery of America—an interpretation that springs from confusing the Reconquest of the Iberian Peninsula, the war against the Moors, with a crusade to expel the infidels and heretics and convert them to the true faith."[5] He emphasized the influence of political considerations in the intense missionary spirit that was manifested at the end of the fifteenth century. The modern state hoped to gain strength by a policy of religious intolerance that would eliminate dissension, whereas the kings of medieval Spain had to allow wide freedom in religious beliefs because of their weakness. This fundamental shift in the religious attitude of the Crown marked the end of the Middle Ages.[6]

This idea comes as a bombshell to those of us brought up in the school that interprets the beginning of the conquest of America in 1492 as but the continuation of the medieval Reconquista that ended at Granada in the same year. The religious head of steam generated during the long centuries required to recover the Peninsula from the Moors was thus available, when Columbus first headed out to sea, for the remarkable attempt the Spaniards made—especially in the early decades of the conquest of America—to convert the Indians. Yet, when one looks more closely at the detailed explanation of Konetzke, does it not appear reasonable to believe that there was indeed a close connection between the political aims of Isabella and Ferdinand and the evangelization of the New World? To Spaniards of that time there was no clear distinction between political and religious motivations; they tended to assume that political advance automatically served religion by extending religious frontiers and that religious expansion strengthened political positions.

The more one studies the European background for the Conquest, the clearer it becomes that there was no single medieval experience but several, at least in Spain, depending on the period and the area. Both the use of force and peaceful persuasion policies were tried. If the counsel of Archbishop Hernando de Talavera had prevailed, even the Moors would have been gently assimilated and not forcibly converted. He had been impressed by Moorish cultural achievements and charitable works and had argued, unsuccessfully: "We must adopt their works of charity, and they our Faith."[7] But force and expulsion were used instead. The history of the conquest of the Canary Islands, the most obvious overseas precedent for the conquest of America, shows a similar situation.[8]

Other elements to consider in the still relatively unexplored history of the Catholic Kings are the messianic ideas and reforming zeal that developed among some Spanish ecclesiastics at the end of the fifteenth century and in the early sixteenth century, which also help explain the fierce determination of some of the friars to convert the Indians.[9] As the conquest in America proceeded and as the Protestant Reformation shattered "the seamless web of Christendom," some friars yearned to establish among the Indians a new Catholic Church, free from the religious dissensions in Europe. Luther and Cortez, it was said, had been born in the same year: one to destroy the ancient Church and the other to build a new Jerusalem in the recently conquered lands across the sea. Abundant evidence proves that many friars undertook the enormous task of converting the Indians with the conviction that they were participating in a great and transcendent labor. As the earliest Franciscans in Mexico expressed it, the conversion of the pagan peoples across the sea was the greatest act of God since the establishment of the early Church.[10]

But did the conquistadores who went to the New World share this vision? Some did, if we may judge from such a classic account as Bernal Díaz del Castillo's history, but we also find in this source examples of Konetzke's view of the exploitative Spaniard, for the conquistador tells how he reproached his companions who "went about robbing the native peoples, taking from them their women and chickens and clothing, just the way they did in Moorish lands." A Peruvian historian has gone so far as to assert, in a recent essay suggestively titled "From the Killing of Moors to the Killing of Indians" ("De Santiago matamoros a Santiago mataindios"), that Spaniards sought exclusively their own interests, not the good of the Indians. Even the struggles to have the Indians recognized as human beings, with souls, were merely a justification of clerical intervention and punishment of Indians, this writer insists.[11]

Perhaps the experience of Las Casas himself helps us understand the attitude of Spaniards during the early years of the Conquest. During his considerable experience on the island of Hispaniola, which began when he arrived in 1502 as a member of Governor Nicolás de Ovando's expedition, he was not much better than the rest of the gentlemen-adventurers who rushed to the New World, bent on speedily acquiring fortunes.[12] He tells, in his *Historia de las Indias*, that he endeavored to convert the Indians—and also reveals that he obtained Indian slaves, worked them in mines, and attended to the cultivation of his estates, which prospered. The sermon of Montesinos evidently did not disturb him, for in the next year, 1512, he participated in the conquest of Cuba and in 1513 received as a reward both land and an encomienda. He continued to play the role of gentleman-ecclesiastic, although in 1514 he was refused the sacraments by a Dominican because he held slaves. The hot dispute that followed left him disturbed but not convinced. Later in 1514 he changed his mind, in 1515 gave up his encomienda, and thenceforth spent his life attempting to protect the Indians.

We do not have many such intimate records of the feelings of Spaniards in the early years of the Conquest, but if Las Casas had difficulty establishing his priorities, it is not surprising that other Spaniards, who were not ecclesiastics, had a similar difficulty, particularly since there appears to have been no strong tradition of conversion of infidels in Spanish medieval experience. As Charles Julian Bishko has written: "What is missing . . . all through the Later Middle Ages in Spain, it seems to me, is either an awareness of the nature of conversion or the development of institutional structures to accomplish it."[13] Does this fact not help us understand how the Spanish struggle to gain justice for the Indians developed in the New World? However one may answer the question raised by Konetzke concerning the medieval background of the evangelization of Spanish America, it is clearly a significant subject that calls for much more research than it has thus far received.

Crown policy in the first years of the Conquest centered on economic expansion, and the key question involved the method. Was colonization to be the aim, or a system based on Italian mercantilism?[14] Missionary objectives began with the papal bull *Inter Caetera* of 1493, and the controversy on Indian liberty developed almost simultaneously.[15] By 20 June 1500 the Catholic Kings formally approved liberty, not slavery, for Indians—a law that led Rafael Altamira to exclaim: "What a memorable day for the entire world, because it signalizes the first recognition of the respect due to the dignity and liberty of all men no matter how primitive and uncivilized they may be—a principle that had never been proclaimed before in any legislation, let alone practiced in any country."[16]

Crown policy in favor of conversion was made clear, however, by a number of early documents. For example, royal instructions to Governor Nicolás de Ovando in 1501 read thus:

Because we desire that the Indians be converted to our holy Catholic faith and that their souls be saved, for this is the greatest good that we can wish for, and because for this they must be informed of the matters of our faith, you are to take great care in ensuring that the clergy so inform them and admonish them with much love, and without using force, so that they may be converted as rapidly as possible.[17]

Instruction and proclamation were one thing; enforcement was another. Therefore if one accepts the interpretation that lay Spaniards were not prepared by their medieval experience for vigorous persuasion of non-Christians, the sermon by Montesinos in 1511 in the straw-thatched church in Hispaniola may be considered not only the beginning of the struggle for justice in Spanish America but also a turning point in the history of Christianity. Henceforth the *people*, not merely ecclesiastics, were expected to participate actively and responsibly in the conversion of the heathen.

The ensuing battle between the Dominicans, who supported Montesinos, and the colonists was carried to Spain, where the Crown listened to the disputants and then, in 1512, promulgated the Laws of Burgos, the first detailed regulations to govern relations between Indians and Spaniards. These laws contained many rules for governing Indian labor and for regulating the food, clothing, and beds to be supplied to them. Most particularly, the laws ordered the Spaniards who had Indian vassals to build churches for them and to take pains to see that they were taught the Christian doctrine and that their children were baptized. This new and rather novel responsibility, laid on Spaniards who enjoyed Indian service and tribute under the encomienda system, must to some extent explain the slowness of the encomenderos in complying with their missionary duties, although we cannot know for certain until we have better histories of the encomienda system, based upon the many manuscripts awaiting the researcher.

Number 24 of the Laws of Burgos also helps us understand the background of custom and attitude against which these laws were promulgated, for it stipulated that "no one may beat or whip or call an

Indian dog *(perro)* or any other name unless it is his proper name."[18] Such treatment shows that some Spaniards, at least, entertained a somewhat low opinion of the Indians. As the Conquest wore on, Spaniards encountered some Indians whose color, culture, religious ideas, and values were so different from their own that they began to doubt that they could be Christianized. There developed during the first half century of Spanish action in America a kind of polarization between the two extremes—what might be called the "dirty dog" and the "noble savage" schools of thought—although there were many different and more subtle shades of opinion in between.[19]

The Las Casas-Sepúlveda disputation of 1550 was the last important event in the controversy on Indian capacity that bitterly divided Spaniards in the sixteenth century and, indeed, has continued to embroil historians in neo-Byzantine discussions. The latest writer on these matters, the Spanish Franciscan Lino Gómez Canedo, recently challenged the view that there were some Spaniards who actually considered the Indians less than men. Were there, he asks, any persons "who sustained the idea that the Indians were not human beings, but animals or something intermediate between men and beasts?"[20] Gómez Canedo answers this question in the negative and calls for more historical documentation before such statements may be accepted.

The following section is designed to provide additional evidence on the subject. And inasmuch as this question has a definite relationship to the argument of Las Casas at Valladolid, it should be treated as an integral part of the background of the *Defense*.

Although questions were raised in the early years of the Conquest on the nature of the Indians, the earliest official inquiry into the subject took place in 1517 on the island of Hispaniola, conducted by the Jeronymite friars, who had been ordered by the Spanish Crown to discover whether any Indians could be found who were capable of living by themselves and to set free all such Indians, as provided for in the Clarification of the Laws of Burgos (1513). The information that was taken down contains much significant detail for anyone interested in the contact of races.[21]

Antonio de Villasante expressed the general opinion of the colonists when he emphatically deposed that neither Indian men nor women knew how to govern themselves as adequately as the rudest

Spaniard. If allowed to run free, he declared, the Indians would revert to their former habits of idleness, nakedness, dancing, eating spiders and snakes, patronizing witch doctors, drunkenness, improvidence, and gluttony. Another colonist, Lucas Vázquez de Ayllón, concluded that it was far better they should become slave men (*"hombres siervos"*) than remain free beasts (*"bestias libres"*). Commenting on these early disputes, the historian Gonzalo Fernández de Oviedo y Valdés observed:

> Great disputes have taken place among famous jurists, canonists, and theologians, as well as among conscientious and skilled prelates, on whether the Indians should serve Spaniards and on whether the Indians are capable or not. . . . But inasmuch as there have been many different opinions expressed in these disputes, no good has come to the land or to the Indians.[22]

Oviedo also reported: "Although some Christians married important Indian women, there were many more who would not marry them under any circumstances because of their incapacity and ugliness."[23]

The first instance of intermarriage occurred in the early years of Ovando's rule in Hispaniola, when a sailor, Cristóbal Rodríguez, served as interpreter in the marriage of an Indian woman and a Spaniard in Concepción. Rodríguez must have been an unusual person for he had acquired a knowledge of the Taino language by voluntarily living for several years among the Indians; he became known as *La Lengua,* and as a Spaniard who favored the Indians and respected their culture. Ovando appears never to have doubted the capacity of Indians for Christianity, but he disapproved Rodríguez's action as interpreter, fined him 10,000 *maravedís,* and expelled him from Hispaniola.[24]

Rodríguez returned to Spain in 1505 and managed to obtain a hearing before King Ferdinand and his Council—much to Ovando's disgust—at which he defended the Indians. Nothing, apparently, came of this early protest, but the question of marriage with Indians continued to agitate Spaniards. In the 4 June 1516 letter that both Montesinos and Domingo de Betanzos signed, along with other ecclesiastics, recommending Las Casas at Court, they denounced the allegation that Indians were "not suitable for marriage, or for the faith. The Christians say this because they consider the Indians only useful for digging gold."[25]

The Franciscan Francisco Ruiz, Bishop of Ávila and close advisor of

Cardinal Francisco Jiménez de Cisneros, whose influence in Indian affairs was great, had this to say on Indian capacity, about 1517:

Indians are malicious people who are able to think up ways to harm Christians, but they are not capable of natural judgment or of receiving the faith, nor do they have the other virtues required for their conversion and salvation . . . and they need, just as a horse or beast does, to be directed and governed by Christians who treat them well and not cruelly.[26]

Not long afterward, in Barcelona in 1519 before the newly elected Emperor Charles V, the Franciscan Bishop Juan de Quevedo declared the Indians to be *"siervos a natura,"* according to Las Casas, who severely criticized the Franciscan's doctrine as based on Aristotle, "a pagan, now burning in Hell, whose principles should be accepted only insofar as they conform to our Christian religion." Finally, in 1520, after a series of discussions, Charles and his Council determined "that the Indians were free, ought to be treated as such, and induced to accept Christianity by the methods Christ had established."

(It should be noted that this first serious argument in Spain on the nature of the Indians had none of the ingenuous attitude manifested by an African Gold Coast king who, when he saw a European [a Dane] in 1661, expressed doubts that this white man was really a human being like himself. An interpreter had explained that the Dane's queue was not really a tail growing out of his neck, but the king remained unconvinced until the European removed his clothes, in private, whereupon the monarch concluded: "Ah, you really are a human being, but only too white, like a devil.")[27]

Spaniards were concerned with other aspects of their Indian problem, and the Crown continued to authorize experiments in the Caribbean islands of Cuba, Hispaniola, and Puerto Rico to determine whether the Indians could in fact live *políticamente* like Spaniards, despite the contrary evidence accumulating from some colonists and some ecclesiastics. In 1525 the Dominican Tomás Ortiz spoke very strongly against Indian capacity before the newly established Council of the Indies. Referring to the "mainland" Indians (but perhaps, as some later writers believed, only to the fierce Caribs), he denounced them in these terms:

They are incapable of learning. . . . They exercise none of the humane arts or industries. . . . The older they get the worse they behave. About the age of ten or twelve years they seem to have some civilization, but later they become like real brute beasts. . . . God has never created a race more full of vice . . . the Indians are more stupid than asses and refuse to improve in anything.[28]

The scene now moves to Mexico, where the first great Spanish mission campaign had begun and where, for the first time, Spaniards came face to face with the imposing New World civilization that had been created by the Aztecs and the Mayas. The foot soldier Bernal Díaz del Castillo, who fought many fierce battles against the Indians during the years following 1519 (when Cortez won Mexico for Spain), was scandalized at their religious practices, but he admired their monuments, the bravery of their warriors, their imposing cities, their impressive ceremonies, and the intelligence of their leaders. These Indians were obviously different from the natives of Hispaniola and the other Caribbean islands he had met before. Bernal Díaz could scarcely believe his eyes when he first beheld the Aztec capital, Tenochtitlán, gleaming on its lake in the morning sun:

Gazing on such wonderful sights we did not know what to say or whether what appeared before us was real; for on the one hand there were great cities and in the lake ever so many more, and the lake itself was crowded with canoes, and in the causeway were many bridges at intervals, and in front of us stood the great City of Mexico, and we . . . we did not even number four-hundred soldiers.[29]

Cortez reported in his Second Letter that "these people live almost like those in Spain, and in as much harmony and order as there, and considering that they are barbarous and so far from the knowledge of God and cut off from all civilized nations, it is truly remarkable to see what they have achieved in all things." A *Times Literary Supplement* reviewer has remarked: "A passage like this compares favorably with any in the works of Las Casas"—which is not quite true, but nevertheless it was a notable opinion by a *conquistador.*[30]

Within the first decade after the conquest of Mexico the battle lines were sharply drawn on how Indians should serve Spaniards; whether the natives had sufficient "capacity" to become Christians and to govern themselves also became emotion-laden issues. During 1532 and 1533 the Council of the Indies sought advice in many quarters, and a flood of sharply contrasting opinions began to inundate the royal councillors. The president of the royal *Audiencia*, Bishop Sebastián

Ramírez de Fuenleal, and the Franciscan Bishop Juan de Zumárraga presided over the first ecclesiastical junta in 1532, at which "all said that there was no doubt that the natives had sufficient capacity, that they greatly love the doctrine of the faith . . . and that they are able to carry on all mechanical and agricultural arts." The junta also recognized that the Indian was a rational being and that he was capable of governing himself.[31] As the principal royal officers, prelates, and friars deposed in 1532: "There is no doubt that the natives have sufficient capacity to receive the faith, and that they greatly love it."[32]

This view soon met a strong challenge, for in late 1532 or early 1533 the Dominican Domingo de Betanzos made a statement on Indian character before the Council of the Indies in Spain that so disturbed some Spaniards that they wrote to Mexico reporting that Betanzos had denied that the Indians were capable of understanding the faith. This written opinion has not yet been found, so that no one knows exactly what Betanzos deposed, but the reports that arrived in Mexico in private letters greatly alarmed the royal judges of the *Audiencia*, and the Franciscans as well. Judge Salmerón on 4 May 1533 wrote to Charles V that the "untrue account *(incierta relación)*" that Betanzos made on the conversion and the capacity of the Indians in New Spain had much disturbed them. He considered it a clever maneuver of the devil to hide under the mantle of an ecclesiastic while giving such opinions.[33]

The Franciscan provincial, Jacobo de Testera, led his entire group, in a letter to Charles V dated 6 May 1533, in denouncing the devil for trying to convince people that Mexican Indians were not capable. At Xochimilco, two Franciscans had baptized some 15,000 Indians in one day, evidently the record, though the Mercedarian friar Francisco Bobadilla was close behind, for he had baptized 29,000 Indians in a few days in Nicaragua. In the face of such missionary triumphs, how could anyone claim that Indians could not understand the faith? Testera roundly asserted that any ecclesiastic who had studied Indian languages knew differently. He may have had Betanzos in mind when he referred to those who were too "fastidious and lazy" to undertake the labor of learning their languages and those who lacked "the zeal to break through this wall of language in order to enter their hearts."[34]

The use of the term "fastidious" is noteworthy, and reminds one of the encounter between the saintly Bishop Zumárraga and certain secular Spaniards in Mexico who urged him to have less to do with the evil-smelling and poorly clad Indians. "Your Reverend Lordship is no longer young or robust, but old and infirm," they warned him, "and your constant mingling with the Indians may bring you great harm." Whereupon the Bishop indignantly replied:

You are the ones who give out an evil smell according to my way of thinking, and you are the ones who are repulsive and disgusting to me, because you seek only vain frivolities and because you lead soft lives just as though you were not Christians. These poor Indians have a heavenly smell to me; they comfort me and give me health, for they exemplify for me that harshness of life and penitence which I must espouse if I am to be saved.[35]

Testera then described the civilization of the Indians in glowing terms, similar to those used by Las Casas in 1550 in the Valladolid dispute:

How can anyone say that these people are incapable, when they constructed such impressive buildings, made such subtle creations, were silversmiths, painters, merchants, able in presiding, in speaking, in the exercise of courtesy, in fiestas, marriages, solemn occasions, receptions of distinguished personages; able to express sorrow, and appreciation, when the occasion requires it and, finally, very ready to be educated in the ethical, political, and economic aspects of life? What cannot we say concerning the people of this land? They sing plainsong and contrapuntally to organ accompaniment, they compose music and teach others how to enjoy religious music, they preach to the people the sermons we teach them; they confess freely and earnestly in a pure and simple manner.[36]

Another Franciscan, Luis de Fuensalida, had an even more emphatic reaction to the opinion of Betanzos. He had received a complete copy of the opinion, and on 26 June 1533 indignantly denounced it in a letter to Bishop Ramírez de Fuenleal as an *"errorem intolerabilem."* If Betanzos were a Franciscan, Fuensalida would have considered that he had "lost his senses." Christianity, he said, is for all people, and those who did not believe this had never learned the language of the Indians, had never preached to them, had never confessed them, and knew only about their sins. Fuensalida lauded their good qualities and referred to their "fear of God, their preparation for death, their confessions, sermons, wisdom, reading, writing, counting, musical ability, repentance for sins, tears of their devotions, fasts, self-punishments, gifts especially at Easter, faithful attendance at church ceremonies: ponder these things, and you will see how much they exceed us in these matters."[37]

Bishop Ramírez de Fuenleal, as we have seen, did not need the spur of Fuensalida's letter; as president of the *Audiencia* of Mexico he had already sent a strong protest to the Crown, on 15 May 1533, against the Betanzos opinion and along the same line as the other letters. He added that Betanzos "agreed to sign the statement drawn up by those who considered the Indians as beasts, because it profited them; on the contrary, the Indians are not only capable with respect to morals but also in speculative matters, and they will become strong Christians. Indeed, some already are."[38]

The battle was now joined, and many of the outstanding figures of the Conquest participated in it. Las Casas, who had retired from the world for about ten years following his entrance into the Dominican order in 1522, was active again. In a long and passionate letter to the Council of the Indies from the island of Hispaniola on 1 January 1531 he had argued for peaceful persuasion in the same terms he was to use in the *Defense* at Valladolid:

This is the true path, gentlemen, this is the way to convert the people in your charge. Why instead of sending among them peaceful sheep |do| you send hungry wolves? Christ did not act in this way. . . . Nowhere in the world are there meeker people or of less resistance or more ready and apt to receive the yoke of Christ as these folk.[39]

Nor did Las Casas content himself with words, for he was a man of action too. The royal judges in Hispaniola reported to the King in 1533 that he refused absolution to encomenderos whose treatment of the Indians he condemned. From Granada, Nicaragua, on 15 October 1535 Las Casas again complained, this time to "a personage at court," against the cruel actions of the Germans in Venezuela:

This is not, my lord, the path Christ followed; this is not the way to preach the Gospel; this is no method to convert souls, but rather a Moslem practice indeed worse than what Mohammed did.[40]

The nature of the Indians became involved in the kind of treatment to be accorded them. The Dominican theologian Francisco de Vitoria, who a few years later was to deliver his classic lectures *De Indis* at the University of Salamanca, in 1535 wrote to his brother Dominican Miguel de Arcos a letter that suggested that some of their contemporaries were indeed questioning whether Indians were men. Commenting on the wars in Peru, Vitoria stated:

I do not understand the justice of this war. . . . In truth, if the Indians are not men but monkeys, *non sunt capaces iniuriae*. But if they are men and our fellow-creatures, as well as vassals of the Emperor, I see no way to excuse these conquistadores nor do I know how they serve Your Majesty in such an important way by destroying your vassals.[41]

Another towering figure of those years was Vasco de Quiroga, who was convinced that the Indians still lived in the Golden Age, whereas Europeans had decayed—a notion not unlike the later declarations of Las Casas at Valladolid on the superiority in certain respects of the Indians over Europeans.[42] Quiroga, then a judge of the *Audiencia*, composed a fundamental *Información en Derecho*, which has yet to be studied sufficiently.[43] Later he was to enter the Church and establish the famous communities for Indians on utopian lines. Later still he was to oppose Las Casas on the perpetuity of encomiendas and on war against the Indians.

But in his *Información*, dated in Mexico, 24 July 1535, he supported the "noble savage" interpretation. "I believe firmly that all the people of this land and of the New World are almost all of one quality, very mild and humble, timid and obedient."[44] They should be brought to the faith by persuasion and by "good and Christian influence," not by war or fear. According to one scholar, the essential sweetness of Indian character, and not the influence of Sir Thomas More, explains Quiroga's plan to bring the Indians to a Christian, civilized life by means of "hospital" communities.[45]

Quiroga opposed the proposal, then being advanced in Spain, that Indians should be enslaved and branded with hot irons. This was an invention of the devil, he maintained: "They should not be considered as beasts rather than men and . . .Spaniards should [not] use them at their pleasure for their service without any hindrance whatsoever."[46] He called it tyranny to have the Indians serve Spaniards "like beasts and animals without reason *(como de bestias y animales sin razón)*, until they are destroyed with work, vexations, and excessive service."[47] Those who allege Indian vices had their own personal profit in mind: "I have never seen verified the abominations charged by those who desire to defame them, nor have I ever been able to verify these charges with the testimony of persons who may not be suspected of self-interest . . . for persons who have Indians serving them use them not as men but as beasts, and worse *(no como de hombres, sino de bestias y peor)*."[48]

But Quiroga also expressed his conviction that no Christian could, in conscience, allow infidels to remain in a state of spiritual ignorance. Alexander VI's bull made it clear that the Christian must try to convert them—even, if necessary, by war. Later, after the Valladolid controversy, Quiroga composed a treatise, *De debellandis Indis,* which has not yet been found but which apparently supported Sepúlveda to some extent.[49]

Polarization of opinions and attitudes on Indians was thus well advanced by 1535, for Quiroga concluded: "Some there are here and there who hate and abominate them, and who speak harshly against them; likewise I am certain that some love them and favor them always, and speak well and truthfully about them and would give their lives and blood on their behalf if necessary."[50]

Quiroga may have had in mind the historian Gonzalo Fernández de Oviedo y Valdés as a representative of those who spoke out against the Indians, for a considerable part of Oviedo's *Historia general y natural de las Indias* had been published in Seville in 1535. Oviedo had a low opinion of Indian capacity, which enraged Las Casas. When Sepúlveda, fifteen years later, relied upon Oviedo as his authority on the nature of the Indians, Las Casas loosed all his wrath upon both Oviedo and Sepúlveda. This bitter and irreconcilable dispute will be analyzed later as an integral part of the Valladolid confrontation.

The Bull *Sublimis Deus*

The most important events of these years relating to the Indians were the issuance in 1537 by Pope Paul III of the bull *Sublimis Deus* and the composition by Las Casas, in the years immediately preceding, of his treatise *De Unico Vocationis Modo*, advocating conversion of the Indians by peaceful means alone, a doctrine he had urged upon the Council of the Indies in his strong letter of 1531 (described above), which was to serve as one of the foundation stones of his argument against Sepúlveda.

A detailed history of the promulgation of this famous papal declaration on the rights of the Indians need not be given here,[51] but it is pertinent to ask whether its publication had not been made necessary by the actions of Spaniards who advocated the incapacity and irrationality of Indians. The Dominican Bernardino de Minaya, who had returned from America in 1535 or 1536 to fight for the Indians, found that the president of the Council of the Indies, Cardinal Loaysa, was influenced—or so Minaya reported in a memorial to the Crown—by the declarations before the Council by Betanzos that the Indians could never be Christians, even though "the Emperor, the Pope, the Virgin, and all the celestial orders intervened on their behalf."[52] Minaya also stated that this opinion of Betanzos had led the Cardinal to issue a law permitting the conquistadores to enslave the Indians, a law that had reached Mexico just as Minaya returned from Peru, where he had confronted Pizarro in an attempt to protect the Indians from slavery and robbery by the Spaniards. These bitter experiences led Minaya to undertake the long journey to Rome in order to fight for the Indians in the highest court of Christendom.

When the law which permitted the enslavement of the Indians arrived, Don Sebastian Ramírez, Bishop of Santo Domingo and President of the Audiencia in Mexico, called in all the ecclesiastics and bade them write to Your Majesty their true opinion of the ability of the Indians. The Franciscans wrote to you but I [Minaya] wished to speak to the cardinal [Loaysa, then president of the Council of the Indies] personally. . . . I embarked on a vessel bound for Spain with no provisions whatsoever, confident that the other passengers would help me. Arriving at Seville, I went on foot, begging, to Valladolid, where I visited the cardinal and informed him that Friar Domingo [Betanzos] knew neither the Indians' language nor their true nature. I told him of their ability and the right they had to become Christians. He replied that I was much deceived, for he understood that the Indians were no more than parrots, and he believed that Friar Domingo spoke with prophetic spirit and, for himself, would follow that friar's opinion. When Dr. Bernal Lugo [a member of the Council of the Indies] asked me what had happened at my interview with the cardinal I told him and added that I was determined to go to the Pope concerning this evil which so endangered the Christianity of the Emperor and the many souls in the Indies; that a more cruel judgment had been rendered against them than against the ancient Hebrews, and that, although merely a poor friar, I should not fear to oppose a cardinal on this matter if I could only get a letter of introduction to His Holiness from the Empress. I will arrange this for you, said Dr. Bernal Lugo. Then I went on foot to Rome with my letter of introduction, which I preserve to this day.[53]

How and when Minaya learned of Betanzos' representations against Indian capacity is uncertain. Betanzos first testified on this subject before the Council of the Indies in late 1532 or early 1533, which led to the previously mentioned counterrepresentations of the *Audiencia* judges and the Franciscans in Mexico in May 1533. A short time afterward Betanzos made—by order of the Council of the Indies, he stated—a long and impassioned statement on the same subject for the Council's consideration. He recalled that he had witnessed many discussions in Hispaniola, in the years following his arrival there in 1514, among the Dominicans, Franciscans, and Jeronymites on the best way to treat Indians. He was defending himself from the charge that he had declared the Indians incapable of the faith, and cried:

A yawning gulf separates the parties to this dispute . . . . If you wish to understand this mysterious situation, look carefully at the opinions given by all those who have treated this subject; they are so diverse and contradictory that never can they be reconciled. What is more, every one is so fixed in his own opinion that he considers any different view is blasphemous and foolish.[54]

Betanzos, too, was convinced that his own views were particularly valid, for as he declared a few years later: "I know that no one is less mistaken in New Spain than myself in Indian affairs."[55]

In his second declaration before the Council Betanzos took note of the opposition in the Council itself and that of the many ecclesiastics and others in Mexico when they learned about it. He wanted to make one point very clear: "I have spoken somewhat on Indian capacity in general, not saying that they were wholly incapable, because I have never said that, but rather that they have very little capacity, like children."[56]

Betanzos also protested that he didn't want to stop the conversion of the Indians and that he had worked hard for their benefit.[57] When he returned to Mexico from Spain in 1536 it is unlikely that his views on the Indians as "children" met with favor among his Dominican brothers, or indeed with many of the other ecclesiastics there. It seems clear that his views were partly responsible for the actions leading up to the bull *Sublimis Deus*. Paul III was led to become interested in the plight of the New World natives not only through the personal intervention of Minaya in Rome but also by an eloquent and erudite letter from the Dominican Julián Garcés, Bishop of Tlaxcala. This letter, quite possibly, was a reaction to the views of Betanzos, which by this time were well-known in Mexico. Alberto María Carreño has printed this letter, in which Garcés wrote:

The time has come to speak against those who have judged wrongly those poor people, those who pretend that they are incapable and claim that their incapacity is sufficient reason to exclude them from the church. "Preach the Gospel to everyone, said the Lord. He who is baptized and believes in me shall be saved." Clearly he was speaking of human beings, not of brutes.

. . . Let us then for the love of God abandon this false doctrine of those who are moved by the suggestion of the devil that these Indians are incapable of our religion. This is truly the voice of Satan, determined that our religion and honor shall be destroyed, but this is a voice that comes from the avaricious throats of Christians, whose greed is such that in order to slake their thirst for wealth they insist that rational creatures made in the image of God are beasts and asses.[58]

Garcés also told the Pope that if some ecclesiastics make such allegations it is because they have "sweated little or not at all in the conversion of the Indians *(sudado poco, o nada en la conversión de los indios)"* and show little zeal in learning their language and their capabilities. Such allegations greatly harmed the miserable multitude of Indians, Garcés felt, because they hindered the preaching of the faith to them and gave some Spaniards an excuse to destroy them by wars, since it was held "no sin to depreciate them, to destroy them, to kill them." On the basis of his ten years' experience he could affirm: "They are justly called rational, they are completely intelligent and possessed of judgment." He stated that their children write in Latin and in Spanish better than the children of Spaniards, and he praised their splendid customs and ability in the same exalted tone used by Testera and the other ecclesiastics in 1533.

The bull *Sublimis Deus* clearly reflected the ideas brought forward by Minaya and Garcés on the nature of the Indians and on the need both to Christianize them and to protect their bodies and their property from the conquistadores. It is, indeed, an excellent example of the way in which theory and practicality are mixed together in the most fundamental and characteristic actions of Spain in America. Pope Paul III declared:

The sublime God so loved the human race that He created man in such wise that he might participate, not only in the good that other creatures enjoy, but endowed him with capacity to attain to the inaccessible and invisible Supreme Good and behold it face to face; and since man, according to the testimony of the sacred scriptures, has been created to enjoy eternal life and happiness, which none may obtain save through faith in our Lord Jesus Christ, it is necessary that he should possess the nature and faculties enabling him to receive that faith; and that whoever is thus endowed should be capable of receiving that same faith. Nor is it credible that any one should possess so little understanding as to desire the faith and yet be destitute of the most necessary faculty to enable him to receive it. Hence Christ, who is the Truth itself, that has never failed and can never fail, said to the preachers of the faith whom He chose for that office "Go ye and teach all nations." He said all, without exception, for all are capable of receiving the doctrines of the faith.

The enemy of the human race, who opposes all good deeds in order to bring men to destruction, beholding and envying this, invented a means never before heard of, by which he might hinder the preaching of God's word of Salvation to the people; he inspired his satellites who, to please him, have not hesitated to publish abroad that the Indians of the West and the South, and other people of whom We have recent knowledge should be treated as dumb brutes created for our service, pretending that they are incapable of receiving the catholic faith.

We, who, though unworthy, exercise on earth the power of our Lord and seek with all our might to bring those sheep of His flock who are outside into the fold committed to our charge, consider, however, that the Indians are truly men and that they are not only capable of understanding the catholic faith but, according to our information, they desire exceedingly to receive it. Desiring to provide ample remedy for these evils, We define and declare by these our letters, or by any translation thereof signed by any notary public and sealed with the seal of any ecclesiastical dignitary, to which the same credit shall be given as to the originals, that, notwithstanding whatever may have been or may be said to the contrary, the said Indians and all other people who may later be discovered by Christians, are by no means to be deprived of their liberty or the possession of their property, even though they be outside the faith of Jesus Christ; and that they may and should, freely and legitimately, enjoy their liberty and the possession of their property; nor should they be in any way enslaved; should the contrary happen it shall be null and of no effect.

By virtue of our apostolic authority We define and declare by these present letters, or by any translation thereof signed by any notary public and sealed with the seal of any ecclesiastical dignitary, which shall thus command the same obedience as the originals, that the said Indians and other peoples should be converted to the faith of Jesus Christ by preaching the word of God and by the example of good and holy living.[59]

This papal bull served as a principal weapon of Las Casas and other

Indian defenders, but its promulgation in 1537 did not stop the disputes. The controversy boiled up again, before and after 1542, when the New Laws were passed to protect the Indians from certain abuses, but in the very next year they were revised in favor of the colonists. It was at the time of the New Laws, too, that the learned Juan Ginés de Sepúlveda first began to give support and comfort to those Spaniards who held the encomienda system and the wars against the Indians to be just. A member of the Council of the Indies learned of these opinions and encouraged Sepúlveda to draw up in treatise form his thoughts on this subject, which set this eminent Aristotelian scholar on the road to the disputation with Las Casas at Valladolid.

Should Indians Be Educated?

Arguments over the nature of the Indians continued to be ventilated in America. One of the questions hotly debated in Mexico in these years was whether they should be given higher education.[60] Augustinians emphasized the importance of learning Indian languages, favored education for Indians, and in general had an optimistic view of Indian capacity, but other friars began to have doubts on the subject.[61] An Indian seminary had been opened by the Franciscans at Tlatelolco, but it did not prosper. According to Bernardino de Sahagún:

> The Spaniards and the monks of other Orders who witnessed the founding of this institution laughed loudly and jeered at us, thinking it beyond all doubt that no one could be clever enough to teach grammar to people of such small aptitude. But, after we had worked with them for two or three years, they had attained such a thorough knowledge of grammar that they understood, spoke, and wrote Latin, and even composed heroic verses [in it]. The Spaniards, both laymen and priests, were astonished. It was I who worked with these pupils for the first four years and who initiated them into all matters concerning the Latin language. When the laymen and the clergy were convinced that the Indians were making progress and were capable of progressing still more, they began to raise objections and oppose the enterprise.[62]

One of the Spaniards in Mexico who most vociferously opposed the friars in their work of higher education was Gerónimo López; he regarded teaching Indians to read and write as "very dangerous."[63] In his letter of 25 February 1545 to the Emperor he quoted, with approval, Montezuma's advice to Cortez to treat the Indians not "with love, but fear," and he reported that Judge Tejada of the *Audiencia* had been providing an excellent example of this policy.[64] But other secular Spaniards, such as Luis de Carvajal, disagreed. He strongly favored the conversion of the Indians, and emphatically did not support the idea that they were not ready for higher education, or even theology.[65] Another Spaniard, accused of mistreating Indians in Guatemala, defended himself in a letter to the *Audiencia* by alleging that they were not capable of becoming Christians.[66] Reports of ecclesiastics for this period contain much similar information on the depreciatory attitudes of Spaniards toward Indians.[67]

Betanzos was among those who opposed the training of Indians for the priesthood. Even Bishop Zumárraga had lost some of his former ardor for their education. Another prominent Franciscan, however, Alfonso de Castro, had prepared a treatise in Spain in the latter part of 1542, titled *Utrum indigenae novi orbis instruendi sint in mysteriis theologicis et artibus liberalibus*, that emphatically supported the idea that Indians should receive higher education.[68] The treatise had been drawn up at the request of the Crown for an opinion and was submitted to the Emperor in early 1543 with the written approval of Francisco de Vitoria and four other theologians.

Castro was a distinguished scholar who taught for thirty years in the Franciscan convent in Salamanca and had become famous for his treatise against Protestantism, *Adversus Haereses* (Paris, 1534). With Francisco de Vitoria, he was considered one of the outstanding theologians of the time. His 1542 opinion in favor of instruction for the Indians is of value in understanding the arguments against teaching them, which were:

1. The Indians are inconstant in the Christian faith;
2. They live obscene lives; because the Indians are like swine, Christians should not throw pearls before them;
3. The sacred texts of the Bible should not be shown to the people.

On the last point, Castro argued that the "mysteries of the Christian faith have value in themselves" and thus the Bible should not be hidden from the people. In this Castro's doctrine coincided with that of

Zumárraga, who in his *Conclusión exhortatoria* favored the translation of the Bible into the popular languages so that it might be read by everyone: "I do not understand why our doctrine should be hidden away from all but those few called theologians. No one can be called a Platonist unless he has read Plato. Likewise, no one may be called a Christian who has not read the doctrine of Jesus Christ." Castro's argument that the scriptures should be made widely available to the people must have surprised some of his contemporaries and perhaps explains why he buttressed his own views with the written support of five other established theologians, including the already famous Dominican, Francisco de Vitoria. These theologians not only approved Castro's doctrine, they also explained in detail why they did so. They had never been to the New World, and they may never have seen one of the Indians brought to Spain by missionaries or conquistadors. But they perceived the deep issues involved in Castro's treatise, and their formal opinions, as drawn up at the time Castro presented his treatise to Charles V, are worth giving in full.

Everything that has been said by the Reverend Father Fray Alfonso de Castro seems to me to have been said in a way that is learned, pious, and religious. I am all the more amazed that anyone should have been the author or inventor of such dangerous (or better, deadly) advice for keeping those barbarians from learning and instruction, both human and divine. Certainly not even the devil could have thought up a more effective means than this for instilling in those peoples a perpetual hatred for the Christian religion.

Many have abandoned Christ the Lord and the apostles after they had received the faith in different places. But it has not been thought for that reason that Christian doctrine should not be taught to others or that anyone should be kept from instruction.

Fray Francisco de Vitoria

Not without reason does the Church complain through the mouth of the prophet, saying, "They have often attacked me from my youth." [Ps. 128:1]. For many zealously but ignorantly attack the Church which they think they are defending and while they take care to meet one danger (and this sometimes a very small one) they run headlong into great and considerable harm.

Of the same type are those who, relying on their own opinion, do not cease to attack, ignorantly and with satanic means, the Church which has recently been born in the western islands and on the newly-discovered continent and which is nowadays growing in a wonderful way. For what battle can be more fierce and frightening than to despoil of their true and real goods those who have entrusted themselves to our faith, to tear out their eyes, to emasculate the strength of their wisdom, and to hurl them bound with the chains of ignorance into the densest darkness of error? But they did not succeed, he tells me, because even if the opponents of the Church increase every day, there is no lack of defenders, one of whom can conquer a thousand. On the contrary, there are more who are with us than against us. This can be seen in a special way in the many divine testimonies and testimonies of holy men. These many and weighty testimonies the Reverend Father Fray Alfonso de Castro cites in this work in a way that is just, pious and learned for the sake of the Church's teaching which has to be held in this matter. To his true and righteous opinion we happily subscribe and we admonish in Christ those who hold the contrary opinion to desist from such a dangerous position lest they be found guilty of such a depraved and destructive teaching on the day of the Lord.

Fray Francisco de Castillo
Fray Andrés Vega

I think that care should be taken that the peoples of the Indies be instructed with the liberal arts and the knowledge of Sacred Scripture. For who are we that we should show the partiality that Christ himself did not have? On the contrary, if these new peoples should see that they are carefully kept away from our mysteries, we would give them the opportunity to form a most deadly suspicion. Further, it is ridiculous to admit them to baptism, to the Eucharist, and to the absolution and forgiveness of sins, but not to the knowledge of Scripture. Now it is indeed true that when the unworthy are admitted to a participation in the sacraments that which is holy is thrown to dogs. But whoever are by right admitted to these are for that reason worthy to share in the mysteries.

The objections of our adversaries arise in part from ignorance of the gospel, in part from human wisdom which is always opposed to the gospel.

I wish everything that I have said to come under the correction of the Church.

Seville, La Rabida, January, 1543.

Fray Luis Carvajal

These declarations were made in Spain at a time when Sepúlveda's views on Indians were being approved by some members of the Council of the Indies who were then engaged in modifying the New Laws that had been promulgated in 1542 to protect the Indians. By 1545 the Council abandoned some of the New Laws; in particular, the encomienda system was continued by which Indians were required to work for Spaniards.

The Council of the Indies had been able to reverse some of the New

Laws partly because opinions contrary to the Indians continued to arrive from America. For example, Domingo de Betanzos and the Dominican provincial Diego de la Cruz sent a letter to Charles V on 5 May 1544 in which they declared:

> Indians should not study because no benefit may be expected from their education, first because they will not be able to preach for a long time inasmuch as this requires an authority over the people which they do not have; moreover, those who do study are worse than those who do not.
>
> In the second place, Indians are not stable persons to whom one should entrust the preaching of the Gospel. Finally, they do not have the ability to understand correctly and fully the Christian faith, nor is their language sufficient or copious enough as to be able to express our faith without great improprieties, which could lead easily to serious errors.[69]

Thus Indians should not be ordained as priests, which meant there was no need to allow them to study. The ecclesiastical council of 1555 forbade the creation of an Indian priesthood, which meant that the *colegio* lost one of the principal reasons for its existence—and the Tlatelolco seminary withered away. But before it perished it produced learned Indians, such as the grammarian Antonio Valeriano, later *gobernador* of Tenochtitlán, and also among its fruits were the Náhuatl-Latin herbal of Juan Badiano and Martín de la Cruz, some of the text and pictures included by the Franciscan Bernardino de Sahagún in his remarkable study of Indian culture. The herbal is "an Indian pictorial text of great beauty and distinction . . . a systematic catalogue of plants, classified in a European tradition, painted in an Indian style, its glosses written in Náhuatl by one learned native commentator and translated into Latin by another . . . which seemed to give promise, thirty years after the conquest, of a combined culture, with enduring Indian values enriched by a European admixture."[70] Both authors had been educated at Tlatelolco.

The consequences of the policy and practice that permitted the Colegio de Santa Cruz de Tlatelolco to fail and that made difficult, if not impossible, the entrance of Indians into the clergy were grave for Mexico and for the Church. As Robert Ricard, whose *La "Conquête Spirituelle" du Mexique* is the best brief treatment we have of the early ecclesiastical history of Mexico, explains, the Church came to be considered a largely foreign institution whose fortunes were dependent upon the favor of the governing power at the capital, the ruling white Spanish group. Indians began to enter the priesthood in the seventeenth century, it is true, but in a sporadic fashion, and they were relegated to humble positions in rural parishes. There came into being, says Ricard, two groups of clergy who knew very little of each other, who loved each other hardly at all, and whose mutual antagonism may be symbolized by the rivalry between the two Virgins: that of the Indians, the *Virgen de Guadalupe,* and that of the Spaniards, the *Virgen de los Remedios,* the *Gachupina.* The Indians were served by a poor and miserable clergy, but the Spaniards had a white clergy that belonged to the ruling class and enjoyed enormous revenues. Ricard concludes that "if the colegio at Tlatelolco had trained only one bishop for the country, the whole history of the Mexican Church would have been far different."[71]

The Retraction of Domingo de Betanzos

Betanzos not only opposed the education of Indians, he apparently believed they were doomed to extinction. In a letter dated 11 September 1545, he held—after some thirty years in the Indies—that all laws promulgated on the supposition that the Indians were to continue to exist "were dangerous, wrong, and destructive of all good in the republic," while laws were sound and good if they were predicated on the assumption that the Indians would all perish very soon![72] No wonder that Betanzos was one of those friars in Mexico who, along with Bishop Zumárraga, yearned to go to China, where the natives were said to be much more intelligent than the Indians.[73] And no wonder that Betanzos found many who questioned his opinions; it appears that he became somewhat unpopular among his fellow Dominicans during the later years of his life, for his first biographer denied that Betanzos returned to Spain because of *"graves persecuciones."*[74] By now, more than half a century after Columbus had first landed, opinions on Indians had crystallized in various ways—as Viceroy Antonio de Mendoza observed in the formal *Relación* he made in 1550 for the guidance of his successor, written about the same time that Betanzos made his retraction in Valladolid.

Viceroy Mendoza had strongly supported Bishop Zumárraga and

the other Franciscans when they established the school for Indians at Tlatelolco. Despite his many viceregal responsibilities, Mendoza liked to visit the school and to discuss in Latin points of grammar with the students to determine how well they were learning their new language. He warmly praised this educational effort, and the ability of the Indians, in his *Relación*. He stated that there would have been even greater success had it not been for the diseases which had taken away many of the most able students and had "passions and jealousies" not arisen among the Spaniards. He denounced as a "great error" the allegations of some that Indians were "incapable" of learning. He did not favor admitting them at once to the priesthood, but he definitely looked forward to the time when they would be sufficiently educated for the priesthood. However, he recognized that the battles over the capacity of the Indians had already created a polarization of attitudes among the Spaniards in Mexico:

Some will tell Your Majesty that the Indians are simple and humble folk, without malice or evil; others will represent the contrary, that they are very rich and are vagabonds who do not want to cultivate the land.

Do not believe either group, but treat the Indians like any other people and do not devise special rules and regulations for them. There are few persons in these parts who are not motivated, in their opinion of these Indians, by some interest, whether temporal or spiritual, or by some passion or ambition, good or bad.[75]

Thus when Betanzos decided to return to Spain in 1548, the "Indian question" was still debated furiously and bitterly in the New World. And he found that the same dispute was being waged in Valladolid, when he arrived there in 1549—just a year before Las Casas and Sepúlveda were to argue whether the Indians were natural slaves according to the doctrine of Aristotle.

As Manuel Giménez Fernández has pointed out, from the standpoint of the Indianist group at Court (led by Las Casas) it was essential to obtain Betanzos' retraction of his reputed earlier opinion on the Indians,[76] for it seems that in 1547, as Las Casas was on his last journey from the Indies to Spain, Rodrigo de Navarrete had informed Las Casas of the results of his Interrogatory on the Indians of Trinidad and Araucas. The tenor of the replies at this inquiry, which Navarrete took down as notary, indicated that the Indians had shown no interest in

Christianity despite fifteen or twenty years of effort by friars.[77] They were *"enemigos capitales"* of the ecclesiastics. The general opinion of the fourteen witnesses recorded by Navarrete was represented by the testimony of the colonist Pedro Moreno: "They are incapable of understanding Christian doctrine because they do not wish to learn it." Navarrete did not belong to either the "noble savage" or the "dirty dog" school, but this Interrogatory must have alarmed Las Casas.

Encomenderos were now present in Spain, vigorously working for the perpetuity of their grants of Indians, while Sepúlveda was actively opposing the *Confesionario* of Las Casas and developing his own doctrine that the encomienda and the wars against the Indians were just. It must have been considered vital, therefore—by Friar Diego Ruiz, prior of San Pablo monastery in Valladolid, by Friar Vicente de Las Casas (a Dominican but not a blood brother of the Bishop), and by other colleagues of Bartolomé de Las Casas—that Betanzos should definitively retract his previous opinions on Indians, made before the Council of the Indies. For many years Betanzos had been a leader among those who held the Indians to be somewhat "incapable" of the faith, who opposed their education, and who certainly did not share the very favorable view of Indian character that Las Casas and others advocated. Las Casas was then living in Valladolid, in the San Gregorio monastery, where he worked surrounded by the archive of manuscripts and books he had accumulated for his battles, at the time Betanzos arrived from Mexico to lodge in the adjoining San Pablo monastery. A few years before, probably in 1545, Betanzos had written Las Casas "a long and public letter, in which he explained why he considered that Las Casas had caused much trouble with his indiscreet zeal and restless, tumultuous nature; especially in Peru where he had been the cause of many scandals and deaths." Betanzos also deplored Las Casas's actions as Bishop in Chiapa, especially his angry altercations with Spaniards over Indians.[78]

Given these antecedents, it is quite possible that Las Casas, in the midst of the final preparation of his voluminous treatise entitled *Defense,* to be used in August 1550 against Sepúlveda, was the master-mind behind the formal retraction by Betanzos that then took place in San Pablo monastery in Valladolid on 18 September 1549. The event must have brought back poignant memories for Las Casas, for it was Betanzos who had persuaded him, a quarter century before, after the failure of his colony in Tierra Firme in 1522, to enter the Dominican Order instead of joining the Franciscans, among whom he also had good friends.[79] This intimate friendship may have cooled when Betanzos departed for Mexico in 1526, in company with the Dominican Tomás Ortiz, author of the diatribe against the Indians that was delivered before the Council of the Indies in 1525, perhaps as a reaction to the destruction (in 1520) of the Chiribichi mission, of which Ortiz had been vicar. For more than twenty years Las Casas must have winced at what he considered the dangerous and erroneous views of Betanzos on Indian capacity—in the same way that Betanzos considered Las Casas's writings and actions both wrong and dangerous. Now, when Betanzos was on the threshold of death, Las Casas and his other Dominican brothers were doubtless determined to have Betanzos cleanse his conscience of what they considered his impious doctrine, by retracting his statements on Indian capacity.

The lengthy legal documents that reveal the solemn drama as Betanzos prepared for death have come down to us, thanks to their preservation in a Bolivian monastery, and they tell a moving and significant story.

In the very noble city of Valladolid on September 13, in the year of Our Lord 1549, before me Antonio de Canseco, notary public of Your Majesties, being in the monastery of San Pablo of the Order of Preachers, in a room in that monastery there was an old man with head and beard shaven, lying in bed apparently ill but in his right mind, called Friar Domingo de Betanzos. And he handed over to me, the aforesaid notary public, a sheet of paper on which he told me he had written and declared certain matters, which concerned his conscience, and which related especially to the affairs of the Indies, which manuscript and declaration he delivered to me.

This declaration referred to a written memorial Betanzos had presented to the Council of the Indies some years before, in which he had declared that the Indians were beasts (*"bestias"*), that they had sinned, that God had condemned them, and that all of them would perish. Now, *in extremis*, he believed that he had erred "through not knowing their language or because of some other ignorance," and he formally retracted the statements in the memorial.[80]

This remarkable document reveals much about Betanzos and the controversies over the nature of the Indians, for this friar had for thirty-five years been a missionary in Mexico and had spoken and written so freely on the Indians' "incapacidad" that many of his ecclesiastical colleagues thought that he did not consider Indians capable of salvation. His Dominican brothers in Valladolid apparently knew all about his reputation for stubbornness in these opinions and were determined to have him repudiate the written declaration he had made before the Council of the Indies almost twenty years before. Even during the last days of his final illness Betanzos exhibited that "profound conviction" in his own beliefs that marked his long life.[81] The dying Dominican did not yield easily, but on the day he died he signed a document with trembling hand which was a formal retraction of his statement before the Council; however, Betanzos still maintained that he did not remember ever having spoken anything "against the Indians."

The interpretation by modern historians of the retraction is another proof—if such were needed—of the complexity and controversial nature of capacity as it pertained to the Indians. The Mexican historian Alberto María Carreño's first reaction was to question the authenticity of the document: "How did this document prepared by a notary public in Spain ever get to Sucre, Bolivia? Is it an original document? Or, if it is a true copy, when was it made?"[82] Carreño even thought that the document might have been prepared by personal enemies of Betanzos, but he decided at last to accept the retraction as authentic and considered it a demonstration that "at the gates of eternity" Betanzos was desirous of defending the Indians. Then Carreño adduced many examples, including Webster's dictionary, to support his interpretation that Betanzos had not meant to term Indians animals when he called them *bestias*; instead, he had really called them "coarse" or "not refined" persons. Betanzos had used the term only to refer to their beastly *customs,* Carreno concluded, and he cited Motolinia and others to justify his assertion that perhaps the majority of the Indians appeared to have "beastly habits" in the eyes of sixteenth-century Spaniards.[83] (Motolinia, however, as Víctor Adib emphasized, lauded the talent and customs of Indians in his *History of the Indians of New Spain.* Motolinia specifically countered the arguments of those who did not want the Indians educated with the comment that no cultivated person could be better occupied than in "showing those who do not know where lies the path to salvation and knowledge of God." And Adib, the modern Mexican commentator on Motolinia, well understood the decisive connection between the arguments over Indian capacity and their liberty or servitude).[84]

The Franciscan scholar Lino Gómez Canedo, the most recent interpreter of the views Betanzos held of the Indians, is puzzled by the attention given to this subject.[85] The problem has been complicated "a little" by the discovery of the retraction, he says, but he also feels that *"bestia"* must not be considered in the literal sense, and he is just as convinced as Carreño that Betanzos' true vision of Indians is best described in the undated memorial in which he denied ever saying that they were "wholly incapable" and stated that his true opinion was that they had "very little capacity, like children." Neither Carreño nor Gómez Canedo attempted to provide a chronological account of the dispute, nor to relate the continuous discussions of Indian capacity to the course of events in the New World. Both of them exhibit that indifference to New World reality that Juan Friede has noted among many Americanists: "They usually pay little attention to the study of the connections between the American reality and the ideas expressed in these controversies."[86]

Thus the story of the retraction did not end with the death of Betanzos. Indeed, the Council of the Indies showed great interest in the retraction, and apparently could not believe that it had been truly made. The Council summoned the notary, Antonio de Canseco, on 20 September, a week after Betanzos signed the document, and had him read it to them word by word. Then the Council ordered Canseco to take evidence from all four friars who had witnessed the document; the Council particularly wanted to know who had transcribed the retraction and who was responsible for its various emendations and erasures.[87] In the fascinating details revealed in these proceedings, which lasted until 10 December, we sense the urgency of the dispute on Indian capacity. Finally, the Council accepted all the documents and placed an official copy in its files. The four Dominican witnesses all swore that Betanzos had been fully aware of the nature of the retraction, including the various emendations and erasures in the document, which had been written in part by Friar Vicente de Las Casas and partly by the prior, Friar Diego Ruiz, because Betanzos' hand had trembled. All deposed that the document had been read to Betanzos several times, to make certain that he understood all of it, and that he had signed it in their presence.

But the retraction and the lengthy legal maneuverings that follow-ed do not answer the fundamental question: Had Domingo de Betan-zos really called the Indians beasts in his first deposition to the Council of the Indies in 1532 or 1533? If he had, exactly what had he meant by this term? And did his Dominican brothers, later in Valladolid, really persuade him that he had been wrong in his previous opinions, or did they merely bring "holy pressure" to bear? We know from the testimony of Friar Diego Ruiz that the final text of the retraction was shown to Betanzos just the day before his death and that he signed it only as he received extreme unction the morning he died, 13 September 1549.[88] Finally, why had Betanzos spent so much time in the New World—more than thirty years of his life—without learning the language of any of the Indians? Did he suffer, as other missionaries have, from what anthropologists term "culture shock" on en-countering so many different kinds of people with whom he could not communicate? Was this the true cause of his apparent inability to reach any firm and clear conclusion on the capacity of the Indians?

On one point we may be certain: the discovery of these documents in Bolivia in a volume of manuscripts titled *Tratado de Indias de Monseñor de Chiapas y el Doctor Sepúlveda* and the contents of the various 1549 depositions required by the Council of the Indies show unmistakably that the retraction at San Pablo monastery was considered part of the Las Casas-Sepúlveda controversy. Moreover, whatever may have been the exact anthropological or philosophical meaning that *"bestia"* had for Betanzos, his Dominican brothers were certain that the propositions he had stated before the Council of the Indies were so "wrong, scandalous, offensive, and unfounded" that they would not allow the friar to die before he had formally retracted them. With this document on file in the archives of the Council of the Indies, Las Casas and his colleagues must have felt that the decks were at least partially cleared for the final battle. Now there was no one of any stature who publicly held such a low opinion of Indian capacity as Betanzos was supposed to have held—except the chronicler Gonzalo Fernández de Oviedo y Valdés. His views afforded great comfort to Sepúlveda, but Las Casas was prepared to cope with these opinions, as we shall see.

At the very time that the retraction of Betanzos was so suspiciously examined by the Council of the Indies, Las Casas must have been hard at work, laboring far into the night in his cell at San Gregorio monastery to prepare his case against his greatest enemy and most skillful opponent, Juan Ginés de Sepúlveda, who also was in Valladolid, busily drawing up his representations. On 23 September 1549 Sepúlveda informed Prince Philip that he had prepared three summaries of his book on the Indies to defend himself from "the calumnies of some passionate friars," with Las Casas as *caudillo,* whom he described as *"homo natura factiosus, et turbulentus."*[89] He awaited royal authorization to publish his own book, but permission was never granted; instead, the Crown determined upon a disputation between these learned and contentious men.

Before considering this significant event in the history of Spain in America—indeed, in the expansion of Europe—we turn to the ideas of Oviedo, for his writings constituted the most powerful arguments in support of Sepúlveda's view of the incapacity of the Indians.

"A Deadly Enemy of the Indians": The Royal Historian Gonzalo Fernández de Oviedo y Valdés

In the passionate *Defense* presented before the Valladolid junta in 1550, Las Casas leveled his heaviest doctrinal attacks on Sepúlveda; he also spoke out sharply and bitterly against his ancient adversary, the royal officer and official historian Gonzalo Fernández de Oviedo y Valdés, whom he considered a "deadly enemy of the Indians."[90] Because historians who discuss the juridical-theological questions raised by the appearance of the American Indian sometimes ignore the American reality involved and because Oviedo's views on Indian nature commanded such a central position in the Valladolid disputation, some detailed attention to Oviedo's life in America and to his views will help put the controversy in proper perspective.[91] Moreover, according to a Spanish historian, Oviedo illustrates—in a particularly convincing way—the perils of studying a man's ideas without reference to his life: "To consider such a person in a vacuum, to speculate on the ideas of a man so pragmatic, opportunistic, and such an able simulator as Oviedo is a very unfruitful activity."[92]

For the purposes of this study, the life of Oviedo began on 11 April 1514, when he first sailed for the New World as a notary and inspector (*veedor*) in the expedition commanded by the notorious Pedro Arias de

Ávila (Pedrarias).[93] It was a large and important company, numbering some 2,000 Spaniards who were transported in twenty-two ships, that included Hernando de Soto, Bernal Díaz del Castillo, Francisco de Montejo, and other conquistadores who were to make their mark in the New World, as well as Martín Fernández de Enciso, who a few years later published the first book on America in Spanish.

The expedition also was noteworthy because so much opposition had been raised against its departure by Spanish friends of the Indians that they had prevailed upon King Ferdinand to hold Pedrarias and his men in Spain until a committee of theologians could draw up proper instructions to make certain that no unjust wars would be waged against the natives. These theologians met in the Dominican monastery of San Pablo in Valladolid, where thirty-five years later Domingo de Betanzos was to sign the much-discussed "Retraction" on the nature of the Indians. In 1513 Fernández de Enciso argued before the theologians that God had assigned the Indies to Spain, by the papal donation to Ferdinand and Isabella, just as the Jews had been given their Promised Land. Therefore "the king might very justly send men to require those idolatrous Indians to hand over their land to him, for it was given him by the pope. If the Indians would not do this, he might justly wage war against them, kill them and enslave those captured in war, precisely as Joshua treated the inhabitants of the land of Canaan."[94]

Then the royal lawyer, Juan López Palacios Rubios, prepared the text of a manifesto, or "Requirement," which was to be read to the Indians before hostilities could legally begin. By its terms, the Indians were required to acknowledge "the Church as the Ruler and Superior of the whole world and the supreme pontiff called the Pope, and in his name the King and Queen Juana in his stead as superiors, lords, and kings of these islands and this Tierra Firme by virtue of said donation." Then Indians were called upon to allow the faith to be preached to them.

If the Indians immediately acknowledged these obligations, well and good. But if they did not, the Requirement listed the punitive steps the Spaniards would take forthwith. They would enter the land with fire and sword and subjugate the inhabitants by force to the Church and the Crown. Lastly, in the words of the document, the Spaniards were to warn the Indians:

We shall take you and your wives and your children, and shall make slaves of them, and as such shall sell and dispose of them as their Highnesses may command; and we shall take away your goods, and shall do all the harm and damage that we can, as to vassals who do not obey, and refuse to receive their lord, and resist and contradict him; and we protest that the deaths and losses which shall accrue from this are your fault, and not that of their Highnesses, or ours, nor of these gentlemen who come with us. And that we have said this to you and made this Requirement, we request the notary here present to give us his testimony in writing, and we ask the rest who are present that they should be witnesses of this Requirement.[95]

One of Oviedo's first official acts after landing on the northern coast of South America (12 July 1514) was to accompany a reconnoitering expedition of some 300 men that set out from Santa Marta and to read the Requirement as provided by law. After marching for more than two leagues without seeing an Indian, the expedition entered a deserted village, where Oviedo declared:

Good Sirs, it appears to me that these Indians will not listen to the theology of this Requirement, and that you have no one who can make them understand it; would Your Honor be pleased to keep it until we have some one of these Indians in a cage, in order that he may learn it at his leisure and my Lord Bishop may explain it to him?

Oviedo then gave the document to the captain, who "took it with much laughter, in which all those who heard the speech, joined."[96]

A complete list of the events that occurred when the requirement formalities ordered by King Ferdinand were carried out in America, more or less according to the law, might tax the reader's patience and credulity. On one occasion the proclamation was made according to the King's instructions, but at the same time the Spaniards cleverly plied the Indians with food, drink, bonnets, cloth, shirts, hoods, and "other little trifles from Castile." This combination of theology and gifts seems to have been effective. The outcome was far different, however, when Captain Juan de Ayora captured a number of Indians, linked them together with ropes tied around their necks, and then read them the Requirement. According to Oviedo:

It appears that they had been suddenly pounced upon and bound before they had learnt or understood anything about Pope or Church, or any one of the many things said in the Requirement; and that after they had been put in chains someone read the Requirement without knowing their language and without any interpreters, and without either the reader or the Indians understanding their language, they had no chance to reply, being immediately carried away prisoners, the Spaniards not failing to use the stick on those who did not go fast enough.[97]

Fernández de Enciso, who had been instrumental in drawing up the manifesto, recorded another Requirement incident in his *Suma de geografía* (1519). The cacique of Cenu, having insisted that an interpreter explain the whole document, thereupon gave his reaction: "The part about there being one God who ruled heaven and earth he approved; as for the pope who gave away lands that he didn't own, he must have been drunk; and a king who asked for and acquired such a gift must have been crazy."[98]

Spaniards themselves, when describing this document, have often shared the dilemma of Las Casas, who on reading it, confessed he could not decide whether to laugh or to weep. He roundly denounced it on practical as well as theoretical grounds, pointing out the manifest injustice of the whole business. Others found it infinitely ridiculous, and even its author, Palacios Rubios, "laughed often" when Oviedo recounted his own experiences and instances of how some captains had put the Requirement into practice, although the learned doctor still believed that it satisfied the demands of the Christian conscience when executed in the manner originally intended. Apologists or semi-apologists, however, are to be found even today. Constantino Bayle, the Spanish Jesuit who vigorously combated the Black Legend of Spanish cruelty, oppression, and obscurantism in America, declared: "What was wrong with the Requirement was that it was intended for men, but read to half-beasts (*medio bestias*)."[99]

As royal official, one of Oviedo's functions was to have charge of the iron that was used to brand Indian slaves and to collect one *tomín* of gold as his fee for each Indian so branded. As the author of the most recent and best analysis of his life observes, Oviedo made no mention of these activities when he wrote his *History*: "Today we are able to see how skillfully Oviedo reported these events in his *History* in such a way as to hide his participation in the business of branding slaves, from which he personally derived profit."[100] But Oviedo described how he had deceived the Indians in Tierra Firme in 1521 by selling them axes of such inferior quality that they did not keep their edge, so that a few months later he had been able to make a profit from the same Indians a second time by charging them for sharpening the axes![101] As Pérez de Tudela remarks, his was an "expert hypocrisy which enabled him to give an impression of personal purity although in reality he was as tainted as any of the conquistadores."[102]

Las Casas probably learned of Oviedo's participation in the fruits of the Conquest during these early years, but it appears that they first came to know, and dislike, each other in Barcelona in 1519, when Bishop Juan Quevedo of Tierra Firme declared before King Charles that the Indians were slaves by nature, according to the Aristotelian concept. Oviedo had not found the Indians as mild and virtuous as Las Casas painted them—but he was also seeking a grant of land. He was granted the land he asked for, Santa Marta, but not the authorization for the one-hundred noblemen of the Order of Santiago he requested, his concept of colonization being distinctly aristocratic. He mocked Las Casas's preference for simple farmers, and later gave an ironical and distorted account of the experiment, as well as Las Casas's entrance into the Dominican Order.[103] Las Casas saw little or no good in Oviedo's work in the New World, twitted him for not knowing Latin, and—above all—profoundly distrusted his pessimistic views on Indian capacity.[104]

Since the encounter in Barcelona, Las Casas remained on the alert against the ideas and influence of a person so inimical to what he considered the well-being of the Indians. For his part, Oviedo continued his career as a royal official in America, in various posts, and devoted some time to literature and to writing a brief work titled *De la natural historia de las Indias* (1526). The first part of his great work, *Historia general y natural de las Indias, islas y Tierra Firme del mar Océano*, was published in part in 1535, and another edition appeared about the time Las Casas returned from America for the last time (1547). Las Casas also learned that Sepúlveda was becoming increasingly active in propagating his view that war against the Indians to convert them was just, and he could not have been surprised to discover that this jurist—who had never been to the New World—was invoking the authority of Oviedo to support his proposition that the Indians were so incapable as to justify their slavery according to the Aristotelian doctrine. Thus Oviedo's concepts of the nature of the Indians and the American reality became a part of the *Defense* expounded by Las Casas in 1550.

These two "giants among the first historians in the New World,"[105] Las Casas and Oviedo, had eyed each other warily since their first clash in 1519. The Colombian scholar Víctor Manuel Patiño has emphasized the fact that Las Casas fought many opponents during his long life— Fonseca, Bishop Quevedo, Gil Quintana, Motolinía, and Sepúlveda— but none of them so absorbed his time and thought as Oviedo:

It was a hidden and mutually felt rancor that existed between Las Casas and Oviedo, not at all a temporary phenomenon, but an antagonism which out-lasted both their lives . . . and as time passed, the whole influence of Spain in America became polarized around fundamentally opposed concepts: the tendency toward Iberian dictatorship and providentialism sustained by Oviedo, as opposed to the more universal and democratic attitude of Las Casas, who saw in Spain the vessel for the transmission of a different, but not necessarily superior, culture to the New World.[106]

Even in their detailed descriptions of such products as the humble peanut they manifested radically different interpretations that reflected social overtones. Oviedo looked upon the peanut, cultivated and eaten by the island natives, as unworthy of Spaniards and suitable only for children and slaves, whereas Las Casas described it as more delicious than any Spanish nut or dried fruit.[107]

For the late Paraguayan writer, Juan Natalicio González, Las Casas was an American in spirit whereas Oviedo represented the Old World.[108] The Argentine Fernando Márquez Miranda is more explicit:

Oviedo was a man of the nobility who represented the opinion of the privileg-ed, or of those who aspired to be, and was full of aristocratic prejudices created by birth and education, while Las Casas is the vibrant popular voice who is able to reach court circles by his will, integrity and talent. Las Casas is, without being aware of it, the first American voice. Oviedo looks at the New World from the outside, whereas his opponent views it from within.[109]

Both of these ancient and experienced antagonists possessed an "electric" quality that either attracted or repelled their contemporaries; and even today's historians are affected by the lively quarrel they carried on in the sixteenth century.

In some respects Las Casas and Oviedo were alike: both were extremely productive writers; moreover, at times Oviedo criticized conquistadores as passionately as Las Casas did, though on a more selective basis. For example, he accused his special enemy, Pedrarias, of being responsible for the death of two million Indians.[110] When Oviedo spoke of thousands of human sacrifices by Indians, Las Casas took him to task for what he believed was an unjustifiable numerical exaggeration. Las Casas included much detail on his enemies in his various writings, but Oviedo rarely did so.[111] They disagreed profoundly, however, on the nature of the Indians and on the kind of sovereignty Spain exercised in the New World. But, as Alberto Mario Salas has declared: "Oviedo did not defend the conquest unconditionally . . . . His words constituted an energetic criticism of some conquistadores rather than a defense of the Indians." Salas also concluded that Oviedo criticized conquistadores largely for personal reasons: "His attitude basically was a negative one, full of antipathy and repugnance, lacking the profoundly Christian spirit which characterized his antagonist, the friar Las Casas."[112] Lastly, it may be observed that Las Casas at times, though rarely, also spoke out on behalf of "old citizens and conquistadores."[113]

Oviedo's Basic Views on Indians

Historians have not yet reached agreement on Oviedo's real views on Indians. Recently, scholars have warned against adopting too simplistic an approach—or against portraying Oviedo's theories without reference to the world in which he lived. Oviedo's views on Indians evolved somewhat, so that a chronological account of his statements on Indian capacity will help explain why, at the time of the confrontation with Sepúlveda in Valladolid, a refutation of Oviedo had become such a significant part of the document presented by Las Casas, his *Defense Against the Persecutors and Slanderers of the Peoples of the New World Discovered Across the Seas.*[114]

Of the major propositions Oviedo set forth, three are of special relevance to this discussion:

1. *The Indies were once under the authority of the Visigothic monarchy in Spain; hence the Castilian kings were merely "recovering" lands that had once been Spanish.*[115]

Oviedo explained this theory in considerable detail, whereas Las

Casas characterized it as "improbable, fictitious, and frivolous,"[116] and a modern historian has described it as "grotesque." But he also observed: "Oviedo's learning may have been a trifle bizarre, but his intent was not obscure. It was to bypass the Alexandrine bulls which in another place he dismissed in one sentence as an injunction to preach the Gospel to the Indians."[117]

2. *The Christian faith had been brought to the Indians centuries before Columbus.*

Oviedo based this remarkable assumption on an unproved declaration by Pope Gregory the Great (590-604) that "the Holy Church has already preached the mystery of Redemption in all parts of the world."[118] According to Oviedo, the consequences for the Indians were clear: Not only had they forgotten the truths of the faith, but when "He remembered them again they had fallen into such evil ways that He consented to their extermination"—except for a few innocent young ones who had been baptized.[119]

This interpretation gives pause to the Spanish historian Pérez de Tudela, who paints a generally favorable picture of Oviedo as "a figure through whose biography we may observe the flowering of the Spanish empire," but who also states: "Oviedo is not wholly crystal clear when he tries to explain the extermination of the Indians on Hispaniola as a divine punishment on account of their crimes and abominable customs."[120]

3. *The Indians are generally incapable of becoming Christians.*

Spanish historians who wrote about the New World paid much attention to the Indians, and Oviedo was no exception. In his first work, *Natural History of the West Indies* (1526), he gave principal attention to plants and animals, but he concentrated on the Indians of Tierra Firme in chapter 10. His treatment was largely descriptive, but he mentioned one matter that he later emphasized in his larger history to indicate how important he considered it:

I also happened to think of something that I have observed many times with regard to these Indians. Their skulls are four times thicker than those of the Christians. And so when one wages war with them and comes to hand to hand fighting, one must be very careful not to hit them on the head with the sword, because I have seen many swords broken in this fashion. In addition to being thick, their skulls are very strong.[121]

Oviedo's opinion, as a royal official with experience in America, had been sought in 1525 by the newly established Council of the Indies, about the time he was getting his *Natural History of the West Indies* ready for the press.[122] The Council was faced with the problem of whether to continue permitting experiments in America for the purpose of determining whether Indians could live by themselves, free of Spanish domination. The text of Oviedo's opinion has not been found, but its tenor apparently was similar to his later pessimistic depositions before the Council of the Indies. Another formal opinion, probably given in 1530 or 1531, recommended that the way to bring peace to Hispaniola was to keep the Indians in subjection and to have them serve Spaniards, as in the past, because one of the reasons for the recent uprisings of the cacique Enriquillo was the fact that the Indians had been given to understand that they were free.[123]

A third opinion—a formal one made by Oviedo before the Council in 1532 in response to an interrogatory answered by other persons as well—also is found in manuscript.[124] Indian supporters had persuaded the Council to issue its declaration against encomiendas (1529) and later, an anti-slavery provision (1530), but in 1532 the dispute boiled again. (It was probably at this time that Domingo de Betanzos delivered himself of that pessimistic verdict on Indian capacity before the Council, which so alarmed Bishop Sebastián Ramírez de Fuenleal and others in Mexico, and which he retracted as he lay dying in Valladolid a few months before Las Casas and Sepúlveda began their disputation.) Oviedo deposed before the Council that some Indians were sodomites, many ate human flesh, were idolatrous, sacrificed human beings, and were vicious people without pity who treated even their friends and relatives like inhuman beasts (*"bestias despiadadas"*). Indian children forgot the good customs taught them; and Oviedo believed that very few of those who reached manhood would be saved.[125]

The dean of Santo Domingo of Hispaniola, Rodrigo de Bastidas, also rendered an unfavorable opinion before the Council, closing with the phrase: "They are all bestial and incapable; thus they live and die bestially."[126] The dean of Tierra Firme deposed that the Indians were "of little capacity and little understanding,"[127] as did the veteran colonist Francisco de Barrionuevo.[128]

Oviedo's views of Indians, however, have been known to the world, principally through his larger and more significant work, the *Historia general y natural de las Indias*, whose first edition appeared in 1535 and comprised the nineteen books of Part I.[129] Sepúlveda found therein what he cited as an authorized and expert opinion, and concluded that the Indians in general were so backward and bestial that they should be converted by force of arms and made to serve the Spaniards as natural slaves, according to the dictates of Aristotle.

Another edition of Part I of Oviedo's history was published at Salamanca in 1547, which may have been why Las Casas devoted so much of his *Defense* to demolishing what he was passionately convinced were recently printed un-Christian, erroneous, and iniquitous ideas. In his *Historia de las Indias,* Las Casas bitterly declared that the world prefers to believe in evil and considers anything printed to be true, and he concluded: "If Oviedo's history carried at the beginning a notice that its author had been a conquistador, a robber and killer of Indians, who had despatched them to the mines—as he himself states and confesses—at least prudent readers would have had little confidence in his history."[130] In any event, Las Casas apparently was successful in preventing the publication of the balance of Oviedo's work, whose complete *Historia* (fifty books) did not appear until the nineteenth century, when the Real Academia de la Historia published it in preference to the *Historia de las Indias* of Las Casas.

In his latter chapters Oviedo somewhat mitigated his harsh judgment on the Indians, and at one point seemed to feel there was even some hope that in time they might become Christians.[131] Was this apparent change the result of his later knowledge about the higher Indian civilizations? Oviedo had slight personal experience of the mainland, which was limited to a few visits (including a slaving expedition to Nicaragua), but he could have acquired much information from the many Spaniards who passed to and from New Spain and Peru by way of Hispaniola during his many years in the Caribbean. As official historian, he would have been eager to obtain as much information as possible. We know that in 1541 he interviewed the survivors of Francisco de Orellana's epic voyage down the Amazon and recorded their names for posterity.

But even if Las Casas had known in 1550 (which of course is possible) the contents of the remaining chapters of Oviedo's *Historia*, which were still in manuscript form, it is doubtful that he would have considered their cautious and tentative remarks on Indian capacity sufficient to wipe out the published, strongly worded denigration of Indians that the royal chronicler had made in the two editions of Part I of the *Historia,* which had become widely known to the world through numerous translations.[132]

In recent years Oviedo's views on the nature of the Indians have been given increasing attention. Alberto Mario Salas, the Argentine scholar who has published one of the most penetrating analyses of the early chroniclers of the Conquest, reached this conclusion about Oviedo:

His undeniable interest in the maintenance of *encomiendas* and *repartimientos,* and that they be made perpetual, led him to look upon the Indians, especially those on the islands, as a poor and detestable people, full of vicious and criminal customs. Sodomy, cowardice, suicide for no reason whatsoever, laziness, lack of gratitude, bestial understanding, are all words and concepts which Oviedo uses with a truly astonishing frequency . . . . His Indians are not the gracious unclothed natives that Columbus saw, nor the exotic beings of Peter Martyr, nor the mild and ingenuous folk of Las Casas. To Oviedo Indians are dirty, lying, cowardly, people who commit suicide because they are bored or because they wish to molest the Spaniards, a people who neither know how to work or wish to. As for their vices, it is preferable not to attempt a catalog of them.[133]

A recent study devoted to Oviedo's Indian concepts, by the Mexican scholar Josefina Zoraida Vázquez Vera, attempted to present the man in a much more favorable light.[134] The author analyzes his thought in a highly theoretical way, without mentioning the "American reality" of Oviedo's life, and draws a fine distinction between Oviedo's attitude on "rationality as essence or nature" and "rationality as accident or history."[135] But even this author concedes that "the Indian, on the supposition that he is a human being, must possess reason; however, Oviedo seems to contradict himself continually by speaking of their irrationality . . . . The basic concept he has of the Indian is truly terrible."[136]

The best solution, Oviedo held, would be for the Indians to disappear from the face of the earth—which links him with the view held by Domingo de Betanzos. Oviedo wrote constantly that "God is going to destroy them soon," and he considered that such extermination would be "an enormous mercy of God."[137] Even an "otherwise high-minded person," according to Alonso de la Vera Cruz, who was apparently referring to Sepúlveda, wanted "to destroy them and hand them over to the power of the Spaniards in the same way as God once handed over the Canaanites to the Israelites."[138]

Oviedo stated in Part II of his *Historia general y natural de las Indias* (1545) that Las Casas eventually became satisfied with the former's writings; but this seems very doubtful.[139] Even today, Oviedo is considered one of the most articulate and influential Spaniards of the Conquest period who—all this notwithstanding—had little use for the Indians. As Professor Benjamin Keen has stated, Oviedo "displayed the same implacable hostility toward the relatively primitive Indians of the Caribbean area, whom he knew at first hand, (as) toward the advanced Aztec civilization, which he knew not at all."[140] Las Casas outlived his opponent—in time as in reputation. In his *Historia Apologética* he denounced Oviedo's accusation of sodomy against the Indians, and he described him as "another one, now dead, who very bitterly defamed these people, in whose history God had little share"[141]—a judgment never altered by Las Casas in any of his writings that have come down to us.

The preceding discussion of the controversy among Spaniards in the first half of the sixteenth century on the true nature of the Indians leads to at least one firm conclusion: no agreement was reached by the many ecclesiastics, colonists, royal officials, jurists, and others who participated in the dispute. Thus it is not surprising that a baffled Crown and its advisors turned to a commission of wise men and experts to hear the argument. It is time, therefore, that we turn to the origin and conduct of the disputation between Las Casas and Sepúlveda, which began in August 1550 in Valladolid.

NOTES

1. Blau (1964), p. 13.
2. Hanke (1935b), p. 21.
3. For the circumstances and the results of this sermon, see Hanke (1965a), pp. 17ff.

4. Chamberlain (1939).
5. Konetzke (1958), p. 182.
6. Konetzke made this statement during the 1957 Washington, D.C. Conference on the Evangelization of America sponsored by the Academy of American Franciscan History. The discussion from which it is taken has not been printed, but Father Antonine Tibesar, O.F.M., was kind enough to provide me with a typewritten copy. For a transcript of Dr. Konetzke's remarks, see appendix 1. For a comment on Dr. Konetzke's remarks by Professor Harold B. Johnson, see appendix 2.

    Jaime Vicens Vives remarked upon the ideal of a crusade, which "seems to conflict with the subsequent tendency of Christians, Moors, and Jews to achieve a harmonious accord within a common social and intellectual abode." He added: "The contradiction does exist; the explanation is that Christian-Islamic integration was an urban event, while the antagonism between Christians and converted Muslims (Moriscos) was a rural phenomenon. Royalty oscillated between the two camps, protecting now one and then the other, until the decision of the Catholic Monarchs—a decision that is dramatic from so many points of view." Vicens Vives (1967), pp. 164-65.
7. Antonio Rumeu de Armas (1967) recently provided an excellent study on this subject in his monograph "Los problemas derivados del contacto de razas en los albores del Renacimiento." See especially the section "El mundo de los neoinfieles americanos" (pp. 93-103). I have not been able to consult his recent *La política indigenista de los Reyes Católicos*. For Archbishop Talavera, see Elliott (1963), pp. 39-40.
8. See the pioneering contribution by Wölfel (1930) and the more general study by Zavala (1935), I, 85-88.
9. For an up-to-date review of the scattered literature on this subject, see Ricard (1968), pp. 232-33. This crucial subject still awaits its investigator. What George Kubler wrote more than twenty years ago still holds: "Singularly little has been written about the European antecedents of the Apostolic Twelve" (Kubler [1948] I, 4). Azcona has recently reached this conclusion: "Todavia no se ha estudiado profundamente el fenómeno misional dentro de la Orden franciscana de cara a la conversión de los moros granadinos y africanos y de los indios americanos" (Azcona [1964], p. 702, n. 112). For a general view of the early reforms, see García Villoslada and Llorca (1967), Vol. III, chap. 18.

    A massive beginning has been made on the early period of the reform in Spain in *Introducción a los orígenes de la Observancia en España. Las reformas en los siglos XV y XVI;* published by the Spanish Franciscan review *Archivo Ibero-Americano,* año XVII (1957), nos. 65-68. See also Bataillon (1959, 1966), Gómez Canedo (1966b), Haubert (1969), López (1930), Martín (1966), Meseguer Fernández (1955), Ybot León (1954), and Zavala (1941, 1965, 1971). Besides the challenge of millions of Indians to be converted and the growing strength of Protestantism, there was great fear in Europe of the Ottoman Turks. In 1555 the French poet Pierre de Ronsard proposed that Europe be saved by abandoning it to the Ottomans and transporting European societies *in toto* to the New World, where they could preserve their values and resume their development unhindered by Moslem attacks (Coles [1968], p. 148).
10. Pou y Martí (1924), pp. 295-96.

11. The Bernal Díaz quotation comes from Vial Correa (1964), p. 90. Was the crusading spirit in the later Middle Ages so faint, or at least so "national," in Spain that it is to be distinguished from that of other European nations? Aziz A. Atiya thought it was (Atiya [1938], p. 481); see also his later summary (Atiya [1962]). But perhaps Spaniards also lacked crusading zeal. According to one writer: "Por fin, con la intervención de bandas de mercenarios aventureros y piratas en las expediciones contra los islamitas, se desvirtúa el original impulso religioso y prevalece el afán de lucro que no distingue entre el enemigo infiel y la sufrida población cristiana de Oriente" (Beinert [1967], p. 48). The Peruvian historian referred to, E. Choy, is controversial rather than convincing; see Choy (1958), pp. 251, 255, 259. The traditional opposing view can be found in the article "El alma critiana del conquistador de América: no veremos en él al guerrero o al hombre de armas, sino al creyente" by Velasco (1964), no. 63, p. 257.

Another interpretation of the Conquest, and of the ideas developed by the theologians as they contemplated the Conquest, has been given by Jaime Concha, who considers such a thinker as Francisco de Vitoria essentially and inevitably a supporter of the conquistadores: "El pensamiento es impotente frente a los poderes del mundo, precisamente porque depende de ellos" (Concha [1966], p. 120).

12. Las Casas (1951), III, 93-95.

13. In a letter to the author dated 15 December 1969. The following passage, quoted by permission of Professor Bishko, gives a more detailed explanation of his view:

"In the case of conversion, what do we have? In 12th- and 13th-century Spain an enormously successful expansion of Christian territory against [the] Muslim and the incorporation of significant numbers of Jews and far more of Muslims into the kingdoms of Castile, Aragon and Portugal. From this point to the Reyes Catolicos, one finds both an actual convivencia of the three creeds (broken down in part by the anti-Jewish massacres of 1391) along with a theoretical intolerance of dissident religion as such. Father Ignatius Burns's 'Social Riots on the Christian-Moslem Frontier, Thirteenth Century Valencia' (*American Historical Review*, LXVI [1961], 378-400), illustrates the resultant situation—an uneasy side-by-side juxtaposition, of irreconcilable beliefs, and a rising intolerance especially visible on the Christian side under the impact of extra-Iberian crusading thought. To be sure, the rise of the mendicants in the 13th century, or of figures like Ramón Lull, lead to interest in missionary enterprise, chiefly, it would seem, at a distance, as in North Africa. What is missing, however, all through the Later Middle Ages in Spain, is either an awareness of the nature of conversion or the development of institutional structures to accomplish it. To be sure, Christians believed strongly that Moors and Jews should accept Christianity; and not infrequently sought to bring this about by force, although this seems to occur not as a regular rule but in isolated or specific places under conditions of intense emotion or immediate popular pressure.

"On the other hand, if one looks to see what the Spanish Church was doing to bring about persuasion of non-Christians, their instruction in the faith, in a word, evangelistic enterprise, one does not find it, at least in any significant degree. Even with the growing success of the Observancia in the 14th and

15th centuries, it is not really until the end of the latter century and the first years of the 16th, that one encounters in the extreme left-wing Franciscans of the Strictísima Observancia people like Juan de Guadalupe throwing themselves into the conversion of the Granadan Moors. It is from this group that the *Doce Apóstoles* of Nueva España come; and similar devoted missionary enterprises in other parts of the Indies. . . . Then, in the case of the Montesinos sermon of 1511, another factor is present which you have no doubt noted. Medieval tradition frowned upon the enslavement of Christians. As Verlinden has said in his *L'Esclavage au Moyen Age* (t. I), medieval slaves, at least when acquired, tended heavily to be pagans, Muslims or—not to be too fussy over details—Eastern Christians. This did not mean that they were not induced by their masters to become Christians of the right Western sort nor did it entail their emancipation when they did; cf. the Negroes brought to Lagos and Lisboa by Dom Henrique's captains, and of whom Azurara speaks as justifiably enslaved because this provided the opportunity to save their souls. But ordinarily one didn't start with enslavement of Christians; and this may have led the encomenderos to take a dim view of conversion *first*.

"It is such factors as these in the whole picture—strongly growing feeling in later medieval Iberia towards uniformity of creed and increasing frailty of the sort of convivencia that one finds in, say, India today as between Hindus and Muslims; failure of the Spanish Church, and thus even more of the laity, to adopt conversionism and missionary enterprise as a positive instrument until the late appearance of the Strictísima Observancia, the non-enslavement of already converted Christians—that must be reckoned with in any comprehensive understanding."

Another question upon which Dr. Bishko asks for more light is the origin of the *doctrina* in the Peninsula before 1492. He adds, in a note to the author dated 12 April 1970: "Much more needs to be done with the historical development of the catechetical literature in the Spanish Church of the fifteenth and sixteenth centuries for the light this may throw upon the attitudes toward, and methods of conversion of, Jews and Moors."

14. Pérez de Tudela (1956), p. 259.
15. For an excellent and detailed exposition of missionary activities in the earliest years, see Olmedo (1953).
16. As quoted by Rumeu de Armas (1967), p. 99.
17. Gibson (1968), p. 55. Some of the royal orders in these early years did not mention conversion (Altamira [1942]), but the general tenor of instructions was to foster conversion and education. The royal order to Ovando of 1503 provided "que se hiziese hazer una casa adonde dos vezes cada dia se juntassen en que haya dos cátedras para que en ellas y en cada uno se pueda leer y se lea gratis . . . todas las ciencias necesarias para reedificación de nuestra santa fe."
18. Laws of Burgos (1960), p. 32. For the best Spanish edition of the laws, see Muro Orejón (1956).
19. See "The Bibliography on the Character of the American Indian," which registers a number of opinions that had been published up to 1935, in Hanke (1935b), pp. 74-81.
20. Gómez Canedo (1966a), p. 157. For a somewhat expanded statement on the same topic, see Gómez Canedo (1967). One of the first writers in this century

to deny that Indians had been called irrational was Pablo Hernández (1913), I, 43. Later, another historian asserted that Indians had not really been characterized as beasts (O'Gorman [1941]). One Spanish authority believes that some Anglo-Saxons, such as the present writer, have not correctly interpreted such expressions as *bestialidad* and *incapacidad* when applied to the Indians; see Pérez de Tudela's remarks in Las Casas (1957), I, xxxi-xxxii.

21. A summary of this inquiry appears in Hanke (1935b), pp. 26-39.

22. Fernández de Oviedo (1959a), I, 95.

23. Ibid., I, 89.

24. Pérez de Tudela emphasizes the actions and ideas of this interesting figure in the earliest years of American history (Las Casas [1957], I, xxvii). Ovando believed, however, in the education of at least some of the Indians, and never abandoned this belief (Lamb [1956], p. 166).

25. D.I.I., VII, 428.

26. Las Casas (1957), I, 1vii.

27. As quoted by Degler (1971), p. 212. For the Council action, see Hanke (1965a), p. 65. The Dominican Pedro de Córdoba greatly influenced Las Casas on behalf of peaceful preaching during these early years (Ramos [1959]).

28. Hanke (1935b), pp. 51-52. As Juan Friede points out, this denunciation by Ortiz continued to have an influence long after 1525. Friar Pedro Simón quoted it in his *Noticias historiales* in the seventeenth century to demonstrate the "bestialidades" of the Indians, and the twentieth-century Jesuit Constantino Bayle believed that the Ortiz statement refuted Las Casas. See Friede (1952), p. 348.

29. Díaz del Castillo (1958), p. 192.

30. Cortés (1971), p. 108. *The Times Literary Supplement* quotation appeared on p. 120 of the 2 February 1973 issue.

31. Llaguno (1963), pp. 14, 151-54. In these early years, too, the Franciscans were sufficiently respectful of the ability of the Indians to engage in colloquies with Aztec priests on religious matters; see Pou y Martí (1924).

32. As quoted by Cuevas (1922), I, 230. A number of manuscripts in the collection recently donated to the Library of Congress by H. P. Kraus clearly show that the Crown believed in the capacity of the Mexican Indians: on 4 February 1531 the Queen informed the *Audiencia* of authorization granted to certain cloistered nuns from Salamanca to travel to Mexico to instruct native girls in the faith; on 17 September 1531 the Queen urged Zumárraga to return to Spain to advise her on the conversion of the Indians; on 3 September 1536 she favored the establishment of a high school in the district of Tlatelolco, inasmuch as the Indian boys who were being taught in monasteries showed "great ability, lively understanding, and excellent memory"; on 7 December 1537 the Queen advised Viceroy Mendoza that Zumárraga had highly recommended the work of respectable Spanish women in teaching the Christian faith to Indian girls.

33. *Archivo General de Indias*, Indiferente General 1530, fol. 452. The letter of Bishop Ramírez, dated 15 May 1533, gave this report on what Betanzos declared before the Council of the Indies: " . . . Hizo Relacion en el consejo que los naturales destas partes no tenian capacidad para las cosas dela fe en lo qual ofendio adios y a V.M.ᵗ gravemente y afirmo lo que no alcanco por que el nunca supo la lengua ni se dio ala entender ny menos dotrino a yndio y como le falto la ynclinacion y devocion delos ensenar no los conocio y acordo de

afirmar lo que dizen los que quieren tener a estos para bestias pues no solo capazes para lo moral pero para lo especulativo y dellos a de aver grandes xpianos y los ay y si por las obras esteriores sea de juzgar el entendimiento exceden a los espanoles y conseruandose hasta que nos entiendan o los entendamos que sera muy presto su Religion y obras humanas de ser de gran admiracion." Ibid. (Mexico), 68.

Besides the formal opinions on Indian capacity there is an impressive variety of reactions of individual Spaniards (*Archivo General de Indias*, Santo Domingo 118). In a memorial of about the same time, Juan de Vellorja, referring to the Indians of Hispaniola, declared, "Son de calidad que no saben, sino dormir y comer. Y otros vicios que no son buenos para el anima ni para el cuerpo hallo." Ibid., 95.

34. *Cartas de Indias*, pp. 62-66. See also the letters of Bishop Sebastián Ramírez de Fuenleal of 11 and 15 May 1533, published by Cuevas (1922), I, 229-30. For statistics on the baptism of Indians, see Borges (1960), 459-63.
35. Mendieta (1870), pp. 631-32.
36. *Cartas de Indias*, pp. 62-66.
37. Paso y Troncoso (1939), III, 93-96.
38. Ibid., XV, 162-65.
39. Las Casas (1957), V, 48.
40. For the letter from the *Audiencia*, see Fabié (1879), II, 59-60; for the Las Casas letter, see Las Casas (1957), V, 68.
41. Carro (1963), pp. 135-36. Those who consider theological questions of little moment should consider how different would have been the history of America if Spanish authorities had decided that the Holy Office of the Inquisition ought to "protect" Indians as well as Spaniards from the "distintegrating spirit of heresy." Fortunately for the Indians, they were, generally speaking, untouched by the Inquisition because of their *rudeza e incapacidad*. For a thorough treatment of this subject, see Greenleaf (1961), p. 42-75.
42. Zavala (1941), pp. 25, 56-57.
43. D.I.I., X, 333-513. See also Burrus (1961), Campos (1965), and Zavala (1941, 1965).
44. D.I.I., X, 348.
45. Miranda (1965), p. 153. Further research is required to assess this opinion, for another competent student of the period holds that the "intellectual leaders of the Mexican colonization were governed by the most novel religious and social ideas of their day in Spain, and they formed a spiritual *avant garde* for the late Renaissance in Spain" (Kubler [1948], I, 15). The most up-to-date and complete information on this subject is given in Bataillon (1966), chap. 1 and the appendix "Erasmo y el Nuevo Mundo." Meanwhile every student concerned with this important question eagerly awaits the "difícil síntesis" promised by Bataillon (ibid., p. 821).
46. D.I.I., X, 351.
47. Ibid., p. 367.
48. Ibid., pp. 383-84.
49. For this treatise, see Bataillon (1966), pp. 225-38, Biermann (1968, 1969), and Zavala (1968, 1969a).
50. D.I.I., X, 471-72.
51. For a detailed account, see Hanke (1968), pp. 57-88.
52. Ibid., p. 76.

53. Ibid., pp. 76-77. Favorable reports on Indian capacity were reaching Spain from Peru, as well as from Mexico. The first bishop in Peru, Fray Vicente Valverde, sent a long report to the King in 1539 in which he strongly urged the importance of defending the Indians from the Spaniards, whom he character-ized as "tantos lobos," and stated: "La gente desta provincia del Perú, como otras vezes he escrito a V.M. es muy abil para recebir la doctrina del santo evangelio" (Santisteban Ochoa [1960], pp. 139, 157).
54. Carreño (1940), p. 383.
55. García Icazbalceta (1896), IX, 382.
56. Carreño (1940), p. 383.
57. Ibid., p. 384. Betanzos appears to have changed his opinions on Indians from time to time, which helps explain how historians today find it difficult to reach a definite conclusion on his views. For example, on 3 December 1540 he wrote a letter to the Council of the Indies reporting happily on the success of peace-ful methods to persuade the Mizteca Indians to become Christians. He de-nounced the previously used methods as "más violenta que voluntaria," declared force to be un-Christian (in terms Las Casas might have used), and particularly lauded the work of Domingo de Santa María. The latter, a devoted friar, learned the difficult Mizteca language and so thoroughly taught these Indians by his preaching and example that, when they were examined, "daban todos tan buena razón de todo, mejor que la sabría dar ningún plebeyo de nuestra nación." As Father Getino, who discovered the letter in the Domini-can archive in Valencia, observed, it is curious that Betanzos—who first attacked the encomienda system in the Caribbean islands and then favored it in Mexico—could have written such a letter (Getino [1945], pp. 56-59).
58. Carreño (1924-1934), pp. 318-319. The John Carter Brown Library has just acquired a very rare or possibly unique item, a Latin version of the Spanish letter by Julián Garcés to Pope Paul III titled *De Habilitate et Capacitate Gentium sive Indorum novi mundi nucupati ad fidem Christi . . . suscipiat* (Rome, 1537).
    Important recent studies of the bull have been made by Hera (1956) and Seco Caro (1967). In the light of this letter by Garcés and the text of *Sublimis Deus*, it is difficult to follow Lino Gómez Canedo (1966a) when he writes: "Paulo III no definió, por lo tanto, que los indios americanos eran hombres; lo que hizo fue declarar que, *por ser hombres, aunque fuesen infieles,* tenían derecho a su libertad y al dominio de sus cosas. Que fuesen hombres no parece que estuviese por entonces en cuestión" (p. 163, emphasis in original).
    If the question of the nature of the Indians was not at stake, why did Paul III include in the bull the charge that some had advanced the idea that the Indians "deben ser tratados como brutos, creados para nuestro servicio, pretendiendo que ellos son incapaces de recibir la fe Católica"? And why had the Pope declared solemnly in the bull: "Consideramos sin embargo que los Indios son verdaderos hombres y que no solo son capaces de entender la fe Católica, sino que, de acuerdo con nuestras informaciones, se hallan deseosos de re-cibirla"? The Portuguese Jesuit in Brazil, Manuel da Nóbrega, in one of the few writings on conversion there, developed the same doctrine that Paul III enunciated in *Sublimis Deus* (see Leite [1954], p. 107).
59. Cuevas (1914), pp. 84-86. For the original Latin text, see Hera (1956), pp. 161-62.
60. Olaechea Labayen (1958), pp. 152-53; Ortega (1929), p. 386.
61. Olaechea Labayen (1958), p. 167. For Augustinian views, see Vera Cruz (1968),

III, 98-101, Ennis (1957), p. 39, and Santiago Vela (1913-1931), I, 34.

62. Ricard (1966), p. 226.

63. Ibid., p. 225.

64. As given by Juan Bautista Muñoz in his *Colección* (t. 66, fols. 71-77) in the Real Academia de la Historia (Madrid).

65. This letter, of January 1543, has been printed in Figuera (1965b), I, 21-38.

66. Professor William L. Sherman has been kind enough to bring to my attention, as examples of this, a report by Tomás de la Torre, companion of Las Casas, who made the report on the journey to Chiapa in 1544, dated 12 November 1552 (*Archivo General de Indias,* Guatemala 168); a letter from the Bishop of Honduras to the Crown dated 1 May 1547 (ibid., 164); the *cargos* 17 and 40 of the *Residencia* of Francisco de Magaña (ibid., Justicia 312); and *cargo* 45 in the *Residencia* of Francisco Brizeño (ibid., 317).

67. Professor Donald Chipman points out, in his unpublished paper "Nuño de Guzmán and the Black Legend," that—in Guzmán's *Residencia* for Pánuco—Indians were referred to in terms usually reserved for domesticated animals.

68. My account of the Castro treatise is based largely on Olaechea Labayen (1958). The English translation of the opinions (ibid., pp. 171-72) of the five theologians who supported Castro's position was kindly provided by Dr. Stafford Poole, C.M.

   After I had completed this section on the Colegio de Tlatelolco, José María F. Kazuhiro Kobayashi of Sophia University in Tokyo was kind enough to give me a copy of his mimeographed doctoral dissertation "La educación como conquista. Empresa franciscana en México" (Colegio de México, 1972). Chap. 4 (pp. 89-465) gives a detailed account of education in sixteenth-century Mexico, with special reference to the Franciscan contribution. The description of the Colegio de Santa Cruz de Santiago Tlatelolco (pp. 318-428) provides a useful survey. The final section, "Opiniones en España sobre la educación superior del indígena" (pp. 428-36), is largely devoted to an account of the 1542 treatise by the Franciscan Alfonso de Castro on higher education for the Indians, which was written at the request of Charles V after the unfavorable opinions of Zumárraga and others had reached the Court. For a résumé of this treatise, based on the text, see Olaechea Labayen (1958), pp. 175-97. Dr. Kobayashi states that the treatise was presented to the Emperor at the beginning of 1543, with the signed approval of Francisco de Vitoria, Francisco Castillo, Andrés de Vega, Constantino Ponce de la Fuente, J. Egichio, and Luis de Carvajal, and that it evidently saved the Colegio for the time being.

   Dr. Kobayashi's report on Indian education in sixteenth-century Spain, however, is incomplete and is based on relatively few sources. He makes no reference to the Valladolid dispute or to Sepúlveda, although Alfonso de Castro's relations with Sepúlveda would have provided important additional information (see Hanke [1970], pp. 60, 63, 65, 117-18). Likewise, in referring to Oviedo, Dr. Kobayashi limits his references to a few well-known sources.

   Ernest Burrus gives additional information on Indian education and the importance of Indian languages, in Vera Cruz (1968), III, 98-101, 120-21, 135, and IV, 23, 87.

69. D.I.I., VII, 541.

70. Gibson (1964), pp. 300, 382, 404. The herbal has been printed with the title *Libellus de medicinalibus indorum herbis* (Mexico, 1948).

71. Ricard (1933), pp. 270-71, 280-81, 340-41, 344. Much information on practices

and attitudes relating to the giving of Holy Communion to the Indians, which involved judgments on Indian capacity, will be found in Bayle (1943); see also Bayle (1931). The hope of developing a strong native clergy did not die easily. When the Jesuits first reached Mexico, a generation after the Tlatelolco failure, they planned (in 1575) to establish schools in which carefully selected Indians could be ordained priests at the age of forty, so as to make certain that the Indians could maintain a celibate life (Ricard [1968], p. 236). In commenting on this episode, Ricard recently stated that he may have given the wrong impression, in the quotation given in the text on the influence of the Tlatelolco failure, that the existence of an Indian clergy would have solved all the problems (ibid., p. 236). For some interesting reflections on why a native clergy developed slowly, see Figuera (1965a), pp. 385-96.

Perhaps the best general presentation of the question of Indian clergy in Mexico, with excellent bibliographic information, is that by Olaechea Labayen (1958). See especially his remarks on Tlatelolco (pp. 108-24). One of the theologians who taught Latin to the Indians at Tlatelolco, the Franciscan Juan de Gaona, later attacked Friar Jacobo Daciano for his *Apologia*, in which Daciano lamented the absence of Indian priests. Gaona was apparently able to induce Daciano to make "una retractación pública en las debidas formas" (Baudot [1968], pp. 614-15).

72. García Icazbalceta (1886), II, 199.
73. Wagner (1967), p. 123. For the interest manifested for the Chinese missions among friars in sixteenth-century Mexico, see Beckmann (1963). Las Casas also seems to have been interested in these missions.
74. Carreño (1924-1934), p. 253, where he quotes the biography of Betanzos by the Augustinian Antonio de Santo Romano.
75. *Instrucciones*, pp. 229-33. The information on Mendoza's visits to the school comes from Olaechea Labayen (1958), p. 142.
76. Las Casas (1962), p. lvi.
77. Ojer (1966).
78. The text of this letter is not known; our knowledge of it comes from the "Carta de Fr. Toribio de Motolinía, 2 enero, 1555" in *D.I.I.*, VII, 263-64, 276.
79. Las Casas (1962), p. lv. Las Casas did not refer to Betanzos' views on Indians when he described his entrance into the Dominican order, although the account was probably written after 1549 (Las Casas [1951], pp. 386-87).
80. Las Casas (1962), pp. 184-86. The manuscript is now in the Academia Nacional de la Historia, Caracas. For the text of the retraction, see appendix 3. Another famous deathbed retraction was that of Fray Gerónimo de Loaysa, first Archbishop of Lima, who reversed his approval to Viceroy Francisco de Toledo for the *mita* system, which compelled Indians to work in the mines.
81. García Icazbalceta (1896), IX, 382.
82. Carreño (1940), pp. 374-76.
83. Ibid., pp. 377-80.
84. Adib (1949), pp. 93-97.
85. Gómez Canedo (1966a), pp. 160-62.
86. Friede (1952), p. 339.
87. Las Casas (1962), pp. 187-92.
88. Ibid., p. 190. We learn, too, from this judicial proceeding, that Prior Diego Ruiz deposed that Betanzos admitted he had spoken about Indian capacity in the presence of the Augustinian Juan de San Román and had given Secre-

tary Samano of the Council of the Indies "ciertos pareceres escritos y firmados de su nombre en perjuicio de los indios" (p. 189).

89. Losada (1949), p. 573.
90. Las Casas (1951), III, 321. For the many references to Oviedo in the *Historia de las Indias,* see the index in ibid., pp. 451-52.
91. Friede (1952), p. 339.
92. José de la Peña y Cámara (1957), pp. 621-22. Peña is referring to studies by Chinchilla Aguilar (1949) and Vázquez Vera (1956).

Other historians have reacted to Oviedo in other ways. The introduction by José Amador de los Rios to the first printed edition of all three parts of the *Historia general y natural de las Indias* (4 vols., Madrid, 1851-1855) was a panegyric, which Peña describes as a "novelita rosa." José Miranda gives a generally favorable view; for him, Las Casas represents a "violento extremismo y dogmático," while Oviedo is a "figura noble y respetable" (Fernández de Oviedo [1950], pp. 69, 73).

The Spanish Dominican Venancio Diego Carro, commenting on Peña's biography of Oviedo, states: "Al final nos habla de su 'simulación y fariseísmo,' para añadir luego en la p. 697: 'Pero hay más: sabe llenar páginas y más páginas, relatando, con espantosos pormenores, lo que el llama "caza o montería interna" de entradas de los capitanes de Pedrarias, "para asolar los indios e robarles e destruir la tierra," acabando con "dos millones de indios . . . en tan poco tiempo," de los cuales gran parte fueron herrados indebidamente como esclavos, sin declarar jamás que él, Oviedo, el mismo Oviedo, que tan espantado se nos muestra de todo ello, quien tenía el oficio de herrar los indios y como tal nombraba tenientes suyos que autorizaban, en cada una de las entradas, la rapiña del oro y los injustos herrajes de anotar, y de su enemiga el protector de los indios por ser el uno de los grandes culpables de los atropellos, que no le impiden el presentarse luego en su historia "cual publicano forrado de farisaíco orgullo," como dice De la Peña y Cámara, y prodigando "su maledicencia agria y egoista" contra los principales eclesiásticos' " (Carro [1966], pp. 235-36).

93. The best general life of Oviedo is that of Juan Pérez de Tudela y Bueso in the introduction to his edition of Oviedo's *Historia general y natural de las Indias* (5 vols., Madrid, 1959); the "Vida y escritos de Gonzalo Fernández de Oviedo" is in ibid., I, vii-clxxv. For a guide to publications by and about Oviedo, see Turner (1966). Works of special value on Oviedo are Salas (1959); "Homenaje a Fernández de Oviedo," *Revista de Indias,* año 17 (1957), pp. 391-705, año 18 (1958), pp. 9-126; Patiño (1966); Esteve Barba (1964); Ramos (1957, 1969); Turner (1963, 1971); and Iglesia (1942) (recently published in English translation by the University of California Press). For an index to the 1851 edition of Oviedo, see Isabel de la Peña y Cámara (1966). For an unusual collection of extracts of manuscripts on Oviedo in the Archivo General de Indias, see Belmonte y Clemente (1886), IV, 114-66.

A curious circumstance is that Sepúlveda rested his interpretation of Indian character so firmly on the word of Oviedo that one wonders whether they ever met and discussed American matters. Although Oviedo had an extensive library, there is no record of any writing by Sepúlveda in it (Turner [1971]). Moreover, they were at Court during the same time, but the outstanding Oviedo specialist Professor E. Daymond Turner has stated that he recalls no reference to Sepúlveda in Oviedo's published work. They were, apparently, rivals for the job of tutor to Prince Philip, but the better-educated Sepúlveda won out (Letter from Professor Turner dated 28 March 1973).

94. Hanke (1965a), p. 32.
95. Ibid., p. 33.
96. Ibid., pp. 33-34.
97. Ibid., p. 34.
98. Fernández de Enciso (1519).
99. Bayle (1942), p. 74.
100. Fernández de Oviedo (1959a), I lv-lvi, of introduction by Pérez de Tudela.
101. Patiño (1966).
102. Pérez de Tudela, in Fernández de Oviedo (1959a), I, cxiv, n. 354. For a recent review of the quarrel between Las Casas and Oviedo on the colonization attempt, see Bataillon (1965), pp. 115-136. Bataillon has this to say (p. 118) on Las Casas's corrections of Oviedo's account: "Tous les documents authentiques mis au jour de notre temps confirment la véracité du recit de Las Casas et justifient sa rectification."
103. Fernández de Oviedo (1959a), II, 199-201.
104. Ibid., I, lxvii.
105. Ibid.
106. Patiño (1966).
107. Ibid.
108. Fernandez de Oviedo (1944-1945), I, 13.
109. Márquez Miranda (1953).
110. Salas (1959).
111. Castillero R. (1957), p. 539. For example, in all the 1,260 folios of his "Batallas y Quincuagenas," devoted to biographies of various minor worthies, there is no article on Las Casas, although Oviedo's remarks would doubtless have been salty and valuable.
112. Salas (1959), p. 134; Salas (1953), p. 33. Neither Las Casas nor Oviedo seems to have recognized the great effects of disease on the Indians.
113. Bataillon (1965), p. 243.
114. Fernández de Oviedo (1959a), I, clii, n. 508.
115. Ibid., Libro I, caps. 3, 8.
116. Salas (1959), p. 288, n. 5.
117. Phelan (1969), p. 228, n. 13.
118. Fernández de Oviedo (1959a), I, cxxii.
119. Ibid., p. cxxiv.
120. Ibid., p. cxxiii.
121. Fernández de Oviedo (1959b), p. 43.
122. Fernández de Oviedo (1959a), I, 68. An earlier report is also available: "Relacion de Gonzalo Fernández de Oviedo veedor que ha sido en Tierra Firme sobre el mal estado en que se hallaban las cosas de aquel reyno," in *Archivo de Indias,* Patronato 193, ramo 9.
123. Fernández de Oviedo (1959a), I, cxvii. The manuscript is in the *Archivo de Indias,* Indiferente General 1624. I have used the photocopy from the Library of Congress.
124. *Archivo de Indias,* Indiferente General 1624. The specific and numbered questions to which Oviedo and the other witnesses were responding were: (1) Should the Indians be given in perpetuity to Spaniards? (2) Should the Indians be divided up as soon as possible to reward the Spaniards who have served

in the New World and for the good of the Indians? (3) Should these actions be taken so as to encourage the Spaniards by letting them know that rewards will be forthcoming promptly? and (15) What is the capacity of the Indians?

125. Fernández de Oviedo (1959a), I, xcvii-xcviii. Oviedo was replying to question 15 on the capacity of the Indians. In replying to questions 1-3 (see n. 124 above) he strongly advised the Council to grant Indians in perpetuity as soon as possible.

126. *Archivo de Indias,* Indiferente General 1624, fol. 812 of the Library of Congress photographic copy.

127. Ibid., fol. 819.

128. Barrionuevo concurred in general. He stated that it was the will of God, and not bad treatment, that explained the decrease in the Indian population. On the basis of his twenty years' experience in the New World, he believed that not a single Indian would be saved unless they were put under Spaniards. He had even see Indians who had been brought up by ecclesiastics backslide after baptism: "Todos los mas yndios destas islas son baptizados muchas veces por tener poca capacidad y ser amigos de novedades." Ibid., Indiferente General 1624, fols. 813-816.

129. Oviedo's views on Indians are scattered throughout Part I, but especially in Book II, chap. 6; Book IV, chap. 2; Book V, chaps. 2-3; and Book VI, chap. 9.

130. Las Casas made this statement shortly after Oviedo's *Historia* appeared in 1547 (Las Casas [1951], II, 518). For a detailed analysis of the circumstances of this 1547 edition, see Ramos (1969).

131. Fernández de Oviedo (1959a), I, clii.

132. Oviedo "boasted that his Primera Parte had been translated into Latin, Greek, Arabic, French, German, Italian, and Turkish"; but apparently "only the French and Italian have found their way into print" (Turner [1963]).

133. Salas (1959), pp. 119-20.

134. Vázquez Vera (1957). See also Vázquez Vera (1962), which is a somewhat larger work on the same subject, in which the author concentrates on Oviedo and the "Relaciones Geográficas" as representative "del pensamiento español en América" (p. 156).

135. Vázquez Vera (1957), p. 497.

136. Ibid., pp. 495, 502.

137. Ibid., p. 512.

138. Vera Cruz (1958), II, 373.

139. Fernández de Oviedo (1959a), IV, 264.

140. Keen (1971), p. 79. Much pertinent material may be found in chaps. 4 and 5 of this work, devoted to "the Aztecs and the Great Debate."

141. Las Casas (1958), II, 530.

II

Prelude to the Battle at Valladolid Between Las Casas and Sepúlveda

Preliminary Skirmishings, 1547-1550

T was possible for Las Casas to be in Valladolid in 1550 to confront Sepúlveda because in 1547, at the age of seventy-three, he had returned to Spain for the last time, after almost half a century of experience in Indian affairs, climaxed by his services as Bishop of Chiapa in southern Mexico.[1] There he had infuriated his countrymen—those who held Indians and enjoyed service and tribute from them under the *encomienda* system—by insisting that such Spaniards could be confessed only according to certain strict regulations that Las Casas himself had drawn up. These regulations required (among other things) restitution to Indians of wealth unjust-

ly taken from them, and this led to a number of deathbed searchings of conscience by *encomenderos*. Some Spaniards in Chiapa refused to obey the *Confesionario* regulations and died pleading in vain for the last rites of the Church. In retaliation, encomenderos brought pressure to bear on Indians not to provide food for friars who enforced the rules so strictly, or not to work on building monasteries; at times they even threatened the Dominicans with physical violence. Passions flared, and dramatic incidents occurred on this far-off frontier of Spain in America as ecclesiastics attempted to apply the ancient teachings of the Church amid the tumult of conquest. No wonder that the *Licenciado* Alonso Maldonado wrote to Charles V from Guatemala, at the end of 1545, that it would be much better if Las Casas were in a monastery in Castile rather than a bishop in the Indies.

During his last months in the Indies Las Casas had also engaged in acrimonious discussion about the application of the principles advocated in his long treatise *The Only Way of Attracting All People to the True Religion,* whose doctrines foreshadowed the arguments he was to use at Valladolid. The method he proposed was peaceful persuasion; one of his principal objectives in 1544 in going at his advanced age to the poor and relatively unimportant bishopric of Chiapa had been to lend his influential support to the attempts of his brother Dominicans to preach the faith in the province of True Peace (Vera Paz) without the use of any force whatever. This attempt, the last great enterprise that engaged his attention in America, embodied what was in many respects his most important concept of the proper relationship between Spaniards and Indians. Indians must be Christianized by peaceful means alone, he insisted—with no soldiers, no force, but only the persuasion of the Gospel preached by godly men. Just before he left America for the last time, Las Casas participated in a turbulent meeting in Mexico City on the nature of Spanish rule in which he condemned war against the Indians, whether to convert them or to remove obstacles to missionaries preaching the faith, as "perverse, unjust, and tyrannical."

During his last year as bishop in America Las Casas learned with horror that some of the famous New Laws for which he had struggled so mightily in 1542 had been revoked. The encomienda system, which the New Laws would eventually have abolished, was to be allowed to continue after all, and the encomenderos were now emboldened to begin a vigorous campaign to make these grants perpetual, together with civil and criminal jurisdiction over the Indians. The struggle over *perpetuidad* now became one of the Indian problems most bitterly debated. Domingo de Betanzos, who had become the center of controversy in Mexico because of his low opinion of Indian capacity, was one of the friars who strongly favored perpetuity.

When Las Casas reached Spain in 1547 he began organizing for the battle. The Indians of Oaxaca in Mexico gave him and his constant companion, Friar Rodrigo de Andrada, legal authority to represent them before the Council of the Indies, and the Indians in Chiapa did likewise. Later, in Peru, Domingo de Santo Tomás organized the Indians to authorize Las Casas to offer Philip II a large sum of money to deny perpetuity. It was, in fact, a blank check, for Las Casas was authorized to offer as much cash as would be necessary to outbid the encomenderos, no matter how much they offered for the privilege of perpetuity.

The veteran *conquistador* Bernal Díaz del Castillo reported on the determined battle that he and others waged in 1550 before the Council of the Indies to win perpetuity for encomenderos in Mexico and Peru. The Council met to "discuss how and in what manner the Assignment might be made in such a way that in every respect the service of God and the Royal Patrimony should be carefully considered and in no way prejudiced." The Indians "would be better treated and instructed in our Holy Faith," and granting perpetuity to those "who have served His Majesty was a relief to his royal conscience, and many other good reasons were expressed."

The Council agreed, at first. Then Las Casas, Andrada, and others began to argue against perpetuity and managed to shake the opinions of some members of the Council. Despite the support of Vasco de Quiroga, Bishop of Michoacán, Díaz del Castillo lamented that "we availed nothing with the Lords of the Royal Council of the Indies." Las Casas and his supporters were able to have the decision postponed until Charles V returned to Spain, a delaying tactic that was successful, and Díaz del Castillo returned to Guatemala. He and his group were not able to gather enough cash or political backing thereafter to convince the Council that perpetuity should be approved: "Such an excellent thing was never effected; and in this manner we proceed, like a lame mule, from bad to worse, and from one Viceroy to another and from Governor to Governor."[2]

Maneuvers such as these have led historians to emphasize Las

Casas's qualities as a politician. Although the veteran friar was described in royal orders in these years as "old and worn out," he never slackened his stern and passionate pace. His zeal in recruiting hard-working and dedicated missionaries continued unabated, and it is clear from the flood of royal orders he inspired and the number of projects he initiated during the five years after his final return to Spain in 1547 that this was one of the most intensely productive and agitated periods of his life. It was then, too, that he put into shape the treatises that were printed at Seville in 1552 and 1553, by which his ideas first became widely known to the world.

The most dramatic and important event of these years, however, was his dispute with Sepúlveda, which led him to prepare the treatise *Defense Against the Persecutors and Slanderers of the Peoples of the New World Discovered Across the Seas.* The question of the true nature of the capacity of the Indians had agitated Spaniards since 1493 (as described in chapter 1), but the argument had become more and more heated after the issuance of the New Laws of 1542, and the revocation in 1545 of the law that would have phased out the encomienda system. These were tumultuous and exciting days, which shook Spanish society in the New World to its core. In Mexico particularly, there was great rejoicing among the friends of the Indians, at least when they first learned of the New Laws. In solemn session on 23 July 1543 the city council discussed the disturbing news that the Franciscan Jacobo de Testera, who had strongly supported Indian capacity, had arrived from Castile and had permitted a great multitude of Indians to receive him.

These Indians bestowed gifts upon him and performed other services, erecting triumphal arches, sweeping clean the streets he was to pass and strewing upon them cyprus and roses, and bearing him upon a litter—all this because he and other Franciscans had informed the Indians that they had come to free the Indians and restore them to the state they enjoyed before they were placed under the rule of the King of Spain. These statements had excited the Indians and they went forth to receive Friar Testera as though he were a viceroy.

In 1546, when the news reached Mexico of the 1545 revocation of certain provisions of the New Laws, the moment arrived for the city council to strew roses in its turn. On 16 December 1546 the members discussed the revocations which had made possible the continuance of the encomienda system and voted to set aside the second day of the

Christmas holiday for a general rejoicing throughout the land. A bull fight was arranged in the lesser plaza of Mexico City, as well as dances in the ancient knightly style, and the *mayordomo* of the town was authorized to buy the necessary vestments for one hundred knights, to have these lordly raiments dyed in sets of orange and white and blue and white, and to procure trumpets for the fiesta, "all at the expense of the town treasury."[3]

In those earlier, agitated years, however, at the time of the discussion of the New Laws, even the right of the kings of Spain to rule over the Indies had been questioned. Indeed, some writers believe that Emperor Charles V was so impressed by Las Casas's views on the sovereignty of the Indians over their lands that he had been disposed to abandon Peru on grounds of conscience, had not the famous Dominican theologian Francisco de Vitoria recommended otherwise.[4]

The close connection of all of Las Casas's principal doctrines becomes evident from a study of the reports that accumulated in the Archive of the Council of the Indies. For example, in 1543 Las Casas and his companion, Fray Rodrigo de Andrada, presented a *relación* to the Council that was a long, impassioned indictment of Spanish cruelty to Indians. Moreover, they urgently recommended that all licenses to conquistadores be revoked and requested that the 1541 decision by Francisco de Vitoria and other Salamanca theologians, which insisted on adequate instruction of Indians before baptism, be promulgated and enforced. They also wanted the King to forbid absolutely that Indians should bear burdens for Spaniards, "because it is against the nature of men that they should be forced to bear burdens for the profit of Spaniards, like beasts."[5]

It was in the tense days of agitation for the revocation of the New Laws that Sepúlveda had been encouraged by the president of the Council of the Indies to compose his treatise "as a service to God and the king." The learned scholar had already demonstrated his ability to defend the interests of empire, at the time of the protest movement of the Spanish university students at Bologna.[6] These elite students from Spain's "best families" had decided in the early 1530s that all war, including defensive war, was contrary to the Catholic religion. How could anyone be a good Christian and a soldier at the same time, they asked? This was dangerous doctrine, and especially at that time, when war against the Turks was one of Europe's principal preoccupations.

The Pope had therefore commissioned Sepúlveda as *visitador general* to handle this protest and other student problems. He had gone to Bologna, which was well known to him from the days when he had studied there the doctrines of Aristotle under Pietro Pomponazzi and had composed a treatise against those who put forward pacifist views. Sepúlveda published the original Latin text of his doctrine, *Democrates Primus,* in Rome in 1535, and in 1541 a Spanish translation, *Diálogo llamado Demócrates,* appeared in Seville, just at the time when similar problems of the New World empire began to agitate Spanish court circles.

It is not surprising, therefore, that when certain groups in Spain wanted the justice of the wars against the Indians explained and justified they turned to the distinguished writer who had already performed a similar service on behalf of the Emperor's wars in the Old World. A Spanish historian has recently argued, though without much evidence, that Cortez himself was responsible for influencing Sepúlveda to compose his treatise.[7] Be that as it may, Sepúlveda set to work at once, and in a few days he had completed his argument, in which he sought to prove that wars against the Indians were just, and even constituted a necessary preliminary to their Christianization. The manuscript version of the treatise rapidly circulated at the Court, and according to Sepúlveda was approved by all who read it.

According to Las Casas in the *Defense,* the Council of the Indies refused to approve the publication of Sepúlveda's treatise, whereupon the latter prevailed upon his friends at Court to have it transferred to the Royal Council of Castile, thinking that "men ignorant of Indian affairs would not notice the poison." Instead, they referred the problem to theologians at the Universities of Salamanca and Alcalá. "After they had argued the point on very many occasions and had given it mature deliberation, they answered that the work was unworthy of the press since the teaching it contained was hardly sound. Some theologians at Alcalá thought it was very dangerous."

We now know that various important thinkers in Spanish university circles, such as Bartolomé Carranza, O.P., and Diego Covarrubias, were lecturing and writing during the years immediately preceding the Valladolid conflict and that none of them supported Sepúlveda's views.[8] Covarrubias, in his doctoral dissertation at Salamanca in 1539, had even declared that empires are not established and maintained by

arms, but by culture. Wisdom and letters are the effective in-
struments, he held, that truly create and defend the greatness of
nations.[9] At the time Sepúlveda's manuscript was being considered by
the group named for this purpose at the University of Salamanca, of
which Covarrubias was a member, the latter delivered some lectures
on the justice of wars against the Indians. While, not mentioning
Sepúlveda directly in his treatise, Covarrubias did attack the idea that
the Indians' supposedly low culture justified war against them. He also
doubted that Indians should be included among those men "born to
obey and to serve others like beasts and fierce animals whom they
resemble."[10] Thus Sepúlveda received no support in university circles.

Sepúlveda was not stopped by these reverses. Previously, he had
sent his work to the Council of Trent, sometime during its first session
(1545-1547), but Las Casas learned that this body had refused to discuss the matter, and he believed that the Council would undoubtedly
have forbidden its publication and imposed silence on its author had it
considered the problem: "A trustworthy man who was present at the
holy council told me this as something well known."[11] In 1548
Sepúlveda reported to his friend Martín de Oliva that discussions of
his doctrine had been held in Córdoba before the provincial chapter of
the Dominicans, and also in Valladolid, where "very famous
theologians" had been involved.[12]

Sepúlveda subsequently sent his manuscript to Rome, Las Casas
stated, "so that it might be printed there, since he knew about freedom
of the press in that city and that there was no one there of a contrary
mind who would fling back his poisoned darts." Sepúlveda's treatise
Democrates Alter never received approval for publication in Spain in the
author's lifetime, nor was even the summary of it permitted to appear
in print. Although he managed to get a résumé and explanation of his
main arguments printed in Rome in 1550, the *Apologia pro libro de justis
belli causis*, Charles V ordered the confiscation of all copies that reached
Spain. Even Las Casas was unable to get a copy of the printed *Apologia*,
so that he had to use one of the numerous manuscript versions
available in Spanish as he put together his arguments against
Sepúlveda's doctrine. Las Casas remarked, in the 1552 résumé of the
disputation, that Sepúlveda had prepared the manuscript summaries
of his book in Spanish, rather than Latin, so that "his ideas might be
pleasant and agreeable to all those who wish to and manage to become

rich, and to acquire wealth and position which neither they nor their ancestors had been able to achieve—all this without any effort on their part but won by the sweat, labor, and even deaths of others." Las Casas, faced with this situation, decided to write a "certain *Apología*, also in Spanish, against the Sepúlveda *Sumario*, in defense of the Indians."[13]

Las Casas did not limit his actions to erudite investigations, though he must have spent many hours searching monastic libraries for ammunition against Sepúlveda. He lobbied actively at Court, but he found conditions not particularly propitious for acceptance of his peaceful approach to Indian affairs. The spirit of the times was such that the unfortunate first viceroy in Peru, Blasco Núñez Vela, who had tried to enforce the New Laws in that violent land, had been captured by angry and independent conquistadores, who killed the viceroy in 1546. The discreet and able royal representative, Pedro de la Gasca, had finally been able to bring peace to Peru and re-establish the king's authority by executing Gonzalo Pizarro and by distributing Indians in encomienda to Spaniards on a carefully calculated basis.

We know the state of mind of Las Casas during this critical period, immediately before the Valladolid discussion, thanks to Marcel Bataillon's discovery in the Archive of the Indies of a letter written by Las Casas, probably in May 1549, to an unnamed correspondent, possibly Domingo de Soto, the confessor of Charles V.[14] Las Casas, in a desperate attempt to convince someone close to the Emperor that the conquests in America must be halted and all Indians incorporated under the Crown, as had been originally prescribed by the New Laws, was answering objections made by his correspondent that the New World was far away and that even pious missionaries offered conflicting advice on the proper action to take. Las Casas pointed out, in pungent language, how some ecclesiastics had been subverted by material support from conquistadores, how others knew nothing about the reality of the Conquest or destruction caused to the Indians, and how still others did not bother to study Indian languages. This last charge, it will be remembered, was often leveled at friars who held that the Indians were incapable; indeed, just a few months later, in September 1549, Domingo de Betanzos was to sign his much-discussed retraction, in which he explained his low opinion of Indian capacity "through not knowing their language or because of some other ignorance." Las Casas apparently never learned an Indian language either, but there is no record of his being sharply criticized on this account.

It was this same September, too, that Sepúlveda wrote to Prince Philip, reminding him that the former's translation of Aristotle's *Politics* had been dedicated to Philip and informing the prince that he was now engaged in defending the book he had composed on the Conquest of the Indies.[15] Sepúlveda explained that he had written three "apologia," which he had sent to various members of the Court, as well as a "summary of the book on Indian affairs," and was hopefully awaiting authorization to print his work. He also awaited word on the fate of the "scandalous and diabolical work on confession" that the Bishop of Chiapa had published against his book.

Sepúlveda stated further: "The *Fiscal* presented this work by Las Casas to the Royal Council and requested that it be burned and the author punished." Thereupon, Sepúlveda reported, the Council called the Bishop before it and reprehended him strongly, but decided that it should consult with Prince Philip, which led Sepúlveda to urge certain authorities to make known their opinion of the *Confesionario* published by Las Casas. Sepúlveda also reminded Philip that it was his duty to favor justice "and not allow imprudent men with fictions and devices to obscure the truth, particularly when the matter concerned the public welfare as well as the fame and conscience of your father and grandfather."

Las Casas meanwhile, in his letter to the unnamed correspondent, bitterly reproached those Franciscans and Mercedarians who had accepted conquistador money and praised the dramatic action of one of the oldest Franciscans in Mexico, probably Francisco de Soto, who had reversed his original decision and had eaten the paper on which he had previously signed his name in support of the perpetuity of encomiendas.[16] The ink has faded on this newly found Las Casas document, and the handwriting is abominable; but the letter, though full of corrections and blottings, and written on the back of another letter more than four centuries ago, still conveys the friar's conviction and eloquence:

Wherever else in the world have rational men in happy and populous lands been subjugated by such cruel and unjust wars called conquests, and then been divided up by the same cruel butchers and tyrannical robbers as though they were inanimate things ... enslaved in an infernal way, worse than in Pharaoh's day, treated like cattle being weighed in the meat market and, God save the mark, are looked upon as of less worth than bedbugs? How can the words of those who support such iniquities be believed?

Las Casas energetically affirmed that the necessary reforms could be achieved if only the necessary laws were made by the Council of the Indies and upright men appointed to execute them in America. He recommended one bishop who would be excellent for the work, and advised that another person under no circumstances be allowed to go. Here we see Las Casas the lobbyist at work. As always, this practical and realistic apostle stressed that the arrangements he proposed would not only redound to the benefit of the Indians and to the increase of Christianity but also to the "incomparable temporal interests" of the king.

In the closing paragraphs of his letter Las Casas urged that further action be not delayed until La Gasca returned from Peru, as his correspondent had evidently suggested. Some good decisions had recently been taken by the Council of the Indies, and more were required. Here Las Casas probably referred to the Council's approval of his own breathtaking proposal, which made conquistadores up and down the Indies grind their teeth in rage, that the licenses of all expeditions then under way be revoked and that no similar grants be made in the future. A drastic step in this direction was actually taken by the Council on 3 July 1549, when it advised the King that the dangers incurred both to the Indians and to the King's conscience by the conquests were so great that no new expedition ought to be licensed without his express permission and that of the Council. Moreover, the Council concluded that a meeting of theologians and jurists was needed to discuss "how conquests may be conducted justly and with security of conscience."

The following statement by the highest board in Spain on Indian affairs is worth quoting. The Council stated that although laws had been issued previously to regulate the conquests,

we feel certain that these laws have not been obeyed, because those who conduct these conquests are not accompanied by persons who will restrain them and accuse them when they do evil.

The greed of those who undertake conquests and the timidity and humility of the Indians is such that we are not certain whether any instruction will be obeyed. It would be fitting for Your Majesty to order a meeting of learned men, theologians, and jurists, with others according to your pleasure, to discuss and consider concerning the manner in which these conquests should be carried on in order that they may be made justly and with security of conscience. An instruction for this purpose should be drawn up, taking into account all that may be necessary for this, and should be considered a law to govern henceforth the conquests approved by this Council as well as those approved by the Audiencias.

The King now took the final step, and on 16 April 1550 ordered that all conquests in the New World be suspended until a special group of theologians and counselors should decide upon a just method of conducting them. Las Casas had won his point; the machinery of conquest was ordered to stop short. Both Sepúlveda and Las Casas agreed that there should be a meeting, and this, too, was decreed by the King and the Council of the Indies to take place in 1550, the same year in which Américo Castro believed that "the Spaniard had attained a zenith of glory." Probably never before, or since, has a mighty emperor—and in 1550 Charles V, Holy Roman Emperor, was the strongest ruler in Europe, with a great overseas empire besides—ordered his conquests to cease until it was decided if they were just.

This was the background against which Sepúlveda and Las Casas began their discussions in Valladolid on the justice of wars waged in far-off America and on the application of Aristotelian doctrine to the Indians.

The Sessions at Valladolid

The sessions began in mid-August 1550 and continued for about a month before the "Council of the Fourteen," which had been summoned to Valladolid by Charles V to sit in judgment on the specific issue: Is it lawful for the King of Spain to wage war on the Indians, before preaching the faith to them, in order to subject them to his rule, so that afterward they may be more easily instructed in the faith?[17] Among the judges were such outstanding theologians as Domingo de Soto, Melchor Cano, and Bernardino de Arévalo, as well as veteran members of the Council of Castile and the Council of the Indies, and such experienced officials as Gregorio López, the glossator of the well-known edition of the Spanish law code, the *Siete Partidas.*

On the first day Sepúlveda spoke for three hours, giving a résumé of his treatise. On the second day Las Casas appeared, armed with his monumental manuscript, which, as he himself stated, he proceeded to read word for word. This verbal onslaught continued for five days, until the reading was completed—or until the members of the junta, as Sepúlveda suggested, could bear no more. The two opponents did not appear together before the Council; instead, the judges seem to have discussed the issues with them separately as they stated their positions. The judges also carried on discussions among themselves.

It is no wonder that the bewildered judges requested one of their members, Domingo de Soto, an able theologian and jurist, to condense the arguments and give them an objective and succinct summary for their more perfect comprehension of the theories involved. This he did in a masterly statement that was then submitted to Sepúlveda, who replied to each of the twelve objections Las Casas had raised. The members thereupon returned to their homes, taking with them copies of the summary. Before departing, the judges agreed to reconvene on 20 January 1551 for a final vote.

Most of the information available on this second session, which actually took place in Valladolid from about the middle of April to the middle of May 1551, comes from the pen of Sepúlveda, who discovered, much to his disgust, that Las Casas had availed himself of the interim period to prepare a rebuttal to Sepúlveda's replies. Sepúlveda made no further rejoinder "because he saw no necessity; indeed, the members of the junta had apparently never read any of the replies."

Nevertheless, Sepúlveda again appeared before the junta and expounded his views on the meaning of the bulls of Alexander VI. It was probably at this time that he composed his paper titled "Against Those Who Depreciate or Contradict the Bull and Decree of Pope Alexander VI Which Gives the Catholic Kings and Their Successors Authority to Conquer the Indies and Subject Those Barbarians, and by This Means Convert Them to the Christian Religion and Submit Them to Their Empire and Jurisdiction." Sepúlveda stated that much of the discussion at this session revolved around the interpretation of the papal bulls of donation, and that the Franciscan judge Bernardino de Arévalo strongly supported his case, but that when he wished to appear again, the judges declined to discuss the issue further.

Unfortunately, whatever records were made of the Council's proceedings have been lost, or at least have not yet come to light, and arguments presented by the two opponents are therefore our only basis for reconstructing the event. Sepúlveda set forth his position from notes, having drawn up no formal brief but closely following the arguments previously developed in his treatise in dialogue form, the *Demócrates Segundo*, which had circulated widely in Spain in the years preceding the disputation. In it, Leopóldo, described by Sepúlveda as "a German who is bringing up again some Lutheran errors out of the disease inherited from his fathers," is a man who believes that the Conquest is unjust, while Sepúlveda, speaking through Demócrates, kindly but firmly opposes Leopoldo's ideas and, in the end, fully convinces him of the justice of wars against the Indians and of the obligation of the king to wage them.

Sepúlveda's Position

Sepúlveda's real doctrine has long been in doubt. Nor was he himself ever satisfied that he was understood. In recent years, however, there has arisen a vigorous school both in English- and Spanish-speaking lands to explain and defend his position.[18] The summary made by Domingo de Soto at the request of the junta and printed at Seville in 1552 by Las Casas presents a concise view of the main points at issue, and Sepúlveda's basic thoughts on just war were included both in a contemporary work issued in Rome and in his *Opera*, which was published in the latter part of the eighteenth century.

If Sepulveda's doctrine has been incompletely understood, this may be due to the fact that his treatise underwent many revisions. Fortunately, a new edition appeared in 1951, prepared by the painstaking Latinist Ángel Losada, and the student who wishes to know Sepúlveda's doctrine on just war against the American Indians will henceforth depend upon this version.[19] It is better organized and more complete than Sepúlveda's earlier versions; it omits some of his harsher expressions on the nature of the Indians; and it corrects what Losada points out as a number of mistranslations in earlier editions. Losada believes that the text he has published represents the true thought of Sepúlveda—and the reader who follows Losada's detailed and exhaustive collation of the four manuscripts is bound to agree.

We will make no attempt to analyze Sepúlveda's theses in detail, except insofar as Las Casas described and combated his views. The reader who wishes to understand all the complexities of this disputation should read the Losada edition, and compare Sepúlveda's argument with the *Defense* of Las Casas. The *Defense*, however, responds to the summary made by Sepúlveda of the more complete argument he elaborated in *Demócrates Segundo*.

The Valladolid scene in 1549 and 1550 was obviously confused, but at least we know that the Council of the Indies was closely concerned with arguments on the capacity of the Indians as they affected royal policy. In September 1549 the Council seemed to be suspicious about the retraction of Domingo de Betanzos, and it ordered a notary public to investigate. After the first confrontation between Las Casas and Sepúlveda, in August and September 1550 before the eminent group appointed by the Council of the Indies to listen to their arguments, the Council immediately ordered, in October, that the "book which Dr. Sepúlveda printed on matters relating to the Indies without a license" not be allowed to be sent to the New World.[20] This book must have been the summary Sepúlveda had issued in Rome in 1550, which served as the basis for the great disputation.

NOTES

1. For more details on these years, see Hanke (1970), chaps. 3-4. The Maldonado citation at the end of the paragraph comes from Fabié (1879), II, 145.
2. Díaz del Castillo (1908), V, 280-85.
3. This discussion of the News Laws is based on Hanke (1965a), pp. 95, 101-2.
4. For a discussion of this idea, and a refutation that seems sound to me, see Bataillon (1965), pp. 291-308.
5. Las Casas (1962), p. 132.
6. This statement on Sepúlveda and the students at Bologna is based on Losada (1970), p. 249.
7. Ramos (1972), p. 199.
8. Pereña Vicente (1956). See also Tellechea Idígoras (1966).
9. Pereña Vicente (1947), pp. 19-20.
10. Pereña Vicente (1956), pp. 154, 168, 205.
11. Poole, *Defense,* p. 343. It is significant that the Council of Trent reached a decision on conversion that was almost identical with that of Las Casas, and this policy of kindness, instead of force, was adopted in Portuguese missions in the East (Silva [1969], pp. 190, 195). Also, it has been stated that the Jesuits, led by Diego Laínez, "made the Council of Trent adopt the thesis that all men,

regardless of their skin color, have souls capable of achieving salvation" (Langnas [1962], p. 345). The person who intervened at the Council of Trent may have been Melchor Cano, according to Losada (1970), p. 284. See also Mateos (1945).
12. Fabié (1879), I, 219.
13. Las Casas (1966), I, 223.
14. Bataillon (1965), pp. 203-23.
15. Losada (1947), pp. 33-34.
16. This section is based on Hanke (1970), pp. 35-36.
17. This section is based on ibid., chaps. 5-6.
18. Quirk (1954). For a recent critique of Quirk, see Korth (1968), pp. 236-37.

My own view is based on Ernest J. Burrus, S.J., the scholar who has most recently examined this controversial topic, in connection with his edition of the works of Alonso de la Vera Cruz. Dr. Burrus has this to say, after examining both the Bekker Greek text and the Latin translation of Aristotle's words by Mauro and Beringer:

"Vera Cruz dared not reject the overwhelming authority of the Greek philosopher; hence, he would show that a more humane interpretation could be given to his theory of natural superiority and natural inferiority of men. The classic text, according to Vera Cruz, did not mean that some were born to be slaves and others to be their masters; it could be taken to mean that some men were naturally superior to others in the sense that they were capable of directing and ruling others, whereas other men were naturally inferior in the sense that they were to be directed and ruled by others.

"It is true that there is such a passage in the first book of Aristotle's *Politics*, but when the sum total of what the Greek philosopher had to say on natural superiority and natural inferiority is taken together, I do not think that it is possible to defend Vera Cruz's benign interpretation." Vera Cruz (1968), II, 72. See also n. 176 on the same page.
19. Sepúlveda (1951). See also Losada (1949).
20. *D.I.U.*, XX, 211-12. The Council also wanted to make certain that no copies remained in America: "El gobernador de Tierrafirme tome los libros que hubiere en aquella provincia de los que el Doctor hizo imprimir sobre cosas tocantes a las Indias sin licencia y los envíe al gobierno." Losada's view, which seems to me reasonable, is that the book referred to was the summary of *Democrates Alter* (Losada [1949], p. 205).

III

Analysis of Las Casas's Treatise

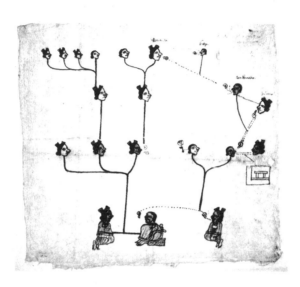

The Two Treatises Prepared by Las Casas to Combat Sepúlveda

 O those who are familiar with the astonishing vigor of Bartolomé de Las Casas it will come as no great surprise that he prepared not only a large treatise in Latin against the doctrines of Juan Ginés de Sepúlveda but also had ready—for the confrontation at Valladolid in 1550 and 1551—a second treatise in Spanish. The Latin work has generally been referred to as the *Apología*, but henceforth will be referred to by the English title, *Defense*, and thus distinguished from the second treatise, in Spanish, and written by Las Casas on the same subject, which he described as an

apología. Las Casas considered both treatises integral parts of his argument at Valladolid for the defense of the Indians. He described his Spanish *Apología* as the "second part" of the *Defense,* though he seems to have read only his Latin treatise to the judges during the first session, in August 1550.

Was this *Apología* the tremendously detailed defense of the character and culture of the Indians that the world has known as the *Apologética Historia?* Ángel Losada, who has done so much to make known the doctrine and life of Sepúlveda, believes that Las Casas's references to the second, Castilian part indicate that it is in fact the *Apologética Historia.*[1] This identification seems doubtful, but it is quite possible that the *Apología* was a prototype of the *Apologética Historia.* Dr. Losada has been the first to study in depth the doctrine of Las Casas in the *Defense,* and my analysis owes much to his pioneer work.

What seems to be reasonably certain is that the information Las Casas provided in the first part, the *Defense,* on the contents of the second part shows that the Spanish second part, the *Apología,* clearly reflects the *Apologética Historia* in purpose and content. Because the question of the exact date when this latter treatise was written has recently been raised in dramatic fashion by Edmundo O'Gorman,[2] it may be useful to examine the *Defense* closely on this point.

Las Casas first mentioned this second part, the Spanish *Apología,* in the *Defense* in connection with his contention that the Indians are not barbaric or dull-witted or stupid, but on the contrary, "very talented in learning, and very ready to accept Christian religion."

Furthermore, they are so skilled in every mechanical art that with every right they should be set ahead of all the nations of the known world on this score, so very beautiful in their skill and artistry are the things this people produces in the grace of its architecture, its painting, and its needlework. But Sepúlveda despises these mechanical arts, as if these things do not reflect inventiveness, ingenuity, industry, and right reason. For a mechanical art is an operative habit of the intellect. . . . So these men are not stupid, Reverend Doctor. Their skillfully fashioned works of superior refinement awaken the admiration of all nations, because works proclaim a man's talent, for, as the poet says, the work commends the craftsman.[3]

Las Casas evidently had not heard of the artistic judgment of Albrecht Dürer, but he would have found much comfort in the words Dürer wrote in his diary in 1520, after he had seen the gifts presented by Montezuma to Cortez which were sent by the *conquistador* to his sovereign Charles V as a demonstration of the riches to be found in the conquered New Spain, and publicly exhibited in Brussels:

Also I saw the things which were brought to the King from the New Golden Land: a sun entirely of gold, a whole fathom broad; likewise, a moon, entirely of silver, just as big; likewise, sundry curiosities from their weapons, armour, and missiles; very odd clothing, bedding and all sorts of strange articles for human use, all of which is fairer to see than marvels.

These things were all so precious that they were valued at a hundred thousand gulden worth. But I have never seen in all my days what so rejoiced my heart, as these things. For I saw among them amazing artistic objects, and I marvelled over the subtle ingenuity of the men in these distant lands. Indeed I cannot say enough about the things that were brought before me.[4]

Las Casas, in the *Defense,* went on to praise the ability of the Indians in other fields:

In the liberal arts which they have been taught up to now, such as grammar and logic, they are remarkably adept. With every kind of music they charm the ears of the audience with wonderful sweetness.[5] They write skillfully and quite elegantly, so that most often we are at a loss to know whether the characters are handwritten or printed. *I shall explain this at greater length in the second part of this* Defense, not by quoting the totally groundless lies of the worst [deceivers] in the histories published so far,[6] but the truth itself and what I have seen with my eyes, felt with my hands, and heard with my own ears while living a great many years among those peoples.

Las Casas then charged that Sepúlveda "should have consulted the honest religious who have lived among those peoples for many years and know their endowments of character and industry as well as the progress they have made in religion and morality."

The basic point Las Casas made was that "not all barbarians are irrational or natural slaves or unfit for government. Some barbarians, in accordance with justice and nature, have kingdoms, royal dignities, jurisdiction, and good laws, and there is among them lawful government." The Indians certainly fall within this class of barbarian:

[They have] important kingdoms, large numbers of people who live settled lives in a society, great cities, kings, judges and laws, persons who engage in commerce, buying, selling, lending, and the other contracts of the law of nations, will it not stand proved that the Reverend Doctor Sepúlveda has spoken wrongly and viciously against peoples like these, either out of malice or ignorance of Aristotle's teaching, and, therefore, has falsely and perhaps irreparably slandered them before the entire world? From the fact that the Indians are barbarians it does not necessarily follow that they are incapable of government and have to be ruled by others, except to be taught about the Catholic faith and to be admitted to the holy sacraments. They are not ignorant, inhuman, or bestial. Rather, long before they had heard the word Spaniard, they had properly organized states, wisely ordered by excellent laws, religion, and custom. *They cultivated friendship and, bound together in common fellowship, lived in populous cities in which they wisely administered the affairs of both peace and war justly and equitably, truly governed by laws which at very many points surpass ours, and could have won the admiration of the sages of Athens, as I will show in the second part of this* Defense.[7]

At various points Las Casas referred to the Spanish *Apologia* in such a way as to show that it was an integral part of his position as set forth in the Latin *Defense*. He commended the Indians' Christian faith, their honor of the holy sacraments, and, at the time of death, "their wonderful concern about their salvation and their soul. . . . *I shall speak at greater length about this in the second part of this apology.*" Later on in the *Defense*, during the long passage against Oviedo, Las Casas stated: "Oviedo's assertion that the Indians are unteachable and incorrigible is false than false, *as will be clear from the second part of this* Defense."[8]

In his summation, made at the close of the *Defense*, Las Casas declared:

The Indians are our brothers, and Christ has given his life for them. Why, then, do we persecute them with such inhuman savagery when they do not deserve such treatment? . . . [They] will embrace the teaching of the gospel, as I well know, for they are not stupid or barbarous but have a native sincerity and are simple, moderate, and meek, and, finally, such that I do not know whether there is any people readier to receive the gospel. Once they have embraced it, it is marvelous with what piety, eagerness, faith, and charity they obey Christ's precepts and venerate the sacraments. For they are docile and clever, and in their diligence and gifts of nature, they excel most peoples of the known world.

The second part of this Defense, *written in Spanish, will set all this before the eyes of everyone with very clear arguments and a true description of that world in order that the wicked plunderers who have defamed that very sincere, docile, moderate, and clever people by poisonous detractions and slanderous lies may be silenced.*[9]

At this point one is led to wonder whether the Spanish *Apología* described by Las Casas as the second part of his argument at Valladolid was not in fact an early version of the *Apologética Historia*, for the first paragraph of this latter work reads as follows:

The ultimate cause for writing this work was to gain knowledge of all the many nations of this vast new world. They had been defamed by persons who feared neither God nor the charge, so grievous before divine judgment, of defaming even a single man and causing him to lose his esteem and honor. From such slander can come great harm and terrible calamity, particularly when large numbers of men are concerned and, even more so, a whole new world. It has been written that these peoples of the Indies, lacking human governance and ordered nations, did not have the power of reason to govern themselves—which was inferred only from their having been found to be gentle, patient and humble. It has been implied that God became careless in creating so immense a number of rational souls and let human nature, which He so largely determined and provided for, go astray in the almost infinitesimal part of the human lineage which they comprise. From this it follows that they have all proven themselves unsocial and therefore monstrous, contrary to the natural bent of all peoples of the world.[10]

Las Casas assured his readers that the truth is the opposite:

Not only have [the Indians] shown themselves to be very wise peoples and possessed of lively and marked understanding, prudently governing and providing for their nations (as much as they can be nations, without faith in or knowledge of the true God) and making them prosper in justice; but they have equalled many diverse nations of the world, past and present, that have been praised for their governance, politics and customs, and exceed by no small measure the wisest of all these, such as the Greeks and Romans, in adherence to the rules of natural reason.[11]

Throughout both the *Apologética Historia* and the argument against Sepúlveda at Valladolid Las Casas devoted many thousands of words to attempting to refute the idea that the Indians were such incapable people that the Spaniards could lawfully wage war against them, and that they fell into the classification of slaves by nature according to the Aristotelian doctrine. It seems reasonable to suppose, therefore, that both the Latin *Defense* and the Spanish *Apología* can be considered essential parts of the immense armory of information about the New World and its inhabitants—together with the learned citations from the laws, ancient history, and Church fathers—that Las Casas had built up over the years in his campaign on behalf of the Indians. The following declaration, by which he explained the sixth reason for the composition of his more general work, *History of the Indies,* might well be taken as one of the main objectives of the last fifty years of his life:

> To liberate my own Spanish nation from the error and very grave and very pernicious illusion in which it now lives and has always lived, of considering these people to lack the essential characteristics of men, judging them brute beasts incapable of virtue and religion, depreciating their good qualities and exaggerating the bad which is in them. These peoples have been hidden away and forgotten for many centuries, and [it has been my purpose] to stretch out our hands to them in some way, so that they would not remain oppressed as at present because of this very false opinion of them, and kept permanently down in the darkness.[12]

If any doubt remains concerning the relationship of the various writings of Las Casas to each other, and specifically the connection between his arguments at Valladolid against Sepúlveda, chapters 142-151 of Book III of his *Historia de las Indias* provide convincing proof. At the end of this work Las Casas was describing the first important public dispute (in 1519 before King Charles and his Court in Barcelona) on the application of the Aristotelian doctrine of natural slavery to the Indians. Las Casas wrote these chapters after 1550,[13] and they constitute a kind of summary of all his thoughts on this subject, as well as another detailed and scathing attack upon the credibility of the historian Oviedo. Las Casas there gave a blow-by-blow account of the encounter he had in Barcelona with the Bishop of Tierra Firme, Juan de Quevedo, in which he used essentially the same arguments and examples he later employed against Sepúlveda.[14] He cited his *Apologética Historia,* which was written in Spanish, on the question of sacrifices and on the bravery of the Indians even in the face of death, a quality that Oviedo did not bother to mention but that Las Casas emphasized in his *Apologética Historia* and also in his *De unico vocationis modo.* One of the basic propositions Las Casas stated over and over again in his various treatises was the grave error of those who depreciated the Indians:

> This charge is not true, but is on the contrary a great falsity and a very pernicious allegation that those make who depreciate the Indians and charge them with a corrupt bestiality. We have disproved this in our *Apología* and in other treatises, and all the world knows it.[15]

Concluding his report on the battle in 1519 against Bishop

Quevedo in Barcelona, Las Casas remarked, referring particularly to Aristotle's definitions of natural slavery:

> This is what the Philosopher says. But it does not apply to the Indians, because they are not stupid, nor without sufficient judgment to govern their households, as has been proved. On this subject we have already written in our *Apología,* written in Spanish, as well as in Latin in our work *De Unico Vocationis Modo*; and in another book in Spanish entitled *Apologética Historia* in which I describe in detail and at length the customs, life, religion, government, and good breeding which all these people have, some more than others as the bishop stated. Some few have not yet reached the perfection of an ordered government, as was the case with all peoples of the world in the beginning, but this does not mean that they lack the necessary reason to be easily brought to an orderly, domestic, and political life.[16]

To those who have read the numerous writings of Las Casas on Indian affairs, and especially those writings composed after he left the monastery in Hispaniola in 1530 and went forth in the world to battle for his ideas, it will come as no surprise that his doctrine is all of one piece—even though some of his treatises may be couched in a largely theoretical tone, such as the *De Unico Vocationis Modo* or parts of the *Apologética Historia*, with relatively few specific references to events in America or to the battles in which they were used. To believe that the *Apologética Historia* was not an integral part of the *corpus* of Las Casas's fundamental doctrine but, instead, was drawn up as the result of his reaction to his alleged polemical failure at Valladolid, as one modern writer believes, seems to me a wrong reading of his *opera*. The abstraction or removal of his theories from the context of the sixteenth-century world in which he lived and fought on behalf of what he considered justice for the Indians seems to me an unhistorical approach, with little possibility of surviving the scrutiny of the years.[17]

An Overview of the Argument

The main lines of the argument Las Casas developed at Valladolid in his presentation to the Council of the Fourteen in August 1550 have been known ever since 1552, when he published a résumé by Domingo de Soto of both his own views and those of Sepúlveda. Soto, the Dominican theologian who was a member of the Council appointed to hear the controversy, and who had been commissioned by his colleagues to prepare a summary of both arguments, never mentioned the second part, the Spanish *apología*.[18] He remarked, however, that Las Casas had once said more than was necessary on a certain point and, at another time, had been "as copious and diffuse as the years of this business," especially in his response to Sepúlveda's charge that the Indians were barbarians and therefore slaves by nature, "to which he did not respond in any one place, but in all his writings may be found his arguments on this topic which may be reduced to two or three main points" (an accurate and perceptive description of Las Casas's writings). At another point Soto stated:

The bishop described at length the history of the Indians, showing that although some of their customs were not particularly civil, they were not however barbarians on this account but rather a settled people with great cities, laws, arts, and government who punished unnatural and other crimes with the death penalty. They definitely had sufficient civilization that they should not be warred against as barbarians.[19]

As Las Casas stated to Prince Philip in the dedicatory letter of the *Defense*, he was responding point by point to the doctrine presented by Sepúlveda in his manuscript *Apología*, which was a résumé of *Democrates Alter*. (It will be recalled that Las Casas complained that several copies of this manuscript were circulating in Spain in the years immediately preceding the Valladolid dispute.) He had to use a summary of this treatise because no copy of the complete text was available to him at the time he was marshaling his hundreds of citations for the *Defense*, which was written, he informed Philip, "at the cost of much sweat and sleepless nights." Las Casas's purpose was a comprehensive demolition of Sepúlveda, "wrong both in law and in fact," and a demonstration of how he "has distorted the teachings of philosophers and theologians, falsified the words of Sacred Scripture, of divine and human laws, and how no less destructively he has quoted statements of Pope Alexander VI to favor the success of his wicked cause. Finally, the true title by which the Kings of Spain hold their rule over the New World will be shown."[20]

Thus did Las Casas, at almost eighty years of age, and after half a century of experience in America, explain how he came to "unsheathe the sword [pen] for the defense of the truth" in one of his most significant writings on the history of Spain in America and on the nature of the Indians. Although the manuscript embodying Las Casas's attack was already bulky, he requested Philip to command Sepúlveda to give him a copy of the complete Latin work so that he could refute his falsehoods even more thoroughly.

Before we enter into the story of this argument it may be useful to have a closer view of the complicated and controversial subject: Is war lawful as a means for spreading Christianity in America? This question has two aspects.

First, its legality: Is war against the Indians ever just, in itself, as a means of attracting them to the true religion? Sepúlveda had expounded his views on this theoretical issue in his Latin treatise *Democrates Alter* and in the summary of this treatise, which Las Casas had read. Las Casas presented his position in the *Defense*, whose text is the basis for this study.

Second, its factual basis: Are the Indians really in such a state of inferiority and barbarism in relation to the rest of the civilized people that this fact alone justifies such war, according to natural law, as a means of liberating them from such inferiority and barbarism? Sepúlveda invoked the testimony of the royal historian Gonzalo Fernández de Oviedo y Valdés in his *Historia general y natural de las Indias,* which had rendered a very unfavorable opinion on Indian capacity and character. To prove the contrary, Las Casas devoted a large part of his *Defense* to expounding his very favorable view of the Indians and to attacking Oviedo tooth and nail. Moreover, he composed the second part of his *Defense,* in Spanish, to demonstrate the truth of his contention that the Indians are not "irrational or natural slaves or unfit for government."[21]

Las Casas divided the Latin part of his argument, the *Defense*, into two well-defined sections. In the first he replied to the four reasons Sepúlveda adduced in favor of waging war against the Indians, and in the second he commented on the "authorities" Sepúlveda cited to substantiate his position.

The imposition of a scholastic organization of thought on the torrential prose of Las Casas does not give the reader a true understanding of the rare combination of passion and erudition that marks the *Defense*. Sarcasm, learning, indignation, and memorable phrases are to be found throughout this treatise, which probably presents a more comprehensive view of Las Casas's thought than any other. Certainly he referred to it so frequently in his printed 1552 treatises as to indicate that he looked upon it as the most detailed exposition of his views.[22] The present analysis, however, will not attempt to tell all; the *Defense* is such a rich and varied combination of his fundamental doctrine and his experiences in the New World that it will doubtless be studied as long as the world maintains its interest in the history of Spain in America and in that procession of remarkable events called the expansion of Europe.

The First Section: Las Casas's Response to Sepúlveda's Four Reasons for Justifying War Against the Indians in Order to Convert Them

Las Casas made it clear at the beginning of the *Defense* that his principal concern was to attack those who condemned *"en masse* so many thousands of people" for faults that most of them did not have. "What man of sound mind will approve a war against men who are harmless, ignorant, gentle, temperate, unarmed, and destitute of every human defense?" He then announced that he would prove Sepúlveda and his followers were wrong in law, a subject he had treated "at greater length elsewhere and in general," and wrong in fact.

For the Creator of every being has not so despised these peoples of the New World that he willed them to lack reason and made them like brute animals, so that they should be called barbarians, savages, wild men, and brutes, as they [i.e., the *Sepúlvedistas*] think or imagine. On the contrary, they are of such gentleness and decency that they are, more than the other nations of the entire world, supremely fitted and prepared to abandon the worship of idols and to accept, province by province and people by people, the word of God and the preaching of the truth.[23]

Then Las Casas plunged into such a detailed rebuttal of each reason, with so many subsidiary arguments, that at times the reader is almost lost in his torrent of words and in the multiplicity of his learned references. A notable characteristic of the disputation at Valladolid was the way in which both Las Casas and Sepúlveda drew upon the immense reservoir of doctrine and example that was represented in the Bible, the writings of Church fathers, and other authorities and events of the past as recorded by historians. Each contestant tried to demonstrate that his opponent misunderstood, and at times twisted, the words of these authorities and the experience of the past to fit his own argument.

Rebuttal of Sepúlveda's First Argument: Indians Are Barbarous

To Sepúlveda's argument that the inhabitants of the New World were in such a state of barbarism that force was required to liberate them from this condition, Las Casas replied that one cannot generalize about "barbarians" in such a loose and broad way. He examined Aristotle's statements on barbarism and found several different kinds:

1. *Those who are barbarians because of their savage behavior.* Las Casas replied that, even those who live in the most highly developed states, such as Greeks and Latins, can be called barbarians if their behavior is sufficiently savage. However, the Spaniards, in their treatment of the Indians, "have surpassed all other barbarians" in the savagery of their behavior.

2. *Those who are barbarians because they have no written language in which to express themselves.* Such persons are barbarians in only a restricted sense, Las Casas said, and do not fall into the class that Aristotle described as pertaining to natural slaves. Spanish missionaries, before and after Las Casas, emphasized the beauty and intricacy of the Indian languages, and the Dominican friar Domingo de Santo Tomás published a grammar of the Peruvian Indians' language to prove their rationality.

3. *Those who are barbarians in the correct sense of the term.* These, Las Casas argued, are the only ones who may properly be placed in Aristotle's category of natural slaves. They are truly barbarians

either because of their evil and wicked character or the barrenness of the region in which they live. . . . They lack the reasoning and way of life suited to human beings. . . . They have no laws which they fear or by which all their affairs are regulated . . . they lead a life very much that of brute animals. . . . Barbarians of this kind (or better, wild men) are rarely found in any part of the world and are few in number when compared with the rest of mankind.

Such men are freaks of nature, "for since God's love of mankind is so great and it is His will to save all men, it is in accord with His wisdom that in the whole universe, which is perfect in all its parts, His wisdom should shine more and more in the most perfect thing: rational nature." To find a large part of the people of the world barbaric in this sense would mean a frustration of God's plan, according to Las Casas, who explained that he had discussed this more fully in his treatise *The Only Method of Attracting All People to the True Faith*, in which he proved that "it would be impossible to find one whole race, nation, region, or country anywhere in the world that is slow-witted, moronic, foolish, or stupid, or even not having for the most part sufficient natural knowledge and ability to rule and govern itself."[24] Even such barbarians should be attracted to the Christian faith by peaceful means; nevertheless, the Indians are not this kind of barbarian, but fall within the second class.

Then Las Casas launched into a description of those barbarians who are "not irrational or natural slaves or unfit for government." They have "kingdoms, royal dignities, jurisdiction, and good laws and there is among them lawful government." Then followed such an optimistic description of Indian culture that one is not surprised that he promised to spell out his views on Indian achievements in greater detail in the second part of the *Defense*. This argument sounds very much like the parallel one developed in the *Apologetic History*.

Las Casas was reacting, of course, to Sepúlveda's harsh estimate of Indian capacity, for Sepúlveda described them thus:

In prudence, talent, virtue, and humanity they are as inferior to the Spaniards as children to adults, women to men, as the wild and cruel to the most meek, as the prodigiously intemperate to the continent and temperate, that I have almost said, as monkeys to men.[25]

Several versions of Sepúlveda's treatise, one of which may have been the text that was available to Las Casas while he was preparing his argument at Valladolid, included the "monkeys to men" phrase in this denunciation of Indian character; however, the most complete and apparently latest version of the text of the treatise prepared by Sepúlveda omits this phrase.[26]

In the definitive text of this treatise (prepared by Losada) Sepúlveda softened his position somewhat, but still had a very low opinion of the Indians' capacity and felt that Spaniards were supremely superior:

Now compare their gifts of prudence, talent, magnanimity, temperance, humanity, and religion with those little men (*homunculos*) in whom you will scarcely find traces of humanity; who not only lack culture but do not even know how to write, who keep no records of their history except certain obscure and vague reminiscences of some things put down in certain pictures, and who do not have written laws but only barbarous institutions and customs. But if you deal with the virtues, if you look for temperance or meekness, what can you expect from men who were involved in every kind of intemperance and wicked lust and who used to eat human flesh? And don't think that before the arrival of the Christians they were living in quiet and the Saturnian peace of the poets. On the contrary they were making war continuously and ferociously against each other with such rage that they considered their victory worthless if they did not satisfy their monstrous hunger with the flesh of their enemies, an inhumanity which in them is so much more monstrous since they are so distant from the unconquered and wild Scythians, who also fed on human flesh, for these Indians are so cowardly and timid, that they scarcely withstand the appearance of our soldiers and often many thousands of them have given ground, fleeing like women before a very few Spaniards, who did not even number a hundred.[27]

Sepúlveda then said that Cortez, whom he greatly admired, had decisively demonstrated the greatness of Spaniards in his conquest of Mexico: "Can there be a greater or stronger testimony how some men surpass others in talent, industry, strength of mind, and valor? Or that such peoples are slaves by nature?" And then Sepúlveda seems to reply to those who, like Dürer, praised the artistic skill of the Indians:

But even though some of them show a talent for certain handicrafts, this is not an argument in favor of a more human skill, since we see that some small animals, both birds and spiders, make things which no human industry can imitate completely.[28]

Even the relatively advanced Mexican Indians fell far short of an acceptable standard:

Nothing shows more of the crudity, barbarism, and native slavery of these men than making known their institutions. For homes, some manner of community living, and commerce—which natural necessity demands—what do these prove except that they are not bears or monkeys and that they are not

completely devoid of reason? . . . Shall we doubt that those peoples, so uncivilized, so barbarous, so wicked, contaminated with so many evils and wicked
religious practices, have been justly subjugated by an excellent, pious, and
most just king, such as was Ferdinand and the Caesar Charles is now, and by a
most civilized nation that is outstanding in every kind of virtue?[29]

Sepúlveda never abandoned the view that Indian culture was vastly
inferior to that of Spaniards. Some years after the Valladolid meeting,
in a political treatise dedicated to Philip II, he returned to this favorite
theme in referring to the justification of wars against the Indians:

> The greatest philosophers declare that such wars may be undertaken by a
> very civilized nation against uncivilized people who are more barbarous than
> can be imagined, for they are absolutely lacking in any knowledge of letters, do
> not know the use of money, generally go about naked, even the women, and
> carry burdens on their shoulders and backs just like beasts for great distances.
> The proof of their savage life, similar to that of beasts, may be seen in the
> execrable and prodigious sacrifices of human victims to their devils; it may also
> be seen in their eating of human flesh, their burial alive of the living widows of
> important persons, and in other crimes condemned by natural law, whose
> description offends the ears and horrifies the spirit of civilized people. They on
> the contrary do these terrible things in public and consider them pious acts.
> The protection of innocent persons from such injurious acts may alone give us
> the right, already granted by God and nature, to wage war against these bar-
> barians to submit them to Spanish rule.

Then he listed the great benefits Spain had conferred on the Indians,
in much the same way as the standard ordinance of 1573, and asked:
"With what behavior, with what gifts will these people repay such
varied and such immortal benefits?"[30]

Las Casas attacked this opinion of Indian culture by charging that
Sepúlveda depended for his knowledge of these matters on Oviedo,
whom Las Casas considered "a deadly enemy of mankind" and utterly
wrong on Indian capacity. Las Casas reproached his adversary for
missing the truth by failing to consult reliable ecclesiastics and such
writers as Paulus Jovius, whose histories gave a more balanced view.
Las Casas could not resist pointing out his own long experience, and
Oviedo's evident self-interest: "The testimony of such a person as
myself, who has spent so many years in America, on the character of
the Indians nullifies any allegation founded solely on the testimony
of Fernández de Oviedo who had a preconceived attitude against
the Indians because he held Indians as slaves."[31]

Las Casas made a final point against the use of force in Spanish treatment of the Indians. Even if it were granted—as it was not—that they had no keenness of mind or artistic ability, they still would not be obliged "to submit themselves to those who are more intelligent . . . even if such submission could lead to [their] great advantage."[32] Here it is evident that Las Casas was aware of Sepúlveda's contention that the Conquest conferred great benefits on the Indians.

Turning to the fourth category, adduced from Holy Scripture, *that those people who are not Christians may be called barbarians and clearly the Indians are barbarians in this sense,* Las Casas recapitulated his analysis of the four classes of barbarians and said that they may be reduced to two large categories, as follows. *Those improperly termed barbarians* comprise the first, second, and fourth classes—together with the Indians— but even Christians are barbarians (of the first class) if they manifest savage customs, and *those properly termed barbarians* comprise only the third class, from which Indians are definitely excluded. Las Casas concluded his exposition of barbarism by observing that Sepúlveda either did not understand or chose not to understand these distinctions with respect to the different classes of barbarians. As if to underline the connection between the *Defense* and the *Apologética Historia,* Las Casas put a long statement on the various kinds of barbarians, based upon the argument in the *Defense,* at the end of the *Apologética Historia.*

Rebuttal of Sepúlveda's Second Argument: Indians Commit Crimes Against Natural Law

To Sepúlveda's contention that war against the Indians may be justified as punishment for the crimes they commit against natural law, with their idolatry and sacrifice of human beings to their gods, Las Casas responded with the following syllogism: All punishment presupposes jurisdiction over the person receiving it, but Spaniards enjoy no jurisdiction over Indians, and hence they cannot punish them.

In the course of his exhaustive study of the nature of jurisdiction Las Casas made a notable statement for a mid-sixteenth-century Spanish Christian. He held that Jews, Moslems, or idolaters who live in a Christian kingdom are under the temporal jurisdiction of the Christian prince, but *not* with respect to spiritual matters (a view that was shared by Vitoria and Vera Cruz). Perhaps Las Casas was following the doctrine he had been familiar with as a young man. As Richard

Konetzke has emphasized, kings in medieval Spain permitted full freedom of worship to their subjects, and as late as 1492 the Catholic Kings Ferdinand and Isabella assured the subjugated Moorish people, after the conquest at Granada, that they could remain in the country and that they would be guaranteed the free exercise of their Islamic religion, their property, and their customs.[33] But in the years after the voyages of Columbus the Crown's authority had steadily tightened, and the modern state which aspires to gain strength by wiping out dissension was well advanced in Spain after 1551, when Las Casas was putting the text of his *Defense* in final shape. Moreover, Las Casas stated that Jews, Moslems, and idolaters who do not live in a Christian kingdom are not under the jurisdiction of the Church, nor any Christian prince, no matter how their crimes may violate natural law. Heretics, however, can be punished if they fail to observe "the obedience promised to God and the Catholic Church in baptism."[34]

Las Casas cited authority after authority to prove his contention that unbelievers do not come under the competence of the Church. Thus the Church cannot punish pagans who worship idols merely because of their idolatry. Nor is it the business of the Church to punish the unbelief of the idolaters, which Las Casas explained in this way:

The worshipers of idols, at least in the case of the Indians, about whom this disputation has been undertaken, have never heard the teaching of Christian truth even through hearsay; so they sin less than the Jews or Saracens, for ignorance excuses to some small extent. On this basis we see that the Church does not punish the blindness of the Jews or those who practice the Mohammedan superstition, even if the Jews or Saracens dwell in cities within Christian territories. This is so obvious that it does not need any proof. Rome, the bastion of the Christian religion, has Jews, as also do Germany and Bohemia. And Spain formerly had Saracens, who were commonly called *Mudejars,* whom we saw with our own eyes.

Therefore, since the Church does not punish the unbelief of the Jews even if they live within the territories of the Christian religion, much less will it punish idolaters who inhabit an immense portion of the earth, which was unheard of in previous centuries, who have never been subjects of either the Church or her members, and who have not even known what the Church is.[35]

The conclusion to this detailed exposition is clear: "There is no crime so horrible, whether it be idolatry or sodomy or some other kind, as to demand that the gospel be preached for the first time in any other way than that established by Christ, that is, in a spirit of brotherly love, offering forgiveness of sins and exhorting men to repentance."[36]

The many examples Las Casas introduced into his text after what must have been a wide-ranging search during those "sleepless nights" of study all pointed to one conclusion: "No pagan can be punished by the Church, and much less by Christian rulers, for a crime or a superstition, no matter how abominable, or a crime, no matter how serious, as long as he commits it . . . within the borders of the territory of his own masters and his own unbelief." Not that Las Casas admitted many "abominations"; rather, he dedicated much space to an exegesis of Pope Paul III's bull *Sublimis Deus* of 1537, which had played such a prominent part in the long struggle, described above, over Indian capacity. Although Las Casas analyzed the declaration in the light of fundamental and unshakable principles, he did not fail to apply them to the Indians. The methods of force and terror used to preach the faith to them had been "contrived by the devil in order to prevent the salvation of men and the spread of the true religion. And, in truth, this is . . . what they did in treating the Indians as though they were wild and brute animals so that they might exploit them as if they were beasts of burden."[37]

Rebuttal of Sepúlveda's Third Argument: Indians Oppress and Kill Innocent Persons

War against the Indians, Sepúlveda argued, may be justified because the Indians oppress innocent persons and kill them in order to sacrifice them to their gods or to eat their bodies, therefore armed intervention against the Indians would prevent an act contrary to natural law, to which all are subject.[38] Here Las Casas entered into the most complicated and subtle questions in the whole treatise, as may be seen from the large amount of space he gave to this argument. Both adversaries, and such eminent authorities of their time as Francisco de Vitoria, accepted the basic premise. Las Casas, however, strove mightily to demonstrate that the Indians did not commit such acts, and that, if they *did* worship idols or engage in human sacrifices to their gods, these acts could be justified.

The methods by which Las Casas and Sepúlveda invoked the Bible to support their respective positions are worthy of more extended treatment than can be given here. Suffice it to say that Las Casas twitted his opponent:

He has not diligently searched the scriptures, or surely has not sufficiently understood how to apply them, because in this era of grace and mercy he seeks to apply those rigid precepts of the Old Law that were given for special circumstances and thereby he opens up the way for tyrants and plunderers to cruel invasion, oppression, spoliation, and harsh enslavement of harmless nations.

What God, centuries ago, commanded the Jews to do to the Egyptians and Canaanites should not be applied to Indians of the New World. Later Las Casas stated that "not all of God's judgments are examples for us." The prophet Elisha cursed forty-two boys who mocked him, calling him a "baldhead," for which they were torn to pieces by bears. If men were to imitate such judgments, "we would commit a vast number of most unjust and serious sins and thousands of absurdities would follow."[39]

Las Casas also denounced as an absurd argument Sepúlveda's invocation of Saint Cyprian because this Church father approved the killing of those who, having heard and embraced the truth of the gospel, returned to idolatry. The Indians, obviously, did not fall into this category. Thus we see the importance of Oviedo's view, had it been accepted, that the Indians had once received the faith and had then reverted to their previous idolatry.

To illustrate his position that the Indians could not justly be punished, because no outside power held jurisdiction over them, Las Casas set forth his ideas in some detail on the conditions under which the Church or Christian princes might have jurisdiction over infidels: (1) when infidels are in fact subjects of the Church or some Christian prince, (2) when the Church or a Christian prince is able to change their potential jurisdiction (*en hábito*) over infidels to actual jurisdiction (*a acto*). Six examples of condition two were given, and Las Casas found that the Indians fit into none of the six cases. But special twists to the argumentation on two of the six circumstances merit attention—the fourth and the sixth.

The fourth circumstance occurs when pagans make obstacles *per se*, and not *per accidens*, for Christian preachers. Las Casas had to admit that missionaries had been killed in the New World, but not because they were preachers *per se* but because the Indians tried to defend themselves from the bad treatment of the accompanying soldiers who waged war against them. His previous treatise, *The Only Method of Preaching the True Faith*, had concentrated on this theme alone, and its doctrine was given in résumé: "What does the gospel have to do with firearms? What does the herald of the gospel have to do with armed thieves?"[40]

The Church has an obligation to preach the gospel to all nations, but Las Casas declared (and illustrated his doctrine with four examples) that it does not follow from this that Christians can force unbelievers to hear the gospel. The conclusion will be no surprise to those familiar with other Las Casas treatises, particularly *The Only Method of Preaching the True Faith:*

> From the foregoing it is evident that war must not be waged against the Indians under the pretext that they should hear the preaching of Christ's teaching, even if they may have killed preachers, since they do not kill the preachers as preachers or Christians as Christians, but as their most cruel public enemies, in order that they may not be oppressed or murdered by them. Therefore let those who, under the pretext of spreading the faith, invade, steal, and keep the possessions of others by force of arms—let them fear God, who punishes perverse endeavors.[41]

The final case brought forward by Las Casas holds unusual interest, for he invoked Erasmus to support his position—probably one of the few times that the sage of Rotterdam was so cited before a royal council in Spain. In this instance Las Casas referred to the doctrine of Alberto Pío, Prince of Carpi, who advanced the idea that the Church may wage war against infidels who maliciously impede the spread of the gospel. Las Casas agreed with this, especially with respect to the Turks, a point on which he was at one with Sepúlveda, who had dedicated a book to Charles V in which he advocated war against the Turks as soon as possible. Las Casas, we know, felt just as strongly as his opponent on this point.

Opposition to the anti-Moslem crusades was considered in Catholic Europe to be a Lutheran error, and one of Sepúlveda's objectives at Valladolid may have been to make the Leopoldo of his treatise, the character who questions the justice of war against the Indians, a quasi-Lutheran, inasmuch as Luther attacked the campaigns against Turkey in his *Resolutiones.* If so, Sepúlveda failed, as Las Casas seems never to have been touched by the Inquisition, despite his strong advocacy of several unpopular doctrines. At any rate, he always held that just war could be levied against the Turks and the Saracens; however, Indians were in an entirely different category, he wrote: they could not be justly warred against because their resistance was purely defensive in the face of conquistador attacks. In adopting this position Las Casas knew very well that the Prince of Carpi had been Sepúlveda's protector when the latter had first arrived in Rome as a young man, and that Sepúlveda had published his *Antapologia* in 1532 to take the part of his protector when the Prince of Carpi was feuding with Erasmus. Las Casas evidently considered Erasmus a Christian thinker in this matter:

Erasmus never dreamed of what Carpi cites against him. In fact [he] very explicitly teaches the Catholic opinion in his commentary on the psalm "Give to the Lord, you sons of God," as well as in many other passages in his writings. Possibly Carpi was seeking glory by attacking Erasmus, to whom our Sepúlveda, in putting together his little book, did not devote much attention, contrary to rumor.[42]

The sixth circumstance occurs when infidels injuriously oppress innocent persons, and specifically by sacrificing them or eating their bodies. Here again Las Casas coincided in principle with Sepúlveda and Francisco de Vitoria in upholding the traditional doctrine of the Church, that all men are obliged to aid the innocent who is in danger of being killed unjustly. But does this doctrine apply to the Indians? Yes, said Sepúlveda, while Vitoria agreed less definitely, and Las Casas argued that such an application must be "the lesser evil." For example, one must refrain from war, and even tolerate the death of a few innocent infants or persons discovered to be killed for sacrifice and cannibalism, if in trying to prevent such deaths one should "move against an immense multitude of persons, including the innocent, and destroy whole kingdoms, and implant a hatred for the Christian religion in their souls, so that they will never want to hear the name or teaching of Christ for all eternity. All this is surely contrary to the purpose intended by God and our mother the Church."[43] Even though some wicked persons would escape punishment, this would be the lesser evil. "Would he be a very good doctor who cuts off the hand to heal the finger?"[44]

When Las Casas got down to cases, he must have had in mind the post-1514 experiences of Oviedo and other Spaniards when they tried to read the requirement to Indians:

Let us put the case that the Spaniards discover that the Indians or other

pagans sacrifice human victims or eat them. Let us say, further, that the
Spaniards are so upright and good-living that nothing motivates them except
the rescue of the innocent and the correction of the guilty. Will it be just for
them to invade and punish them without any warning? You will say "No,
rather, they shall send messengers to warn them to stop these crimes." Now I
ask you, dear reader, what language will the messengers speak so as to be
understood by the Indians? Latin, Greek, Spanish, Arabic? The Indians
know none of these languages. Perhaps we imagine that the soldiers are so
holy that Christ will grant them the gift of tongues so that they will be understood by the Indians? Then what deadline will they be given to come to their
senses and give up their crimes? They will need a long time to understand
what is said to them, and also the authority and the reasons why they should
stop sacrificing human beings, so that it will be clear that evils of this type
are contrary to the natural law.

Further, within the deadline set for them, no matter what its length, they
will certainly not be bound by the warning given them, nor should they be
punished for stubbornness, since a warning does not bind until the deadline
has run out. Likewise, no law, constitution, or precept is binding on anyone
unless the words of the language in which it is proposed are clearly understood, as the learned jurists say. . . .

Now, I ask, what will the soldiers do during the time allowed the Indians
to come to their senses? Perhaps, like the forty monks Saint Gregory sent to
convert the English, they will spend their time in fasting and prayer so that
the Lord will be pleased to open the eyes of the Indians to receive the truth
and give up such crimes. Or, rather, will not the soldiers hope with all their
hearts that the Indians will become so blind that they will neither see nor
hear? And then the soldiers will have the excuse they want for robbing them
and taking them captive. Anyone who would foolishly and very unrealistically
expect soldiers to follow the first course knows nothing about the military
mind [45]

Human sacrifice required much explanation. Las Casas held that
the Indians were "in probable error" for such actions, but added:
"Strabo reminds us that our own Spanish people, who reproach the
poor Indian peoples for human sacrifice, used to sacrifice captives and
their horses." Ancient customs are hard to eradicate: "There is no
greater or more arduous step than for a man to abandon the religion
which he has once embraced." Las Casas concluded that proving the
sinfulness of human sacrifice to those who practice it is very difficult, a
basic question to which he applied four "principles":

1. No nation is so barbarous that it does not have at least some
   confused knowledge about God.
2. By a natural inclination men are led to worship God according

to their capacities and in their own ways. We must offer Him whatever we have—our wealth, energies, life, and our very soul—for His service.

3. There is no better way to worship God than by sacrifice.
4. Offering sacrifice to the true God or to the one thought to be God comes from the natural law, while the things to be offered to God are a matter of human law and positive legislation.[46]

From these principles one may adduce that Las Casas recognized the good faith of the pagan in his religion, even if it were idolatrous, and justified the pagan's human sacrifice as a natural act because he was offering his most valuable possession, his life, to the God he considered the true one. Neither Sepúlveda nor Vitoria, nor indeed few theologians then or later, adopted a similar view. Thus Las Casas respected, perhaps more than any of his contemporaries, the beliefs, rites, and customs of the Indians as appropriate and proper for them, but in the minds of many of his contemporaries he must have seemed to be teaching something very close to heresy, although the Inquisition never called him to account. For him, the religious beliefs of the Indians were valid—for them at that time—and in no wise indicated atheism. He even considered them more truly religious than those Spaniards who tried to attract Indians to their civilization and their religion by "fire and sword": "If Christians use violent methods to impose their will on the Indians, it would be better for them to maintain their own religion; indeed, in such a case the pagan Indians would be those on the right path and Christians should learn from them how to conduct themselves."

He closed his argument on human sacrifice with these words:

Thus it is clear that it is not possible, quickly and in a few words, to make clear to unbelievers, especially ours, that sacrificing men to God is unnatural. On that account, we are left with the evident conclusion that knowledge that the natives sacrifice men to their gods, or even eat human flesh, is not a just cause for waging war on any kingdom. And again, this long-standing practice of theirs cannot be suddenly uprooted. And so these entirely guiltless Indians are not to be blamed because they do not come to their senses at the first words of a preacher of the gospel. For they do not understand the preacher. Nor are they bound to abandon at once their ancestral religion, for they do not understand that it is better to do so. Nor is human sacrifice—even of the innocent, when it is done for the welfare of the entire state—so contrary to natural reason that it must be immediately detested as something contrary to the dictates of nature. For this error can owe its origin to a plausible proof developed by human reasoning.

The preceding arguments prove that those who willingly allow themselves to be sacrificed, and all the common people in general, and the ministers who sacrifice them to the gods by command of their rulers and priests labor under an excusable, invincible ignorance and that their error should be judged leniently, even if we were to suppose that there is some judge with authority to punish these sins. If they offend God by these sacrifices, he alone will punish this sin of human sacrifice.[47]

As Las Casas stated over and over again during the course of his disquisition on sacrifice: "It is not altogether detestable to sacrifice human beings to God from the fact that God commanded Abraham to sacrifice to Him his only son."

Anyone who is familiar with the genuine horror produced in the Spaniards by human sacrifice, from foot soldiers to priests, as evidenced in the many chronicles of the Conquest, must reckon the attitude of Las Casas to such ceremonial sacrifices—especially in Mexico—as one of the most remarkable of all his doctrines.[48] It was, moreover, a doctrine to which he was firmly committed, as may be seen from his even more extensive treatment of it in the *Apologética Historia,* in which he used the same authorities and examples to reach the same conclusions on the justification for human sacrifice by the American Indians. Toward the end of his long life, in a letter to his fellow Dominicans in Chiapa, he proudly referred to the arguments he presented against Sepúlveda in Valladolid: "In this controversy I maintained and proved many conclusions which no one before me dared to treat or write about." And the only specific doctrine he mentioned was his defense of human sacrifice by the Indians.[49]

Rebuttal of Sepúlveda's Fourth Argument: War May Be Waged Against Infidels in Order to Prepare the Way for Preaching the Faith

In this section Las Casas argued against Sepúlveda's use of the parable of the wedding feast, when the Lord commanded his servants to go into the highways and byways and "force them to come in." He had treated this subject in other writings, but in refuting Sepúlveda he used language reminiscent of his bitter attacks on the Conquest in his *Very Brief Account of the Destruction of the Indies:*

At this point I would like Sepúlveda and his associates to produce some passage from sacred literature where the gospel parable is explained as he explains it; that is, that the gospel (which is the good and joyful news) and the forgiveness of sins should be proclaimed with arms and bombardments, by subjecting a nation with armed militia and pursuing it with the force of war. What do joyful tidings have to do with wounds, captivities, massacres, conflagrations, the destruction of cities, and the common evils of war? They will go to hell rather than learn the advantages of the gospel. And what will be told by the fugitives who seek out the provinces of other peoples out of fear of the Spaniards, with their heads split, their hands amputated, their intestines torn open? What will they think about the God of the Christians? They will certainly think that [the Spaniards] are sons of the devil, not the children of God and the messengers of peace. Would those who interpret that parable in this way, if they were pagans, want the truth to be announced to them after their homes had been destroyed, their children imprisoned, their wives raped, their cities devastated, their maidens deflowered, and their provinces laid waste? Would they want to come to Christ's sheepfold with so many evils, so many tears, so many horrible massacres, such savage fear and heartbreaking calamity? Does not Paul say, "Treat each other in the same friendly way as Christ treated you"?[50]

Sepúlveda's fourth argument also provided Las Casas with an opportunity to deliver one of his fundamental statements on the nature of man, based on one of his favorite authorities, Saint John Chrysostom:

"Just as there is no natural difference in the creation of men, so there is no difference in the call to salvation of all of them, whether they are barbarous or wise, since God's grace can correct the minds of barbarians so that they have a reasonable understanding. He changed the heart of Nebuchadnezzar to an animal mind and then brought his animal mind to a human understanding. He can change all persons, I say, whether they are good or bad: the good lest they perish, the bad so that they will be without excuse."

Therefore Las Casas concluded that "since the nature of men is the same and all are called by Christ in the same way, and they would not want to be called in any other way."[51]

The wedding parable was then explained in familiar terms, after which Las Casas turned to Sepúlveda's use of Constantine the Great's wars against unbelievers so that once subjected to his rule, "he might remove idolatry and the faith might be introduced more freely." Historical data was produced on the Goths and the barbarian Irish to show "how great an opportunity is given to pagans to blaspheme Christ if war is waged against them and how great a hatred for Christian religion is implanted in the hearts of pagans by war. . . . Pagans, therefore, must be treated most gently and with all charity." If not, the results will be disastrous:

Now if Christians unsettle everything by wars, burnings, fury, rashness, fierceness, sedition, plunder, and insurrection, where is meekness? Where is moderation? Where are the holy deeds that should move the hearts of pagans to glorify God? Where is the blameless and inoffensive way of life? Where is humanity? Finally, where is the meek and gentle spirit of Christ? Where is the imitation of Christ and Paul? Indeed, thinking about this pitiful calamity of our brothers so torments me that I cannot overcome my amazement that a learned man, a priest, an older person, and a theologian should offer deadly poisons of this type to the world from his unsettled mind. Moreover, I do not think that anyone who fails to see that these matters are clearer than the noonday sun is truly Christian and free from the vice of greed.[52]

Christ did not arm his disciples and authorize the use of force to teach the truths of Christianity: "How does it agree with the example of Christ to spear unknowing Indians before the gospel is preached to them and to terrify in the extreme a totally innocent people by a display of arrogance and the fury of war or to drive them to death or to flight?" Preaching the faith by massacres and terror was an Islamic practice that must not be emulated by Christians.

Las Casas aimed to meet, and defeat, every one of his adversary's arguments:

Sepúlveda says that he does not want the Indians to be baptized unwillingly or to be forced to the faith. But what greater compulsion can there be than that which is carried out by an armed phalanx, shooting rifles and cannon, so that, even if no other effect should follow, at least their flashes of light and terrible thunder could dishearten any strong person, especially one not accustomed to them and ignorant of how they work? If pottery shakes because of the cannon, the earth trembles, the sky is hidden in heavy darkness, the old, the young, and women are killed, homes are destroyed, and everything resounds with warlike fury, shall we still say that these persons are not really driven to the faith? Is this not a just fear? Once they have been affected by these measures, what will the Indians refuse? Or what freedom of mind is left for embracing Christ's faith sincerely, so that they may persevere in it?

I should like the reader to answer this question: What will the Indians think about our religion, which those wicked tyrants claim they are teaching by subjugating the Indians through massacres and the force of war before the gospel is preached to them? When I speak of the force of war, I am speaking about the greatest of all evils. Furthermore, what advantage is there in destroying idols if the Indians, after being treated this way, keep them and adore them secretly in their hearts?[53]

The parable's phrase "force them to come in," therefore, must never be interpreted to apply to unbelievers who had never heard the truths of the faith. For them, only "the urgings of reason and human persuasion or spiritual and interior persuasion attained through the ministry of angels" should be used.

The *"compelle eos intrare"* parable was used frequently in sixteenth-century disputes on the conversion of American Indians. Mendieta felt it meant only peaceful actions, but others followed Sepúlveda's interpretation.[54] Even the saintly Jesuit in Brazil, José de Anchieta, who worked hard for the Christianization of the natives, in 1563 advocated the use of force "because for this kind of people there is no better way to preach the Gospel than by fire and sword." The Brazilian historian who recalls these early evangelization attempts concluded that there were more supporters there of the "dirty dog" than of the "noble savage" school.[55]

But what of infidels—how should they be treated? Here Las Casas followed the general thought of his time: "It is lawful for the heretic to be forced by the Church to keep the faith, offer obedience, and live according to Christ's law, which he vowed and freely promised" to obey. Las Casas went into this subject in some detail in order to establish the fundamental distinction, based on Saint Augustine: "Heretics must be judged differently from pagans, who must be attracted and invited to the faith with kindness and mildness, but not forced."[56] Las Casas charged that Sepúlveda had twisted Augustine's teaching, and also that he misunderstood Gregory on this point, for Gregory approved war only for the purpose of recovering provinces that had once been under Christian jurisdiction.

Thus we see again how the treatment of the Indians would have been drastically affected if Oviedo's two suppositions had been upheld: (1) the faith had been preached to them before; they had accepted it, and then fell back into idolatry, and (2) Spain's jurisdiction over the New World had been established centuries before. If Oviedo had been able to convince the Crown on these crucial points, the Indians would surely have been classified as heretics and subjects in revolt. There would then have been no occasion for the king and the Council of the Indies to consider using peaceful persuasion rather than force.

Las Casas also made a long excursion into history, because Sepúlveda cited Augustine and Thomas Aquinas as "teaching that the Romans had a just cause for subjugating the world because God wanted the world to be ruled by them since they were superior to other peoples in skill and justice." Las Casas argued that God allowed the Romans to conquer and execute peoples whose crimes had angered them, but they too had perished because their wars were not pleasing to the Lord: The tyranny of the Romans does not justify Spanish tyranny towards the Indians, which has been called *conquista*.[57]

The multiplicity of citations and repetition of basic thoughts in a bewildering variety of situations leads the reader to believe at times that one of Las Casas's methods was to wear down his opponent by the very weight and reiteration of his arguments. But his conclusion is never in doubt:

In regard to other nations or unbelievers that, along with their rulers, never heard anything about the faith nor inflicted any offense on the Church by means of any of the cases previously mentioned and never had even the smallest suspicion of what the Church is or whether it really exists, and therefore were completely outside the Church, it is perfectly clear that none of the conditions mentioned before are verified in them. In fact, all the conditions are exactly the opposite. Therefore, the status of all unbelievers is completely different, no matter how given over to idolatry they may be, provided they are not guilty according to any of the six cases already mentioned. It is quite different, I say, from the situation that motivated Gregory, Ambrose, and Augustine to exhort Christian rulers to destroy idolatry and to commend their Christian laws concerning this matter.

From the foregoing, then, the true interpretation of the original opinions of the holy doctors of the Church is obvious, as well as their interpretation of human laws, whose arguments the Venerable Doctor Sepúlveda ineptly introduces in support of his position, although they clearly militate against his position.[58]

The Second Section: Las Casas's Comments on the Authorities Cited by Sepúlveda to Support His Argument

At the close of his formal presentation of the dispute (outlined above) Las Casas appended a series of analyses of some of the principal authorities that was, in effect, a reprise of the matters he considered

most essential. These analyses constitute a short but significant portion of the *Defense*, and may in part have been elaborated after 1551,
when the sessions ended, inasmuch as the adversaries continued to
think about and sharpen their arguments for some years.

John Major

Las Casas quoted and then with great care dissected this Scottish
theologian's opinions on the Indians, for he suspected that this was
where Sepúlveda obtained some of "his poisons" with respect to the
doctrine of natural slavery. Besides, Major had never been to the New
World or seen an Indian, yet he dared to write about Indian affairs
"without an exact knowledge of the facts and the law."[59] Las Casas
characterized his views as confused, mistaken, and wrong, and went
over Major's points one by one. Major's remarks on the Conquest,
embedded in his *Commentaries on the Second Book of Sentences* of 1510,
probably constitute the first extended theoretical treatment of Spain's
actions in America. He had censured the abuse of indulgences and
defended the doctrine that "kings who comport themselves unjustly
may be deposed by the people." Major and his theories, however, seem
to have had no great influence on the course of events in the New
World or the development of the legal battles in Spain. Francisco de
Vitoria and Alonso de la Vera Cruz, as well as Las Casas, referred to
him in their manuscript works, but his ideas did not play a principal
role at the time of the Valladolid dispute.

"A king must be deprived of his rule if his people are converted to
the faith and he refuses to accept it." Las Casas commented that this
statement of Major merely demonstrated that he knew nothing of the
attitude of the Indians whom he has never seen. "No one accepts the
faith more willingly or quickly, if they are correctly instructed, than do
the kings and rulers of those nations." And, of course, "not even a king
should be forced to the faith."[60]

A king "should be deprived of his authority so that his subjects can
freely profess the Catholic faith." Las Casas replied by saying that just
as Christians are commanded to obey their rulers, even unbelievers
should do likewise. If pagans are converted to Christianity, they still
owe their ruler "reverence and obedience as to their master in matters
that are not contrary to God's law. . . . Rather, his subjects should
pay taxes to him." A ruler does not deserve to be deposed if his subjects
do not accept the faith, nor if they accept it. Major's opinion that those

who are baptized are free from all obligations, including taxes, smacked of heresy, according to Las Casas, who quoted Saints Paul and Thomas Aquinas and several jurists who had commented on their doctrines.[61]

"If a people who have embraced the faith of Christ have embraced it wholeheartedly, they ought to want their ruler to be deposed if he persists in his paganism." Las Casas retorted that it is as difficult for a people to admit a new, especially a foreign, ruler as it is for them to accept a new and strange religion: "One must not be astonished that a recently converted people does not have such a great evangelical strength as to enable them [then] to strip themselves of all their feelings and hate their former ruler whom they have known through many years' habit. Therefore something must be allowed for and conceded to their feelings, although those feelings may not be purely Christian."[62]

At this juncture in the argument, Major's most grievous error—in the eyes of Las Casas—came to the fore:

John Major goes on to speak falsely about the Indians in these words: "There is yet something else. Those people live like beasts on either side of the equator and between the poles men live like wild beasts, as Ptolemy says in his *Quadripartite*. And now this has been discovered by experience. . . ." He also brings forward the statement of the Philosopher in the first book of the *Politics* that the Greeks should rule over barbarians.[63]

Las Casas loosed all his sarcasm and ridicule on these ideas, advanced by a theologian "without an exact knowledge of the facts and the law." He showed how the people Ptolemy referred to as "bestial" lived in Moorish Africa, and that of course Ptolemy had no knowledge of America. But the argument of the geographer on the importance of climate impressed Las Casas, and it was this, perhaps, that led him to devote so much attention to this subject in the *Apologética Historia*. Las Casas admitted that those peoples living in cold and severe climates, those farthest from the equator, "would almost lack human reason." He inquired:

What has this to do with the Indians of the New World who live very close to the equator? All of their provinces are twenty or twenty-five or thirty degrees distant from the Arctic and a little more from the Antarctic, both to the north and to the south. Now since the days and nights on the equator are equal in length, it is very temperate. From this we infer that the Indians live in the most favorable regions of the whole world—a fact which we not only know theoretically but have experienced in practice. Consequently, according to the ideas of Aristotle, Vegetius, and Ptolemy, the Indians are clever and most capable of reasoning. We ourselves are witnesses to this fact for we have traveled for very many years through those regions, thoroughly observed those peoples, have considerable information about their practices and capacities, and know far more than what John Major foolishly writes in his ignorance about the happy nature of the people and of the equator. If he knew only this, it would be enough to make him reject the slanders and lies of those who, on invading those provinces, did most monstrous damage to a gentle, sincere, and decent people—something which can hardly be told without tears.[64]

As for Major's other gross error, in applying Aristotle's dictum on natural slaves, Las Casas told the story of Major's disciple in the early days of Spanish rule in Hispaniola—of Don Carlos de Aragón, who served as a vicar of the bishopric of Concepción and in 1513 dissolved a marriage between an Indian woman and her Spanish husband because "he judged that she was stupid and lacking in reason."[65]

Las Casas gave many more details about Don Carlos in his *Historia de las Indias*.[66] It appears that he was an Aragonese in Hispaniola, where most of the royal officers also were Aragonese. He also was a spirited preacher, with a doctor's degree from Paris, in a relatively primitive society that considered him vain and arrogant. He frequently quoted his master while he was in the pulpit, and on each occasion he doffed his bonnet and said with great reverence: "The Doctor John Major says this." Even worse, he held little reverence for Saint Thomas Aquinas, and when he referred to him would say "Let us pardon Saint Thomas, who did not know what he was saying." This, of course, did not sit well with the Dominicans and others, who began to question his statements. He went back to Spain, where the Inquisition condemned him for his many errors; he publicly recanted, was sentenced to life imprisonment, and "since then, nothing more was heard of him. See what these absurd or, I might say, wicked, incantations of John Major have done!"[67]

As always, Las Casas mixed theory with the American reality. Major, declaring that a large army would be required to make the Indians listen to the faith, was utterly mistaken, "not knowing what the situation really is. For the Indians are very meek and when the Spaniards first penetrated their provinces, an enormous number of them quickly boarded the ships of the Christians with a sincere attitude and entertaining the Spaniards in their homes, they paid them the highest honor as godlike men sent from heaven."

Away, then, with John Major and his dreams! He knows neither the law nor the facts. Now it is ridiculous that this theologian should say that, even before a king understands the Spanish language and even before he understands the reason why the Spanish build fortifications, he should be deprived of his kingdom by reason of expenses if he does not accept the faith. If the unfortunate king does not understand the Spanish language, how will he grasp or believe Christ's truth and abandon his own religion, approved by so many centuries of acceptance? Would not the man be insane to do this? Or are Christian dogmas like the principles which nature itself teaches and demonstrates by a special light implanted in every pagan and unbeliever? Who is so blind as to fail to see that to despoil an innocent and thoroughly ignorant ruler and to lead him, after he has been deprived of his property, into captivity under the pretext of expenses, are wiles of Satan? What does this have in common with the charity of Christ or common sense? Does the Indian who has never heard the name of Christ believe any less, at least in a human way, that his religion is true than the Christian does of his religion? John Major adds that the Indian king should reasonably put up with this. I certainly do not think that John Major would tolerate such evils and crudities, supposing he were an Indian. If Hungarians or Bohemians, of whose language he would be ignorant, were to despoil him of his dignity or rule if he were a king, when they first approached him, upsetting everything and terrifying his provinces with the tumult of war, even if they were motivated by a good cause, would he graciously and joyfully accept that good cause? And would he gladly pay the expenses when, after the passage of time, there would be a mutual grasp of both languages? I do not think so. What is forced faith, if not this? Nor is it simple force, but it involves massacres and the terror of war, the worst of all. In a passage quoted previously, Gregory says, "Preaching which exacts faith by punishment is novel and unheard of."[68]

One part of Las Casas's analysis deserves special notice: his view, which was shared by Vitoria and Vera Cruz, that "the power of election by the people" supersedes even the power of the king. Citing Peter of Paulus, he said that "if the pope deposed a king for some just cause, he cannot substitute another in his place, for the right of choosing a king, which belongs to the people by natural law, cannot be taken away from them."

A modern commentator has observed: "For Las Casas, then, the fundamental proposition is the right of the entire people (*communitas*), from whom all power is derived, to participate in the election. He thus establishes the basis for the modern parliamentary system, and we may justifiably say that he anticipated the modern system of universal suffrage." However, this interpretation seems somewhat forced, for it rests upon the view that "the people" of today may be equated with the medieval *communitas*. Las Casas's doctrine in this respect was not modern but, rather, essentially conservative, for in this argument he was drawing upon that portion of medieval political theory that emphasized the essential and residual political power of the people.[69]

Francisco de Vitoria

Had not this great theologian and political thinker died in 1546 he might well have been appointed one of the judges at the Valladolid disputation, and might even have been stimulated by the argument to compose a sequel to his classic treatise *On the Indies*. We know that he signed his approval of the 1542 treatise of the Franciscan Alfonso de Castro, which argued that the Indians were indeed capable of learning, and that this treatise probably helped the Mexican Colegio de Tlatelolco continue to receive royal support for a time despite the pessimistic reports on Indian capacity by Bishop Zumarraga and others.[70] Moreoever, the exact relationship between Vitoria's doctrine on wars and that of Las Casas has attracted the attention of modern writers, which makes the discussion in the *Defense* of special interest.

Las Casas denounced Sepúlveda's statement that Vitoria approved war against the Indians. Vitoria, in the first part of his *Prima Relectio,* "proposes and refutes, in a Catholic way, the seven headings by which war against the Indians would seem to be just." In the second part, the situation is different:

He introduces eight titles by which, or by some of which, the Indians could come under the jurisdiction of the Spaniards. In these titles he presupposes, for the most part, that certain reasons for judging this war to be just are very false and that they have been appealed to by those plunderers who overflow far and wide that whole [new] world. He is a little more careless, however, regarding some of those titles, since he wished to moderate what seemed to the Emperor's party to have been rather harshly put, although for lovers of the truth, nothing he discussed in the first part is harsh; that is, it has not merely been true in the past, but is Catholic and certainly very true. He indicates this well enough by speaking conditionally, fearing that he might suppose or make false statements instead of true ones. Now since the circumstances that this learned father supposes are false, and he says some things hesitantly, surely Sepúlveda should not have thrown up against us [Vitoria's] opinion which is based on false information.[71]

Las Casas concluded his brief but significant allusion to Vitoria by indignantly denying that four Dominicans (Miguel de Arcos, Herrera, Esbarroya, and Diego de Vitoria) supported Sepúlveda's position, as the latter had claimed. These ecclesiastics voluntarily wrote to Las Casas to complain against Sepúlveda. Even in the sixteenth century there were ample opportunities for scholars to misunderstand each other, for

they complain that you attribute to them what they have never said. Others, furnished with false information and wicked lies, have answered conditionally that this war can be just, but only on the basis of all those criminal lies of which they were persuaded when they were consulted. They have added, however, that your work which contains these outrages, should under no circumstances be published, so that this highly touted little book of yours should not give added encouragement to the wicked, who lack only the excuse to plunder and murder. In fact, this is what, unsolicited by any letters of mine, they have voluntarily written to me. So stop covering up your error with the names of so many men; rather you should aid the cause of Christ, as befits a scholar.[72]

Gonzalo Fernández de Oviedo y Valdés

Sepúlveda's reliance upon Oviedo as an authority on Indian capacity infuriated Las Casas, who, as we have seen, had known and distrusted the royal historian for more than thirty years.

He [Sepúlveda] offers a confirmation of his most contagious opinion, that is, a work on Indian matters which its author, a certain Oviedo, calls *A General History*. In book 3, chapter 6 of this work, this Oviedo writes that the people on the island of Española are undependable, idle, untruthful, inclined to evil and given over to many vices, inconstant, forgetful, cowardly, ungrateful, and hardly capable of anything. Then he says that although they are somewhat virtuous during adolescence, when they enter the age of manhood they fall into abominable vices. Then, in chapter 9 of book 6, speaking about the inhabitants of the mainland, he calls them wild, fierce, incorrigible, unable to be corrected by severity or led to virtue by inducements or friendly warnings, that they are shameless, prone to evil, harsh, and that they do not know how to show mercy. He also writes that their baptized children can attain eternal happiness but that once they become adolescents, they have little concern about the Christian religion even if they receive baptism at that time or have received it previously, both because the Christian religion seems burdensome and bothersome to them and because, being forgetful, they immediately forget whatever is taught them. Oviedo is not shamed to write these lies, scattered in various passages of his history, from which he stupidly promises himself immortality.

[The practical consequences of holding such views are obvious]: by his most virulent slanders, this utterly empty trifler has encouraged very wicked plunderers to destroy a nation totally undeserving of such treatment and has lessened the zeal of godly men who thought that they were preaching the gospel, not to men, but to wild beasts. If false defamation of one person is a sin worthy of eternal death—the more serious in proportion to the loss of property or honor that results from it—and if a sin of this type is scarcely forgiven by recantation, what must one think of or who can worthily exaggerate the sin of this very unhappy man who reviles almost the entire human race and from whose sin so many massacres, so many burnings, so many bereavements, and, finally, such an ocean of evils result?[73]

Las Casas then explained that Oviedo reviled the Indian people with such slanderous lies "because he himself from 1513 had participated in the conquest and shared the loot." In their raids, the conquistadores

spared neither women, children, nor the aged, and even burned men alive so that they might steal their gold, and divided the other men among themselves, that is, enslaved them. At that time, when Oviedo was in charge of inspection the King's accounts, his office was that of the person we call in Spanish the *veedor*. To him belonged a share of the loot that was taken during those detestable raids. The poor Indians were asleep, unsuspecting—and behold, before dawn, those savage men, plunderers rather than soldiers, rushed to attack the Indian huts, which are made of straw, put them to the torch, and burned men alive, together with their homes. After the flames died out they looked for the gold melted down by the fire. Not content with this, they most cruelly tortured the Indians they had captured alive so that they would tell where a greater supply of gold might be hidden.[74]

Naturally, Las Casas said, one must be suspicious of a person who engaged in such nefarious activities, for how could his word be trusted?

If Oviedo was a member of this wicked expedition, what will he not say about the Indians? With what vices will he not charge them in his writings? But what trust is to be given an enemy, one who has fabricated all that history from absolutely shameless lies? Because of these brutal crimes, God has blinded his eyes, along with those of the other plunderers who were infamous for their pride, greed, brutality, lust for power, and ambition, in order that he should not be allowed by God to know that those naked people were mild, simple, and meek.[75]

Las Casas also attacked Oviedo for alleging that the Indians were guilty of sodomy and "other heinous crimes," a charge Las Casas said Oviedo fabricated from stories told him by a sailor: "God willing, I shall teach at greater length in the history which I shall write about Indian affairs" that the Indians of Hispaniola and the other islands were completely free of sodomy, nor did they offer human sacrifice or eat human flesh. It sounds as if Las Casas, in mentioning "the history which I shall write," is referring to the *Apologética Historia*, or perhaps to the *Historia de las Indias*. In any case, this projected work seems to be closely connected with his argument at Valladolid, for he concluded his remarks against Oviedo by saying that his "assertion that the Indians are unteachable and incorrigible is false than false, as will be clear from the second part of this *Defense*."[76]

The Papal Bull of Alexander VI

Las Casas condemned Sepúlveda's assertion that Pope Alexander exhorted the kings to subjugate the Indians by war, and to prove his own position he analyzed the bull in detail, making much of the Pope's reference to the "meekness, sincerity, and simplicity of the Indians, as well as their capacity and receptiveness for [accepting] God's word." It was unthinkable that the Pope believed that such a gentle people had to be overcome by war against them, which was "evil and essentially unchristian." The Pope's intention, clearly, was that the Indians "should be led to the truth by a holy and Catholic instruction. Therefore the assertion that the Pope advised the Kings of Castile to wage war against the Indians is false." Queen Isabella, "the ornament of her century," well understood what the Pope had in mind, as demonstrated by her will, in which she commanded her heirs not to consent to any action whereby the Indians would "suffer any harm in their persons or goods."[77]

Las Casas concluded his voluminous *Defense* with a passionate exhortation to Sepúlveda and the "other enemies of the Indians . . . to listen to and respect the traditions of the holy Fathers, and fear God who punishes perverse undertakings." He also declared that the second part of the *Defense*, the Spanish *Apología*, would provide "very clear arguments and a true description of that world in order that the wicked plunderers who have defamed that very sincere, docile, moderate, and clever people by poisonous detractions and slanderous lies may be silenced."[78]

NOTES

1. Losada (1968), p. 206. Dr. Losada and I have corresponded on this subject, and at my request he prepared the following note and has authorized its reproduction:

"Para mí está fuera de duda que, cuando Las Casas preparó su larga 'Apologia' la dividió en dos partes: *una originalmente en latín* (el actual manuscrito de París) en la que exponía *los argumentos de derecho* y respondía parte por parte a la 'Apologia' de Sepúlveda, *y otra originalmente en castellano* en la que exponía *los argumentos de hecho* (concretamente para demolir la argumentación de Sepúlveda a este respecto basada en F. de Oviedo: el indio no entraba en la condicion aristotélica de esclavo).

"Para mí es también casi seguro que (como hubo versiones en castellano de la 'Apologia' de Sepúlveda, y tal vez también del *Democrates II*) se hizo también una traducción castellana del manuscrito de París, aunque desgraciadamente no se ha descubierto (¡y es una verdadera lástima pues nos hubiera ahorrado muchas horas de traducción!). Ello es muy lógico, pues el contenido de dicho manuscrito debió hacerse muy popular con motivo de la Junta de Valladolid y había interés en que llegase al mayor número de lectores incluso a los que no dominaban tanto el latín.

"Pasemos ahora a la cita que V. me transcribe del libro III, cap. 151 de la *Historia de las Indias*.

"En primer lugar yo creo que el original debía decir: ' . . . en nuestra Apologia escrita en lengua castellana y en latín' (es decir suprimiéndose la coma puesta sin duda por los editores entre 'castellana' y 'y en latín'). No creo que esta coma existiera en el original lascasiano; no tiene sentido decir solamente 'en lengua castellana' pues es evidente que lo fue en latín, a menos que haciendo tal cita en un libro escrito en castellano (*Historia de las Indias*) creyese Las Casas más indicado *citar solo la versión castellana* de su 'Apologia' (primera parte). Por otra parte no hay que olvidar que el texto del manuscrito de París contiene alguna página en castellano: la larga cita del testamento de la Reina Isabel; ello, aunque dificilmente justificaría en cierto sentido la frase 'en lengua castellana y en latín.' Yo sigo creyendo que hubo dos versiones del texto del manuscrito de París: latina y castellana.

"Sigo también creyendo que la segunda parte en castellano a que el propio Las Casas se refiere en el manuscrito de París constituyó el elemento esencial de lo que después él llamó 'Apologética Historia'; sin duda en un principio no con este nombre; y sin duda también que lo que después fue 'Apologética Historia' recibió muchos añadidos (el mismo nombre 'Apologética' viene a indicar que formaba parte de su gran 'Apologia' y sobre todo la propia afirmación de Las Casas en el manuscrito de París sobre el contenido de su segunda parte y sobre el hecho de estar escrita en castellano.

"Lo que, a mi juicio ocurrió, es que Las Casas, después de la Junta de Valladolid siguió trabajando tanto en la primera como en la segunda parte hasta ofrecernos esta segunda parte como su Apologética'; conforme a su método añadió aquí y allá infinidad de pegotes un poco sin ton ni son (así por ejemplo en la 'Apologética' tal como nos la dió en definitiva versión introdujo el capítulo sobre 'las diferentes clases de siervos' que aparecía ya *in extenso* en la primera parte (manuscrito de París) y no es por tanto lógico que estuviese en la primera versión de la mencionada segunda parte). Esto plantea otro importante problema: el de la versión definitiva de todas las obras de Las Casas tal como hoy de nos presentan: V. sabe que muchas de ellas: *De Thesauris, De unico vocat., Apologia, Apologética* . . . son en buena parte un conglomerado de añadidos y de repeticiones de lo mismo."

2. Las Casas (1967), I, xvi-lv. As an example of the interest aroused by the *Apologética Historia*, one may cite the manuscript résumé of this treatise in the Vatican Library (Reg. Lat. 659), discovered by the Peruvian Jesuit Rubén Vargas Ugarte (1935), I, 118. I am deeply indebted to Dr. Antonio de Egaña, S. J., of the Institute of Jesuit History in Rome, for the following note on this manuscript: "No es copia sino resumen libre sacado de la obra del P. Las Casas, omite o abrevia todo lo relativo a las largas descripciones de Las Casas sobre los pueblos clásicos, lo mismo que los pasajes, donde se trata de discursos filosóficos o jurídicos. Se nota en el abreviador su plan de dar lo elemental de Las Casas, con el mismo ideario de éste, defensor de los indios. No se divide su resumen ni en capítulos ni en libros. . . . Al fin (fols. 188-216) se añade: 'Caso propuesto para salir de cierta duda.' Se trata de un español que habría ido a Indias en tiempo de la conquista, y después habría quedado de regidor de un pueblo, por mandato del governador, sin seguir la guerra, y habría percibido 5,000 ducados o màs; y se pregunta si está obligado a la restitución. El autor consultado responde afirmativamente. . . .

"En resumen: no se trata de una copia fiel, se trata de una reducción. Esto se hace omitiendo capítulos y párrafos enteros, reduciendo otros, explicando los mismos conceptos ad sensum. No se altera el pensamiento de Las Casas, sí se conserva su letra materialmente en casos, y en otros se abrevia su pensamiento ad sensum." (Letter from Dr. Egaña dated 29 March 1973.)

3. Poole, *Defense,* p. 44.
4. Hanke (1970), p. 49. See also Torre Villar (1956). A most dramatic and curious example of disregard for the American reality may be seen in the recent treatment by Sakari Sariola (the Finnish scholar) of the Las Casas and Sepúlveda doctrines; he devotes much attention to their differences but uses fancy sociological language and theorems that mystify rather than enlighten (see Sariola [1972], pp. 46-126). Also, he has devised several curious graphic illustrations (figures 1-7) by which he attempts to summarize, in schematic fashion, what the Las Casas-Sepúlveda dispute signified in the light of his interpretation of the nature of power in the Spanish Empire.
5. This is one of the relatively rare instances when Las Casas referred to the musical ability of the Indians. See Stevenson (1966), p. 114, for Spanish attitudes toward Indian music.
6. Las Casas probably refers to Oviedo here. Emphasis added.
7. Poole, *Defense,* pp. 42-43. Emphasis added.
8. Ibid., pp. 255, 348. Emphasis added.
9. Ibid., p. 362. Emphasis added.
10. Las Casas (1967), I, 3.
11. Ibid., p. 4.
12. Hanke (1970), p. 113.
13. Giménez Fernández (1953), I, 763. The 1519 dispute is given in some detail on pp. 753-65.
14. Las Casas (1951), Libro III, caps. 142-156.
15. Ibid., cap. 144.
16. Ibid., cap. 156.

17. For a note on this new interpretation by Dr. Edmundo O'Gorman, see appendix 4.

18. As referred to above (p. 64). Las Casas once stated that sometime before 1550 he had considered composing an *apología* in Spanish to oppose Sepúlveda's *Sumario*, but he did not say that he actually wrote such a work. Moreover, from Las Casas's description, the treatise he had in mind apparently would have concentrated more on doctrine than on Indian culture and thus might have been a prototype of the *Defense*. We know, however, that among Las Casas's papers were "un libro, en romance, entitulado Sumario del libro que el Doctor Sepúlveda compuso contra los indios" and "parte de una apología que contra él hizo el obispo de Chiapa, de 94 hojas escritas en folio" (*D.I.U.*, XIV, 166).

19. Las Casas (1966), I, 283.

20. Poole, *Defense,* p. 22.

21. Ibid., pp. 41-42.

22. Las Casas (1966), II, 931, 951, 973, 981, 997, 1001, 1017, 1041, 1053, 1137, 1147.

23. Poole, *Defense,* p. 28.

24. Ibid., p. 38.

25. Sepúlveda (1951), p. 33. For additional information on his views on Indians, see ibid., pp. 34-35, Sepúlveda (1963), pp. 35-43, and the *Defense,* chap. 4.

26. Sepúlveda (1951), pp. xxvi-xxxii. For an English translation of one of these earlier versions, see Sepúlveda (1973).

27. Sepúlveda (1951), p. 35.

28. Ibid., p. 36.

29. Ibid., p. 38.

30. Ibid., pp. 78-79.

31. Losada (1968), p. 210.

32. Poole, *Defense,* pp. 46, 48

33. Konetzke (1958), p. 517.

34. Poole, *Defense,* p. 55.

35. Ibid., pp. 78-79.

36. Ibid., p. 96.

37. Ibid., p. 102.

38. Ibid., chap. 13.

39. Ibid., p. 121.

40. Ibid., p. 173.

41. Ibid., p. 181.

42. Ibid., p. 184. Marcel Bataillon commented thus on how little *Erasmistas* in Spain participated in the great debate over Indian problems: "En esta España de Carlos V que combatía a la vez en tantos campos de batalla, en que muchos letrados persistían en la ilusión de una paz cristiana impuesta por las armas del Emperador, no hubo un solo erasmista que tomara contra Sepúlveda la defensa del pacifismo radical y utópico. Cuando el *Democrates alter* planteó, después de las *Relectiones* de Vitoria, el problema de la guerra justa a propósito del caso concreto de la conquista de América, no se vio tampoco que los erasmistas interviniesen en el debate. . . . En suma, lo que hay que consignar es la ausencia del erasmo español, despues de la muerte de Alfonso de Valdes, en los grandes debates sobre la guerra y la paz" (Bataillon [1966], p. 633).

43. Poole, *Defense,* p. 190.

44. Ibid., p. 214.

45. Ibid., pp. 217-18.

46. Ibid., chap. 35.

47. Ibid., pp. 241-42.
48. Padden (1967) gives much information on human sacrifice among the Aztecs.
49. Las Casas (1957), V, 471.
50. Poole, *Defense,* p. 270.
51. Ibid., p. 271.
52. Ibid., pp. 279, 285-87, 288.
53. Ibid., pp. 297-98.
54. Pike (1969), pp. 59-60. For more complete information on Mendieta's views, see Phelan (1969).
55. Buarque de Holanda (1969), pp. 292-303. See also Leite (1962). Indeed, there seems to have been no idealization of the Indian in Brazil until the early nineteenth century (Boxer [1962], p. 22). In the colonial period the Indians were generally depreciated and treated cruelly, as may be seen in detail in Azevedo (1930). Boxer (1962) has summarized the views of two representative Portuguese in Brazil, Domingos Jorge Velho (1694) and Paulo da Silva Nunes (1724). The latter stigmatized the Indians in Brazil as "squalid savages, ferocious and most base, resembling wild animals in everything save human shape." He agreed with those authorities who considered them "not true human beings, but beasts of the forest incapable of understanding the Catholic faith." Boxer (1963), pp. 94-96. For a recent authoritative overview, see Alden (1969).
56. Poole, *Defense,* pp. 305, 307.
57. Ibid., pp. 321, 325.
58. Ibid., pp. 320-21.
59. Ibid., pp. 331.
60. Ibid., p. 330.
61. Ibid., pp. 330, 333.
62. Ibid., pp. 337, 338.
63. Ibid., p. 339.
64. Ibid., p. 383.
65. Ibid., p. 340.
66. Las Casas (1951), II, 554-55.
67. Poole, *Defense,* p. 340.
68. Ibid., p. 329.
69. See Losada (1968), p. 243. For additional views of Las Casas on the election of kings, see Las Casas (1969), pp. 34, 48. For a general view of Las Casas's political doctrines, see Hanke (1935a).
70. For information on the Castro treatise, see Olaechea Labayen (1958), pp. 175-97, and Kobayashi (1972), pp. 430-35.
71. Poole, *Defense,* pp. 340-41.
72. Ibid., p. 341. The true position of Diego de Vitoria requires further study; he certainly seems to have signed an approbation of the *Democrates,* but he may have changed his mind later.
73. Ibid., pp. 343-44.
74. Ibid., p. 345.
75. Ibid., p. 346.
76. Ibid., pp. 347, 348. Las Casas returned to Oviedo in his *Historia de las Indias,* in which he again refuted his allegations on the Indians in pungent detail:
    "Dice Oviedo que cuando alguno se casaba, señor o principal o de los plebeyos y bajos, todos los convidados, primero que el novio, habían de tener con la novia mala parte; yo creo que el que lo dijo a Oviedo no le dijo verdad, porque

nunca hobo tiempo para que aquello de los indios se alcanzase. Y si verdad fuese, naciones hobo entre las antiguas que vivían sin cognoscimiento de Dios, que acostumbraron lo mismo, como a la larga en nuestra *Apologética Historia* mostramos." Las Casas (1951), Libro III, cap. 24.

Las Casas could not contain his indignation in recounting the many dreadful qualities Oviedo attributed to the Indians, including the remark about their heads being so hard and thick that Spaniards broke or blunted their swords when they struck them:

"¿Qué más puede decir, aunque fuera verdad, en infamia de todo este orbe nuevo [donde tan infinitas naciones hay], y engañado a todo el otro mundo viejo por donde anda su historia? Si infamar una sola persona, puesto que se dijese verdad, descubriendo sus pecados, de donde le puede venir, e peor si le viniese, algún gran daño, es grande pecado mortal y es obligado el tal infamador a restitución de todo aquel daño, ¿qué pecado fue el de Oviedo y a cuánta restitución será obligado, habiendo infamado de tan horrendos pecados a tan sin número multitúdines de gentes, tanta infinidad de pueblos, tantas provincias y regiones plenísimas de mortales que nunca vido ni oyó decir, por la cual infamia incurrieron todas en odio y en horror de toda la cristiandad, y los que a estas partes han pasado de los nuestros y de los de otra nación, en las guerras que se hallaron, no hicieron más cuenta de matar indios que si chinches mataran, y hicieron por esta causa en ellos tantos géneros y novedades de crueldades, que ni en tigres ni bravos osos y leones, antes ni los mismos tigres y bestias fieras, hambrientas, en otras de otro género no las hicieran tales como ellos cometieron en aquestas gentes desnudas y sin armas?" Ibid., cap. 143.

As he continued his strong and sustained attack on Oviedo in the *Historia de las Indias*, Las Casas referred to greater details on this or that matter in his *Apologética Historia* (ibid. caps. 144-145). He rightly understood that the opinions of the Oviedo, the royal chronicler, as printed in the two editions of Part I of his *Historia*, might well influence the Council of the Indies and others, in 1550 or later, to support the learned Sepúlveda's application to the Indians of Aristotle's doctrine of natural slavery. Hence his fierce onslaught on Oviedo in his writings against Sepúlveda in both Latin and Spanish, as well as in his later *Historia de las Indias*.

77. Poole, *Defense,* pp. 353, 355-56, 357.
78. Ibid., p. 362.

IV

The Aftermath of the Conflict

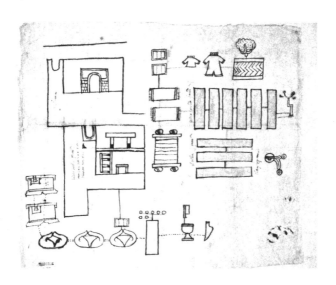

Echoes of the Controversy to 1573

HE judges at Valladolid, probably exhausted and confused by the sights and sounds of this mighty conflict, fell into argument with one another and reached no collective decision.[1] Las Casas later stated that the decision had been favorable to his viewpoint, "although unfortunately for the Indians the measures decreed by the Council were not well executed," and Sepúlveda wrote to a friend that the judges "thought it right and lawful that the barbarians of the New World should be brought under the dominion of the Christians, only one theologian dissenting." The dissident was perhaps either the Dominican Melchor Cano, who had previously combated the ideas of Sepúlveda in systematic fashion in one of his works, or Domingo de Soto.

The available facts do not conclusively support the claim of either contestant. The judges went home after the final meeting, and for many years afterward the Council of the Indies struggled to get their opinions in writing; as late as 1557, a note was sent to Cano explaining that all the other judges had rendered their decision and that his was wanted at once. These written opinions have not yet come to light, except for one: Dr. Anaya's statement approved the Conquest in order to spread the faith and to stop the Indians' sins against nature, provided that the expeditions be financed by the king and be led by captains "zealous in the service of the king who would act as a good example to the Indians, and who would go for the good of the Indians, and not for gold." The captains were to see that the usual peaceful exhortations and warnings were made before force was used. Another judge, the jurist Gregorio López, largely supported Las Casas's ideas on the main issue in the notes to his 1555 edition of *Siete Partidas.*

Immediately after the last meeting, Las Casas and his companion, Rodrigo de Andrada, made arrangements with the San Gregorio monastery in Valladolid to spend the rest of their lives there. According to the contract drawn up on 21 July 1551, they were to be accorded three new cells—one of them, presumably, for the large collection of books and manuscripts Las Casas had amassed—a servant, first place in the choir, freedom to come and go as they pleased, and burial in the sacristy.

Las Casas, however, did not settle down to a life of quiet contemplation. The failure of the Valladolid disputation to produce a resounding and public triumph for his ideas may have convinced him that his efforts on behalf of the Indians needed a more permanent record. He was seventy-eight years old, and weary from half a century of battle on Indian affairs, and perhaps desirous of using the printing press to get his propositions and projects before Spaniards whom he could not otherwise reach. At any rate, he left San Gregorio and in the next year, 1552, went to Seville, where he spent many months recruiting friars for America and preparing the series of nine remarkable treatises that were printed in Seville in 1552 and early 1553. It is possible, however, that he had no intention of publishing these bold tracts for all the world to see, for they included the inflammatory *Very Brief Account of the Destruction of the Indies,* denouncing Spanish cruelty to the Indians, and the series was a limited edition, intended only for the eyes of Prince Philip and the royal councillors. Whatever his intentions, the treatises were sent across the Pyrenees, where they were eventually issued in numerous English, Flemish, French, German, Italian, and Latin translations.

The treatises—among them the *Confesionario* and the résumé of the Las Casas-Sepúlveda dispute—were immediately shipped to the New World, much to the disgust of those Spaniards who held Indians and of others who deeply resented the wholesale attack by Las Casas on the *conquistadores*. The tracts also served as manuals and textbooks to guide the friars scattered over the vast stretches of America as daily they confronted the problems of conscience. The full story of these heroic and little-known attempts to enforce Las Casas's doctrines—some of which have been revealed through the patient archival work of the Colombian historian Juan Friede—will eventually provide another valuable chapter in the history of the struggle for justice in the Spanish conquest of America.[2]

The publication of these passionately argued doctrines may have been a direct result of the Valladolid debate. Perhaps Las Casas came to realize that his whole life's work was profoundly jeopardized and he wanted to be sure that the *corpus* of his doctrine would be readily available to his successors (in one of the treatises he noted that his life expectancy was short).[3] The preparation and publication of this collection of controversial writings constituted, as Manuel Giménez Fernández stated at the end of his brilliant reconstruction of Las Casas's life in Seville in 1552 and 1553 while he saw the treatises through the press, a "solemn profession of political and religious faith."[4] Their publication also transformed what had been a bitter but private feud in Spanish intellectual and court circles into an ever more widely discussed subject in Europe and elsewhere.

Publication of the résumé of the controversy did not, however, stop the dispute. Both Las Casas and Sepúlveda continued to sharpen their arguments and seek supporters for their views. Perhaps this continuing debate on the complex issues debated at Valladolid helps explain why the Council of the Fourteen never rendered a collective decision. The *Defense* itself, in its present form, was drawn up by Las Casas in the years following the publication of the treatises in Seville. During these years Las Casas also completed two of his greatest works, the *Historia de las Indias* and the *Historia Apologética*. These remarkable compositions include almost all of his fundamental views on Spain's conquest of America. Las Casas refers to one of his most essential doctrines—that the Indians are not to be considered slaves *a natura*—over and over again in all three treatises. Toward the end of the *Historia de las Indias,* completed about 1559, he devotes much attention to Bishop Juan de Quevedo's first application of Aristotle's doctrine to the Indians in the presence of the young Emperor Charles V at Barcelona in 1519. Las Casas declares that the doctrine could not and should not be applied to the Indians: "They are very capable of the Christian faith and of all virtue and good customs; by their nature they are free and have their own kings and natural lords who govern them."[5]

Here we see Las Casas setting forth his views on Indian capacity in his principal treatises, and he may have been putting the finishing touches on the *Defense* at about the same time he was bringing the *Historia de las Indias* to a close. In 1562 we find the Dominican Bartolomé de la Vega trying to convince the Council of the Indies that the *Defense* should be published, and describing its author as "the discoverer of truth in Indian affairs and the father of all the inhabitants of that new world." Las Casas had not only been the first to show the justice of the Indians' cause but had "fought a war by debating and examining this matter with certain doctors who have attempted with all their energy to defend what is the exact opposite to every truth and to this very day refuse to retreat from their insane opinions." And Vega, in his concluding plea, emphasized the universal significance of the doctrine Las Casas expounded in the *Defense*:

> Unless I am mistaken, there is certainly no other matter that can surpass this business of the Indies in magnitude. For what is at stake is nothing less than the salvation or loss of both the bodies and souls of all the inhabitants of that recently discovered world. Rightly, then, is this work to be regarded as supremely important, for it is vitally necessary for the whole world. On it the author has spent so much labor. He has grown old from many anxieties and sleepless nights. He has read through many books, as anyone can easily see for himself in the result.[6]

Nor had Sepúlveda and his adherents been idle after the Valladolid dispute. The popular historian Francisco López de Gómara, who had been so pessimistic on Indian capacity, did not trouble himself to justify the Conquest but recommended that his readers "consult Sepúlveda, the emperor's chronicler, who wrote most elegantly in Latin on this topic, and thus you will be completely satisfied on the matter."[7]

Spaniards, however, were not "completely satisfied," and the battle of words continued. Sepúlveda kept the pot boiling by writing, soon after the galaxy of treatises by Las Casas appeared in 1552-1553, a blast that was titled *Rash, Scandalous and Heretical Propositions Which Dr. Sepúlveda Noted in the Book on the Conquest of the Indies Which Friar Bartolomé de Las Casas Printed Without a License.* In this vigorous complaint against the wiles and stratagems of Las Casas, Sepúlveda repeatedly accused his opponent of heretical views. He maintained his position that it was just and holy to subject the barbarians to Spanish rule to make them abandon their idolatry and obey the laws of nature, whether they wanted to or not. Then the gospel should be preached with Christian mildness, and the Indians were not to be killed, or enslaved, or deprived of their haciendas—a doctrine and a program that would be difficult to deduce from the treatise Las Casas had attacked at Valladolid.[8]

During the years that followed the disputation, Sepúlveda's rich correspondence was filled with information and reflections on his dispute with Las Casas. In a letter to Francisco de Argote he indignantly denied that he supported the enslavement of the Indians:

I do not maintain that the barbarians should be reduced to slavery, but only that they should be submitted to our rule; I do not maintain that we should deprive them of their property, but only conquer them without committing any unjust acts against them; I do not maintain that we should abuse our power over them, but rather that our dominion should be noble, courteous, and useful for them. Thus we should first of all root out their pagan customs and then influence them with kindness to follow natural law, and with this magnificent preparation for the acceptance of Christian doctrine attract them with apostolic kindness and charitable words to the Christian religion.[9]

His emphasis here was not the same as during the Valladolid discussions, but he still felt that Spanish dominion should be considered a simple act of generosity on the part of his countrymen that would benefit both the conqueror and the conquered:

Natural law therefore provides a justification for those people who, by pure motives of generosity, undertake to establish their rule over barbarous peoples, not to the end that they thereby profit or that they treat them unjustly or reduce them to slavery, but rather to comply with a duty of mankind by trying to root out their customs so contrary to natural law [that] they make them change their lives and adopt the obligations of natural law. By this process a double benefit will be achieved; moreover, there will be an interchange of favors between the dominant nation and the conquered peoples.[10]

After the Valladolid debate Sepúlveda also corresponded with the Franciscan Alfonso de Castro on the means by which just war might be waged against the Indians. In his earlier writing Sepúlveda seems to have favored something like the Requirement, the remarkable document that was drawn up in 1513 and was first read to the Indians by the historian Oviedo. Now, at another decisive moment in the history of just war in the Indies, the same question was raised—how, or even whether Indians should first be invited or warned to accept the Christian faith and Spanish domination. Castro had drawn up the 1542 treatise supporting the view that Indians could be educated, and subsequently had composed the important *De Justa Hereticorum Punitione*. Now, in correspondence with Sepúlveda, he supported Sepúlveda's doctrine in general but stated in his book that some kind of exhortation or preliminary warning was necessary. Sepúlveda pointed out, in his letter to Castro, that no warning had been given in biblical times, nor had Pope Alexander VI mentioned any such warning with respect to the Indians. He believed that such a warning would be very difficult to give, and in any case quite useless, as it was clear that "no people will abandon the religion of their ancestors except by force of arms or by miracles." (On an earlier occasion he had made it clear that he expected few miracles.)

Castro seems to have vacillated on Indian questions. Known principally in legal history for his contributions in penology, he held doctrines similar to those of John Major, who had been the first to apply Aristotle's doctrine of natural slavery to the Indians. But he believed that even war against idolaters would be unjust unless it were preceded by a period of intense apostolic labor to convert them. One of his earlier opinions, on which Vitoria commented favorably, was that Indians could and should be instructed in all the liberal arts and ordained by the Church. In later correspondence with Sepúlveda (referred to previously) he reversed his position on the need for exhortations and missionary labor before waging war, for he agreed that if by "prudent conjectures" it could be determined in advance that the idolaters were in fact "pertinacious," they could be warred against justly, even without the warning. All this would be in conformity, wrote Castro, with what theologians had said with respect to *correctio fraterna*.[11] He also strongly supported giving *encomenderos* control over Indians in perpetuity, in a long and detailed opinion written and delivered to Philip II in London on 13 November 1554.

The publication of the treatises in 1552-1553 ensured that Las Casas's doctrines would be discussed overseas as well as in Spain. Alonso de la Vera Cruz, the Augustinian who became one of Las Casas's disciples during his later years, preserved a number of other writings by Las Casas, which according to Henry R. Wagner, "are our main source for the closing chapters of Casas' life."[12] On 16 August 1566 the notary Gaspar Testa delivered to Vera Cruz the 1,511 *reales* that had been provided for him in Las Casas's will as a bequest, possibly for the purpose of having his writings copied. Las Casas also entrusted a considerable portion of his manuscripts to his close Augustinian friend, but Vera Cruz was never able to get either his own or Las Casas's treatises on justice for the Indians published.

Only recently has Dr. Ernest J. Burrus, S. J. been able to print Vera Cruz's views on the defense of the Indians, to which the latter had devoted his first theological course at the University of Mexico in 1553-1554. One of Vera Cruz's fellow professors, Francisco de Cervantes Salazar, described him as "the most learned professor of arts and theology that our province has, the foremost interpreter of this most sacred and divine science, a man of varied and manifold erudition, in whom the highest virtue vies with rare and admirable learning." In his treatise Vera Cruz did not mention Sepúlveda by name, but he opposed the application of Aristotle's doctrine of natural slavery to the Indians. Likewise, Vera Cruz did not accept the charge by Sepúlveda and others on the incapacity of the Indians; instead, he insisted on their innate ability. In most respects he was close to Las Casas's views, though never so dogmatic or doctrinaire. The publication of his treatise more than four centuries after its composition enables the world at last to appreciate the learning and courage of this outstanding scholar who occupied himself with the defense of the Indians in the years immediately following the Valladolid disputation.[13]

University professors were not the only Spaniards in Mexico who were concerned with Sepúlveda's thesis. His treatise afforded comfort to the town council of Mexico City, the richest and most important city in all the Indies; indeed, the town fathers voted on 8 February 1554 to buy "some jewels and clothing from this land to the value of 200 pesos" as a grateful recognition of what Sepúlveda had done on their behalf and "to encourage him in the future."[14] Sepúlveda complained bitterly that he had been accused of being corrupted by conquistador gold, and a modern admirer of his doctrines defends him from the charge.[15] A few years later the Mexico City town fathers employed the famous humanist scholar Francisco Cervantes de Salazar as their official chronicler, and he devoted a few scornful lines to the Tlatelolco seminary, which had been established to train Indians for the priesthood, concluding that "the Indians cannot and should not be ordained, because of their incapacity."[16]

Treatises for or against Sepúlveda's doctrine continued to be written. Bishop Vasco de Quiroga, the Franciscan Bernardino de Arévalo, Bartolomé de Albornoz, the Dominicans Miguel de Arcos and Pedro de la Peña, and others denounced or supported the idea that wars against the Indians were just.[17] Although the manuscripts of the principal protagonists remained unpublished, their arguments lived on—long after Las Casas died in 1566 (at the age of ninety-two) and Sepúlveda in 1573.

By this time the Crown had evidently reached its decision on how conquests should be conducted.[18] All regulations for conquistadores, beginning with the Requirement of 1513, were superseded by a general ordinance promulgated by Philip II on 13 July 1573 and designed to regulate all future discoveries and conquests by land or sea. The president of the Council of the Indies, Juan de Ovando, knew of Las Casas's doctrines and in 1571 caused his manuscripts to be brought from Valladolid to the Court in Madrid for use by the Council. Thus this standard law may have been drawn up in such generous terms because of the battle Las Casas fought at Valladolid. Ovando, one of the most important but least-studied Crown officials, probably was much influenced by Las Casas's ideas. Las Casas himself could not have more forcibly expressed the support for peaceful action toward the Indians that was contained in the basic law of 1573.

Detailed examination of these provisions indicates how far the

King had departed from the early requirement policy and from the proposals of Sepúlveda at Valladolid. The Spaniards were to explain the obligation resting upon the Crown of Spain and the wonderful advantages that had been bestowed upon those natives who had already submitted—a sort of justification by works—so perhaps Sepúlveda's arguments at Valladolid also found echo in the 1573 ordinances. The Spaniards were charged, furthermore, with emphasizing that

the king has sent ecclesiastics who have taught the Indians the Christian doctrine and faith by which they could be saved. Moreover, the king has established justice in such a way that no one may aggravate another. The king has maintained the peace so that there are no killings or sacrifices, as was the custom in some parts. He has made it possible for the Indians to go safely by all roads and to carry on their civil pursuits peacefully. He has freed them from burdens and servitude; he has made known to them the use of bread, wine, oil, and many other foods, woollen cloth, silk, linen, horses, cows, tools, arms and many other things from Spain; he has instructed them in crafts and trades by which they live excellently. All these advantages will those Indians enjoy who embrace our Holy Faith and render obedience to our king.[19]

The Crown had long ruled, however, that "all these advantages" must be paid for by the Indians. The tribute exacted of Peruvian Indians at the time of the Valladolid disputation, for example, was heavy; they were required to deliver money, food, and manufactured goods to their encomenderos, who might live forty leagues away.

The 1573 ordinances do not refer to such tribute by Indians or to their obligation to pay the cost of the benefits bestowed on them. On the contrary, unpleasant topics were avoided, and the law decreed particularly that the word "conquest" no longer be used; the new, authorized term was "pacification." The vices of the Indians were to be dealt with very gently at first, "so as not to scandalize them or prejudice them against Christianity." If, after all the explanations, the natives still opposed a Spanish settlement and the preaching of Christianity, the Spaniards might use force, but they were to do "as little harm as possible." No license was given to enslave the captives.

This general order governed conquests as long as Spain ruled her American colonies, even though some Spaniards could always be found who thought that the Indians should be subjugated by force of arms because they were not Christians. The disputes that led to the 1573 law were responsible for a fundamental cleavage among those who wrote on the work of Spain in America, so that Spanish historiography became polarized around two extreme and apparently ineradicable points of view. Many historians either condemned Spain or exalted her contributions to the Indians, depending upon whether they followed the arguments of Las Casas or Sepúlveda.

The general ordinance governing conquests was only one of the basic laws devised in the early 1570s to strengthen royal authority. The Council of the Indies was reformed and a new set of regulations was devised for it; the office of official chronicler and cosmographer was established (perhaps because of the Las Casas-Sepúlveda dispute);[20] the Crown was increasingly concerned to see that "true history" was written, and Philip II personally took a hand in censorship;[21] the system of gathering economic and geographical information from the Indies was improved; and the *Patronazgo* law of 1574 put all ecclesiastics, even the hitherto free-wheeling mendicant friars, more closely under royal supervision and direction.[22] The heroic days of the Conquest were over, but discussion on Indian capacity did not cease.

Continued Conflict on the Capacity of the Indians

Although the Valladolid disputation did not end the arguments over the nature of the Indians and their aptitude for entering a Christian civilization, it did tend to change the terms and intensity of the battle. The idyllic "noble savage" vision was continued by such outstanding friars as Gerónimo de Mendieta, who "Franciscanized" the Indians in this way:

Some of the Indians, especially the old people and more often the women than the men, are of such simplicity and purity that they do not know how to sin. Our confessors, who are more perplexed by some of these Indians than they are by notorious sinners, search for some shred of sin by which they can grant them the benefit of absolution. And this difficulty does not arise because the Indians are stupid or ignorant, for they are well versed in the law of God. They answer well all the questions, even the trifles, that they are asked. The fact is, because of their simple and good nature they do not know how to hold a grudge, to say an unkind thing of anyone else, to complain even of mischievous boys, or to forget to fulfill one particle of the obligation that the Church has imposed on them. And in this case I do not speak from hearsay but from my own experience.[23]

Mendieta also lamented the "miserable fall and the catastrophes of our Indian Church," especially after the end of the early "golden age," which he believed terminated with the death of such figures as the Emperor Charles V (1558) in Spain and Viceroy Luis de Velasco (1564) in Mexico. The Franciscan's denunciation of Spanish greed rivaled that of Las Casas:

At this time the high wall of very saintly laws, *cédulas*, and commands that the fortunate and invincible Emperor Charles V and his good governors had constructed for the defense, aid, and protection of the vineyard was surrounded by wild animals and beasts of prey who were eager to seize, ravish, and destroy it; but a little door was opened in the wall with the arrival of a *visitador* [Valderrama] who came to increase the tributes [of the Indians] and to shout for money and more money, and suddenly the wild beast of unbridled avarice and the wild boar entered the vineyard. Every day they increased—so rapidly that they have now occupied and seized the whole vineyard. The wall has been torn down so that all kinds of animals of prey can enter. Not only have the fruits of the Indians' Christianity and the branches of their temporal prosperity disappeared, but even the few stocks of the vine that are still left are sick, lean, worm-infested, sterile, and profitless. The vineyard has turned into an uncultivated pasture.[24]

But even Mendieta did not go so far as to favor ordaining the newly converted Indians as priests, for they might return "to the vomit of their heathen rites." He judged them to be the best pupils in the world, but not fit to command or rule—fitted, rather, only to be commanded and ruled.[25] He even declared that had it not been for his firm belief in the original unity of human beings, "he would have believed that the Indians belonged to a different species."[26]

Nor did the "dirty dog" school disappear. Francisco López de Gómara, secretary-biographer of Cortez and great admirer of Sepúlveda, contributed to the debate on Indian nature with the publication in 1552 of his popular *Historia general de las Indias*. As one writer today describes his views:

The author despised the Indians and filled his volume with outrageous characterizations of them. He stated that their principal god was the devil; that they engaged in public sexual intercourse like animals, and were "the greatest sodomists," that they were liars, ingrates, and the source of syphilis. He further contended that many were cannibals and knew nothing of justice; that they went shamelessly nude; that they "are like stupid, wild, insensate asses," prone to "novelties," drunkenness, vice, and fickleness; that, in short, they were the worst people God ever made. López de Gómara wrote his book in part "to persuade the Council of the Indies that they do not deserve liberty" and, consequently, decided they should be enslaved.[27]

Other writers of the time, recognizing that a polarization of opinions had developed, attempted to find a middle position. One of these was the Dalmatian Dominican Vicente Palatino de Curzola, whose 1559 treatise on just war against the Indians has not yet been fully published or adequately analyzed. This relatively obscure friar is the only known Dominican who in the lifetime of Las Casas composed a treatise against the doctrine of the Bishop of Chiapa. Palatino de Curzola had served several years (ca. 1533) as a soldier in the conquest of Yucatán and had later entered the Dominican order. His "Tratado del derecho y justicia de la guerra que tienen los reyes de España contra las naciones de la India occidental" was considered by Bartolomé de Albornoz, the first professor of civil law at the University of Mexico, to be the best on the subject, but it never became well-known because the Crown prevented its publication.[28] Juan Bautista Muñoz, who abstracted this treatise in the eighteenth century, wrote that the Dalmatian Dominican had this to say on Indian capacity:

> The published writings of Bishop Casas, injurious and prejudicial as they are, motivated the writing of this work which seeks to prove that the kings of Spain, by virtue of the papal donation, may occupy the Indies by force in order to propagate Christianity.
>
> The author sets forth the two extreme views held concerning the Indians: one is that inasmuch as they are idolatrous, barbarous madmen *(locos)*, incapable of reason, they are natural slaves *(siervos a natura)* and therefore they may be deprived of their property and their liberty. The other opinion is that they are rational, mild, pious, etc., and thus there is no justification to war against them. The author favors an intermediate position and speaks of the Indians on the basis of what he himself has seen.[29]

Palatino de Curzola made it clear which view he supported in describing the treatment of Francisco de Pizarro's ambassadors by Peruvian Indians:

They killed the ambassadors cruelly, sacrificed them to the devils, and afterwards ate their bodies. These are the Indians described by the Bishop as innocent, hospitable, mild, and humble. The prudent reader may judge how hospitable they were when they killed the Spaniards who had treated them well and had freed them from captivity by their enemies. What innocence did they manifest when they sacrificed them to the devils? What humility, what humanity did they have when they ate those dead bodies like wild beasts? They obeyed no divine or natural law, not even following the law of ferocious animals, who sometimes are domesticated by praise and good treatment.[30]

The Dalmatian Dominican held some curious ideas on previous governments in America, for he maintained that Rome and Carthage had previously ruled there, which helped to explain, he felt, the imposing Mayan monuments in Yucatán. He denounced the killings of friars by Indians and their sodomy and cannibalism:

In the time of Montezuma in Mexico alone more than 100,000 men, women, and children . . . were eaten publicly, and everywhere else the same was done. I saw with my own eyes the Indians committing these crimes of sodomy and other crimes against nature. I saw the Indians going into battle with painted figures *(machos)* with which they sinned, and they had many other such sculptures *(bultos)* in their houses. These are the innocent, holy, and humble people of the Bishop and other ingenuous persons who call what is bad, good, or what is good, bad. And they persist in these opinions, either because they do not understand what is going on or are influenced by gifts that the Indians give them, or to acquire honor, fame, and bishoprics, alleging that they are moved by charity. These Indians are drunken, lying, traitorous, enemies of all virtue and kindness, and they will never abandon these evils unless they are first punished and subjected by force and wars, and afterwards preached to.[31]

A wide variety of opinions on how to convert Indians continued to exist. The Franciscan Motolinia, in his vehement letter of 1555 against Las Casas, strongly recommended the use of force in bringing Christianity to them: "It is convenient to Your Majesty that the Gospel be preached in all these lands, and those who do not wish to listen to the holy Gospel willingly should be forced to do so, for the proverb applies here: it is better to achieve good by force, than evil by degrees."[32] Yet, at about the same time, other Franciscans, perhaps inspired by the doctrine and example of Las Casas, were attempting to preach the faith peacefully in northern South America.[33]

The Dominican Domingo de Santo Tomás, a great admirer of Las Casas and his colleague in the struggle against the perpetuity of encomiendas, continued to fight for the Indians with the same weapons that Las Casas had developed.[34] He denounced the conquistadores in similarly strong terms: "They only rob and kill the Indians and treat them like vagabond animals. The condition of the Indian is worse than that of a donkey in Spain." He had studied the language of the Peruvian Indians and published both a dictionary and a grammar to demonstrate to King Philip II how intelligent the Indians were and how ready to receive the Christian faith.[35] The tone of the introduction to his *Gramática* is very similar to the arguments developed and used by Las Casas against Sepúlveda at Valladolid:

My principal objective in offering this little work to Your Majesty has been so that it may demonstrate clearly and emphatically how false is the opinion of the many persons who have wished to persuade you that the natives of the kingdom of Peru are barbarous and unworthy of being treated with kindness and liberty as are your other vassals. Your Majesty will clearly understand how false this opinion is when you see by means of this work the great organization that this language has, its abundance in words, and its flexibility. One may also see the diverse and curious ways their language permits them to speak. The soft and pleasing sounds it produces, the facility it permits in writing it with our characters and letters.[36]

The author of this *Gramática* went on to laud the declinations, many verb forms, and the ability of the language to express many thoughts and feelings briefly. It was a very polished and delicate language, worthy of being compared with Latin. And he concluded: "As Aristotle has often said, there is no better way to judge the genius of man than in the words and language that he uses. You may thus rest assured, Your Majesty, that the natives of Peru are people of great culture and order."[37]

Yet the experiences of such a competent student of Indian culture as the Franciscan Bernardino de Sahagún did not bear out these enthusiastic views. He had examined Aztec history and literature more systematically than any other sixteenth-century Spaniard and had long been familiar with the work of conversion. His considered opinion on the results of the work of the friars in the conversion of the Indians must be given much weight: "While they all publicly go to receive the sacraments and to celebrate the Christian holy days, deep inside they do not give up their gods as gods and they continue to pay them service, through clandestine offerings and celebrations—all this taking place in secret."[38] Given this attitude, it is not surprising that the Inquisition, formally established in Spanish America in 1571, took one of the most important decisions ever made about Indians. They were exempted from the Inquisition because of their "incapacity and lack of understanding concerning Christian doctrine."[39]

A contemporary of Sahagún and a fellow Franciscan, Diego Valadés, had a much higher opinion of Indian capacity. Valadés, the *mestizo* son of a conquistador, had labored some thirty years in the mission field, principally among the Chichemecas, and then had gone to Italy, where he published his important *Rhetorica christiana* (1579), which included much detail on the ancient rites of Mexican Indians as well as an impressive knowledge of Renaissance learning. He lauded the temples, music, and dances of the Indians. Charles V spent a whole afternoon watching their dances at Valladolid, he reported, with his nobles of highest rank in attendance. Valadés devoted considerable effort to defending Indians from "the thoughtless accusation of some who assert that the Indians are no more Christian than the Moors in Granada. Many question the conversion of the Indians with harsh and bitter words, attempting with all their strength to deny them their Christianity." He rejected the idea that Indians attended religious ceremonies like monkeys who imitated what they saw others doing. Although he was proud of the achievements of Spaniards in the Indies, Valadés vigorously refuted the opinion of some that the Christianization of the Indians was no more genuine than that of the Moriscos of Granada. In every respect were the Indians more thoroughly converted, and—unlike the Moriscos—they had suffered no violence.[40]

The fundamental questions on how to preach the faith and on the Aristotelian doctrine of natural slavery continued to be argued, as is demonstrated by the deliberations at the Third Mexican Council in 1585. This body of notable ecclesiastics refused to approve the "fire and sword" method of converting the Indians, even the warlike Chichemecas, and also rejected the argument that the "Indians, being inferior, should serve the Spaniards"—Aristotle and his *Politics* notwithstanding. Dr. Stafford Poole has emphasized the striking similarity of thought, attitude, and even expression of the ecclesiastics in 1585 to the doctrine of Las Casas.[41] Even in the far corners of the Spanish Empire these matters were discussed—on the frontier in

Chile and far across the Pacific in the Philippines, where defenders of the doctrines of Las Casas were vehement and powerful.[42]

Spanish settlers, as well as theologians, governors, and scholars, had reactions to Indians and held various views on their nature. Those responsible for drawing up the "Relación Geográfica" for Sanct Joan de la Frontera de Guamanga (Peru) in 1586 exhibited an attitude that was not radically different from the attitude manifested by some of the earliest colonists on Hispaniola. As citizens Pedro de Ribera and Antonio de Chaves y Guevara reported:

Everything they [the Indians] do is slowly done and by compulsion. They are malicious, lying, thievish; only for malice have they any sharpness of wit. They are dissemblers, and they are revengeful—not getting their revenge like honorable people, but cautiously and on the sly. They lack charity. By condition they are cowardly, and for that reason they are all the more cruel when they may safely be so. They are very ungrateful. They have the appearance of Christians, but while they easily receive baptism, with difficulty do they keep to the things they promise in it. They are capital enemies of the Spaniards. All farm, although by force, and they are content with very little; they do not store up things for their children. Their wives make their clothes and drinks and do part of the sowing of their crops. In order that they may take their ease and drink, of which they are so fond that they consider it an honor to be generally drunk, the Indians make their wives work excessively and treat them like slaves. There has been no remedy found for this.[43]

Thus far in the historical record most of the opinions on Indian capacity and their conversion have been delivered by ecclesiastics, but in the generation after the Valladolid confrontation several *Audiencia* judges of unusual experience and wisdom formulated views on Indians and how they should be treated. These judges were the mainstay of Spanish administration in the New World. Generally trained lawyers, they were expected to maintain the Crown's authority, and usually did so. As Clarence H. Haring emphasized, the *Audiencia* "was the most important and interesting institution in the government of the Spanish Indies,"[44] but its history largely remains to be written. Fortunately for our purposes, several sixteenth-century judges of outstanding intelligence and integrity wrote detailed accounts, based on their life in America, in the form of treatises that paid much attention to Indian affairs—Tomás López, Alonso de Zórita, and Juan de Matienzo. Of all the functions of *Audiencia* judges, that of supervising the treatment and taxation of the Indians was one of their most significant tasks.

Tomás López served fifteen years (1549-1563) in the *Audiencias* of Los Confines in Central America and Santa Fe in northern South America. During this period he traveled widely, and often to remote provinces, as *visitador* or inspector and regulator of local practices, and thus he became familiar with the seamy side of colonial life. In one of his early letters to the King, dated 9 June 1550, he emphasized the harshness of life in the new land, and said that even some ecclesiastics were affected by it: "They have become brutalized by these mountains, and they must be civilized anew."[45]

At the time that Las Casas and Sepúlveda were engaged in their second session in Valladolid, López was in Guatemala to punish those who had mistreated Bishop Las Casas and other friars there in the tumultuous years 1545 to 1547. He found some Spaniards who had not confessed for five or six years, and some had died pleading in vain for confession from friars who followed to the letter Las Casas's injunction in his treatise *Confesionario* not to administer the Church's sacraments to those who held Indians unjustly.[46]

After López returned to Spain (in 1563) he drew up a treatise on the natural history of the regions he had visited and lived in, the *Tratado de los tres elementos*, which still remains in manuscript in the Real Academia de la Historia in Madrid.[47] His conclusions on the greed and oppression of Spaniards in their treatment of the Indians often coincide with the accusations of Las Casas.[48] He spoke out against those who considered the Indians incapable of becoming Christians in a strongly-worded sermon (for he was also a priest) on returning to Spain. The *Apología, o sermon defensorio*, which he composed, was designed to combat "those false ideas that they could not have conceived without help from the devil himself."[49] In the *Tratado* he drew up a balance sheet of the good and evil wrought by Spain in the New World—a subject that has been endlessly debated by Spaniards and others from the sixteenth century until today—and entered the following charge on the debit side: "Although it has been falsely stated that the Indians are beasts, it is the Spaniards who are changed into wild animals; the latter care for their own beasts so well that the Indians suffer lack of food on that account."[50]

López also shared Las Casas's concern for the essential unity of all mankind, for he stated in the *Tratado*: "All the world is one, and if the Indians were worthy of reproach for their manner of government, much more are we." López considered Spaniards more culpable: Indians "sinned as barbarians and people separated from God and did not know it." He concluded: "There is no excuse for our bad example."[51]

Alonso de Zorita, also a well-trained lawyer, had even broader geographic experience than Tomás López for he had worked in Santo Domingo, New Granada, Guatemala, and Mexico.[52] His treatise on life and labor in Mexico provides such important information on ancient and colonial Mexico that it has been translated into English.[53] This "major source," composed by an *Audiencia* judge of "massive integrity," provides important testimony on how one responsible and disinterested royal official looked upon Indians after he retired to Spain in 1566 at the end of nineteen years of officeholding in the Indies. He had journeyed on foot through some of the most rugged regions in America. He was also a scholar, for during his last ten years as a judge of the prestigious *Audiencia* in Mexico he was admitted with the degree of doctor of laws to the University of Mexico cloister or governing body.

Zorita proved to be a man of action, too, for in 1561 he joined in a project to peacefully preach the faith with Fray Jacinto de San Francisco, who had first reached Mexico as a soldier even before Cortez and had been rewarded for his service in the Conquest by a grant of Indian towns and slaves who mined gold for him. But just as in the life of Las Casas, "God had illumined his spirit and had showed him that his encomiendas and slaves were putting him in the way of perdition." So Fray Jacinto had abandoned his encomiendas, freed his slaves, and entered the Franciscan order. After thirty-three years as a friar, he proposed to save Indians by sending an expedition into the land of the Chichemeca and the mysterious regions beyond. The only person deemed worthy of leading such an expedition, Fray Jacinto and the other Franciscans felt, was Zorita, whose memorial to Philip II embodied ideas proposed by Las Casas at Valladolid: "to win the Indians to Christianity and civilization by the methods of Las Casas, by kindness, good works, and good example."

Messengers of their own nation would be sent to invite the Indians to settle in towns; from these all lay Spaniards would be barred. A religious would have charge of the conversion and religious instruction of the natives in each Indian town. Zorita was convinced that the Indians were disposed to pursue a peaceful agricultural life, were it not for their fear of the Spaniards, from whom they had received much injury. There should be no encomiendas; the Indians were to be subjects in perpetuity of the Crown, and should be exempt from tribute for a number of years.[54]

The Crown did not see fit to accept Zorita's proposal but instead adopted a "fire and sword" policy, which did not succeed during the years it was tried, 1570-1585. After this failure the Crown put into effect a peaceful policy, which resembled the projects of Fray Jacinto and Zorita and which at long last brought peace.[55]

Zorita's retirement years, 1566-1585, were passed in Spain. During this time he continued to correspond with friends on Indian affairs and to write about them. He defended the moral and intellectual character of the Indians in an epoch when such humanist scholars as Sepúlveda in Spain and Francisco Cervantes de Salazar of the University of Mexico were charging Indians with inferiority and all manner of wickedness.[56] Zorita described the plight of the Mexican Indians as one of intolerable misery, a view that his modern editor judges to be in conformity with the views of most of his contemporaries. He idealized both the Aztec past and the rustic simplicity and innocence of the Indians of his own time, and was a "worthy representative [of] that exalted Spanish humanism and *Indianismo* whose dominating personality was Fray Bartolomé de Las Casas."[57]

Zorita's defense, which was based on a manuscript by Motolinía, followed the same line as that of Las Casas at Valladolid: the Indians had a perfectly respectable culture.

There are among the Indians many singers and musicians who play flutes, flageolets, sackbuts, trumpets, and violins. These Indians know how to read and write, and very skillfully compose books of plain song and songs with organ accompaniment, with very beautiful large letters at the beginning, and they bind these books. Many of them know Latin.

The Indians generally know all they need to know to earn their living; they know how to perform both rural tasks and those of the town. An Indian does not have to look for someone to build his house for him, nor does he have to search for materials, for everywhere he finds the wherewithal to cut, tie, sew, and strike a light. Almost all, including the boys, know the names of all the birds, animals, trees, and herbs, knowing as many as a thousand varieties of the latter and what they are good for; they also know many edible roots. All know how to work stone, build a house, twine a cord, and where to find the materials they need. They know all the other crafts that do not demand much art or complicated tools.[58]

Then Zorita roundly criticized Cortez for calling Indians barbarians, and he followed Las Casas explicitly in this well-worn argument. Indians are simple in some respects, but so are Spaniards, Italians, and others:

If this can happen among such enlightened folk as ourselves, in such well-ordered commonwealths, why should we wonder at the innocence of the Indians? Nor is there any reason for calling them barbarians, for there is no doubt that they are a very able people who have learned very easily and quickly all the mechanical arts known to the Spaniards who live in New Spain. Indeed, some Indians learned these arts in a few days simply from looking on at Spaniards. For the rest, I have said there are among them good Latinists and musicians. Let those who call them barbarians consider that by the same token they could call "barbarians" the Spaniards and other peoples famed for great ability and intelligence.[59]

Zorita also referred to the widespread idea that the Indians were believed to be human only in appearance and stated that this "popular error" was even supported in the Spanish edition of the works of Saint Jerome, though readers could not be sure whether Saint Jerome or a later editor was responsible for the idea. In conclusion, Zorita harshly reproached those Spaniards who "give not a rap whether these poor and miserable Indians live or die," though the whole being and welfare of the country depended upon them:

God has closed the eyes and darkened the minds of these Spaniards, so that they see with their eyes what is happening yet do not see it, so that they perceive their own destruction, yet do not perceive it, and all because of their callousness and hardheartedness. I have known an oidor to say publicly from his dais, speaking in a loud voice, that if water were lacking to irrigate the Spaniards' farms, they would have to be watered with the blood of Indians. I have heard others say that the Indians, and not the Spaniards, must labor. Let the dogs work and die, said these men, the Indians are numerous and rich. These officials say such things because they have not seen the Indians' sufferings and miseries, because they are content to sit in the cool shade and collect their pay.[60]

A third judge, Juan de Matienzo, was equally distinguished and knowledgeable on Indian affairs in Peru, where he worked for many years as one of the principal royal officers during the rule of Viceroy Francisco de Toledo. In his *Gobierno del Perú* (1567) he gives a much more pessimistic view of Indian nature than López or Zorita and is much closer to the opinion of Sepúlveda:

All the Indians discovered thus far are timid and weak-minded, which results from their being naturally melancholy. They are filthy, and eat on the ground. Their toe nails and finger nails are very long. Men and women alike eat the lice which they take from each other's heads. All this indicates that they were born and reared to serve. It is more beneficial for them to serve than to rule. As Aristotle says, nature has given stronger bodies and less understanding to those born to serve, while those who are free have less physical force and greater understanding.

They participate in reason to some extent, but not to follow its dictates. In this they are the same as animals, which are ruled by their passions. This may be seen clearly since for them there is no tomorrow.

They are, thus, born to serve and to learn mechanical trades, in which they have ability. They are very good weavers and painters. They are tailors, shoemakers, silversmiths, rope makers, blacksmiths, ironmongers, and very good farmers. . . . Idleness is the mother of all evils, especially in these parts where . . . the people have so little reason.[61]

Matienzo urged that Indians be severely restricted in their activities; they should not be allowed to make gunpowder, ride on horses, or dress like Spaniards. They had "little understanding." Nature created them to obey and to serve, not to rule themselves or others.[62]

Thus opinion during the second half of the sixteenth century continued to diverge on Indian capacity. Optimists still were to be found, as well as those Spaniards described in 1569 by Luis López, one of the first Jesuits in Peru: "They are very cruel to the Indians, they seem to them not to be men but beasts because they treat them thus to achieve their end, which is silver."[63] The idea persisted that Indians were "people of slight ability." Or at least so deposed the leaders of the Augustinians, Dominicans, and Franciscans in Mexico in a petition to the Inquisition on 16 September 1579 to justify their proposal that the Bible not be translated into Indian languages lest it cause confusion among Indians and imperil their conversion.[64]

On the whole, however, the Jesuits held to a more moderate position of "appreciation and respect but with limitations."[65] The great José de Acosta probably represented the views of many in his order, and his writings reveal a more sophisticated view of Indians than did the writings of the earlier participants in the dispute over their capacity. Significantly, the first chapter of his treatise on how to preach the faith to the Indians (*De Procuranda Indorum Salute*, 1588) was devoted to "Why there is no reason to give up Hope for the Salvation of the Indians."[66] Chapter 2 explains "Why the Salvation of the Indians seems Difficult and Unimportant to Many Persons." Acosta states that some believe the Indians are not sufficiently intelligent to understand the faith, and in another chapter he reproves those who insist on Indian rudeness and incapacity.

He also specifically repudiates the idea that war may ever be waged justly against barbarians because of their crimes against nature or because of the Aristotelian theory of natural slavery. He describes this doctrine and then refutes it.[67] At this point he appears to refer to Sepúlveda, without mentioning his name, for he remarks that this doctrine was condemned by the universities of Alcalá and Salamanca, as well as by the Council of the Indies, which "prescribed very different methods for new expeditions." In these pages Acosta strongly supports the essential doctrines of Las Casas on peaceful preaching, but he does not use his name or cite his books. Perhaps this caution may be explained by the fact that one of his brother Jesuits, Luis López, was then under accusation by the Inquisition in Peru for holding various opinions, one of which was akin to that of Las Casas on Spanish rule in America.

Acosta may have found it prudent not to enter directly into the Las Casas-Sepúlveda dispute, but his viewpoint was quite clear. He emphatically believed that the Indians were capable of understanding the faith and that the way to Christianize them was by peaceful methods. He supported the encomienda system, in theory at least, but he well understood the reality, for the only time the earnest Jesuit curses in *De Procuranda Indorum Salute* is in describing the results of the system: "Looked at in itself, it is a goodly system and very honest: but when we see how it actually works, my God, what disorder, what ugliness!"[68]

He returned to the subject in his other principal work, the *Natural and Moral History of the Indies* (1590), which was composed in much the same spirit exhibited by Las Casas in his *Defense* against Sepúlveda at Valladolid:

Having treated before of the religion the Indians practiced, I plan to write in this book of their customs, policy, and government for two purposes: one is to refute the false opinion many ordinarily hold of them as being brutish and bestial people or that they have so little as scarcely to merit the name [of people]. From this delusion derive the many excesses against them, for they use them like brute beasts and consider them unworthy of any respect. This is a very common and pernicious error, as those persons know well who with any zeal or consideration have travelled among them and come to learn their secrets and counsels. The most ignorant and presumptuous in depreciating the Indians are usually the ones who know the least about them.

The best way I know to counteract this pernicious opinion is to explain the order and way they live according to their own laws. Although they showed many traits of barbarians, many others were worthy of admiration which indicates clearly that they have a natural capacity for learning from good instruction. In many respects they surpass our own people. It is not surprising that they manifest some serious errors, as did the most respected lawgivers and philosophers, among such were Lycurgus and Plato. And in even such wise republics as those of Rome and of Athens we find laughable ignorance, as we do now among the Mexicans and the Incas.[69]

Nor did the disputes end with the coming of the seventeenth century, for the valorous Don Bernardo Vargas Machuca, governor and captain general of Margarita, prepared a hot attack on the writings and ideas of Las Casas. Despite the fact that his treatise was prefaced by laudatory sonnets by four Dominicans, Spanish authorities did not permit the publication of this compendious treatise, which was completed in 1612. He ridiculed the favorable opinion Las Casas held on Indian capacity and believed that the devil had deprived the Indians of their reason and had converted them into *"brutos animales"*:[70]

They are the cruelest people in the world and are as brutish as they are cruel. It is my opinion and that of many who have known them . . . that they are even more brutish than irrational animals. . . . No one who knows the lies and deceptions of the Indians considers them rational beings.[71]

Captain Vargas Machuca therefore concluded that Indians must be forced to receive the Christian doctrine:

These people are by their nature barbarians and without any prudence whatsoever, for they are contaminated by barbarian vices of the kind one reads about in the history books. Therefore the war against them is just by natural law, because their nature is such that they cannot be brought to accept Christian doctrine by words. They must be put under the yoke like beasts and compelled with all the rigor of the laws.[72]

At about the same time that Captain Vargas Machuca was vainly trying to get his treatise printed the Franciscan Juan de Silva was preparing a set of memorials supporting peaceful preaching, but in this case the Council of the Indies arranged for the printing of his *Advertencias importantes acerca del buen govierno y administracion de las Indias assi en lo espiritual como en lo temporal*. Silva had served the king forty years, first as a soldier in Malta, Flanders, and against the Turks and then for twenty years as an ecclesiastic converting the Indians in Mexico and Florida. His views coincide with those of Las Casas at Valladolid. He cited Pope Paul III's bull, denied that barbarians could not be converted, and met the argument that missionaries would be killed unless soldiers accompanied them by admitting that the faith had never been preached without shedding the blood of some preachers. The Conquest must be made without force—"with mildness and kindness, not with arms, soldiers, or any kind of force. Ecclesiastics should alone carry on the work, not secular persons accompanied by armed soldiers as has been done up to now, for this is to contravene evangelical truth as has been proved at length."[73]

Another evidence of the deep schism on Indian character appears in the writing of the Peruvian poet Diego Dávalos y Figueroa, whose *Miscelánea austral* (1602) contains strong attacks on Indians. He was replying to "a certain modern author," quite possibly Las Casas, and to his statement that the Indians were "civilized people, capable of government, and with other good qualities." Dávalos considered this opinion a "notorious deception, because what good can there be in a people who lack prudence, letters, truth, charity, and honor?"[74]

We know about this particular quarrel because an eighteenth-century historian of the Villa Imperial de Potosí, Bartolomé Arzáns de Orsúa y Vela, was so affronted by the poet's derogatory remarks that he never allowed his readers to forget that the glorious story of the "imperial city" depended upon the labor of the Indians: "Without Indians, the Indies could not exist."[75] Early in his *History* he interrupted his account of the conquest of Mexico to indignantly deny that the Indians were "brutes incapable of reason," a falsehood, he said, spread by the enemies of Spain to diminish the importance of the astonishing victories Cortez and his soldiers had won over the hosts of Monte- zuma. The Indians were truly astounded by the color, dress, and weapons of the bearded Spaniards, but "mere ignorance does not presuppose incapacity," and he pointed out that the Araucanian and Paraguayan Indians fought courageously and successfully against the best Spanish soldiers, including those with battle experience in Flanders.

He early stated his fundamental position: although most Indians could not read or write, the reason was not their stupidity but because "they do not concern themselves with such matters." The Indians of Peru, he said, show "rare ability, clear understanding, and decided perseverance." They were able to practice all the professions, artistic as well as mechanical, and Indian craftsmen could build an altarpiece, a doorway, a tower, and even an entire building without knowing either arithmetic or geometry, let alone reading and writing—all of which caused great astonishment among the Spaniards. So notable was their capacity that King Charles II issued an order permitting the sons of Indian chieftains, governors, and nobles to be ordained to the priesthood after university education and theological training. This attitude colored all of Arzáns's subsequent comments on the Indians. Here we see clearly that the struggle to ensure justice for the Indians was a live issue long after the great champions of the sixteenth century had asserted Indian rationality.

Dávalos denigrated Indian culture in his 1602 poem in a way that is familiar to all who have read Ramón Menéndez Pidal's depreciatory interpretation of the life of Las Casas, published in Madrid in 1963. In boldly praising the capacity of Indians and in defending them from the charge of being brutes, Arzáns manifested an attitude not at all com- mon among the Spaniards of his time. Even today, in Andean coun- tries, some people believe the Indians to be "subhuman," and in their treatment of Indians conduct themselves accordingly.

Arzáns indignantly rejected this low conception of Indian capacity and directly attacked Dávalos in his description of the construction of the new church in Potosí. He marveled, too, at the skill of the Inca emperor Yupanqui the Good in building the great Temple of the Sun in

Cuzco, and he praised the ancient temple on an island in Lake Titicaca—even asserting that the opulence of the Inca monarchs surpassed that of the Egyptians, Persians, and Greeks. The Inca empires lasted longer, too, he pointed out, in a passage reminiscent of Las Casas. Arzáns condemned the opinion of some Spaniards that the impressive Inca monuments (still standing in Peru) were the work of the devil, and he scorned Dávalos for believing that they were constructed by giants of the past, not Indians. He admitted that the Indians had learned much from the Spaniards—which proved to him their innate ability. He recorded the names of the Indian artists whose work enriched the Franciscan church, and especially lauded Sebastián de la Cruz, who had died while on the job. Though illiterate, this Indian "was a remarkable craftsman in stone," who had also built the great tower of the Jesuit church, judged then and later as one of the architectural glories of Peru.

Most historians of the time felt obliged to make some reference to Indian capacity. Juan de Torquemada, the eminent Franciscan, felt it necessary, in his *Monarquía Indiana* (1612), to defend the Indians by making known "all the things preserved by these people, which excuses them from being called *bestial* as our Spaniards have termed them."[76] Other writers, such as the Augustinian Antonio de Calancha in his *Crónica Moralizada del Orden de San Agustín en el Perú* (1639-1653), compared native practices with both the mythologies and superstitions of the Romans and the customs of pagan Spain to the general advantage of the Indians, and defended Indians "of certain areas from general attacks upon their rational nature and their supposedly barbaric customs."[77] And as late as the closing years of the eighteenth century the exiled Jesuit Francisco Javier Clavijero, looking back over the history of the Conquest, once more felt it necessary to defend the Indians from the charge of irrationality: "Their souls are fundamentally the same as those of other men, and they are endowed with the same faculties. Never have Europeans manifested less honor to their own reason than when they doubted the rationality of the Indians."[78]

Viceroys, friars, archbishops, colonists, and indeed many Spaniards in Europe and America continued to speak and write about the capacity of Indians and how to civilize them. Even as the years of Spanish domination in America were drawing to a close, these questions were still discussed. Two widely read Spanish travelers had this to say in 1745:

It is no easy task to exhibit a true picture of the customs and inclinations of the Indians, and precisely display their genius and real turn of mind; for if considered as part of the human species, the narrow limits of their understanding seem to clash with the dignity of the soul; and such is their stupidity, that in certain particulars one can scarce forbear entertaining an idea that they are really beasts, and even destitute of that instinct we observe in the brute creation. While in other respects, a more comprehensive judgment, better-digested schemes, and conducted with greater subtilty, are not to be found than among these people. This disparity may mislead the most discerning person: for should he form his judgment from their first actions, he must necessarily conclude them to be a people of the greatest penetration and vivacity. But when he reflects on their rudeness, the absurdity of their opinions, and their beastly manner of living, his ideas must take a different turn, and represent them in a degree little above brutes.[79]

The "initiator of the study of the history of ideas"[80] in Mexico, Juan José Eguiara y Eguren, took up the cudgels against a certain Manuel Martí, dean of Alicante, "who had denied the most elementary level of culture to the people (ancient and modern) of the New World in general and of New Spain in particular." Eguiara y Eguren defended the Indians' culture, praised their cultivation of history, poetry, rhetoric, arithmetic and astronomy, and provided "the first attempt to synthesize the most valuable elements of Náhuatl culture and thought."[81]

A detailed account of these eighteenth-century discussions on Indian capacity might well fill a volume, and need not be set forth here,[82] but enough has been said to demonstrate that the subject remained important as long as Spain ruled the Indies. Thereafter the historians took up the controversy.

Peanuts, Polarization, Polemics, and Paranoia

The story of the struggle—over the centuries—on the true nature of the Indians, as first conceived by sixteenth-century Spaniards, becomes a vast account of controversy over subjects large and small. Las Casas and Oviedo disagreed not only on whether the Indians were civilized or beastly but even on whether the peanut was a tasty food.

Polarization of opinion on all the major issues developed, as Viceroy Mendoza pointed out in his official report to his successor in 1550. Moreover, so many Spaniards and foreigners have participated in the dispute about the Indians that this topic has engendered many of the most profound and persistent polemics on the nature of Spanish rule in America.

Whatever position the reader has taken on this review of the enormous literature on the Las Casas-Sepúlveda confrontation at Valladolid, the above discussion illustrates the doubts and difficulties that arise when historians of today try to find out exactly what Spaniards in the sixteenth century meant when they wrote and spoke about Indian capacity. Probably doubts and disagreements will continue to be voiced concerning the actions of Spain in America, and especially when Bartolomé de Las Casas enters the scene. For example, the most dramatic event of all the many commemorations associated with the 400th anniversary of his death was the publication of the biography by Ramón Menéndez Pidal, *El Padre Las Casas. Su doble personalidad.*[83] In this notable work Don Ramón, the oldest and most distinguished Hispanist of his time, wrote that Las Casas, although in some respects a normal person, was a propagandist (rather than a thinker) who incorporated in his works (though at times incorrectly), some Christian ideas. Menéndez Pidal employed his rich Castilian vocabulary in an attempt to convey his idea of Las Casas's defects, and a compilation of his phraseology as applied to Las Casas must surely merit some kind of prize for variety:

Anti-Christian, austere and vehement exaggerator, conceited egotism, presumptuous vanity, ostentatious megalomania, he lacked entirely the moral force of a St. Francis of Assisi or a Savonarola, childish vanity, delirium of grandeur, tendentious inaccuracies, eccentric whimseys, disorderly, aggressor, systematic delirium, intemperate impetuosity, arrogant truculence, pleasure in describing bestialities, furious language, shocking imprudence in speech, an irresistible pathological tendency, a staggering magnification, an irrepressible habit of tremendous overstatement, maniacal preoccupation, unconscious victim of his own incriminating delirium, totalitarian prejudice, medieval canonist, backward, attacks the citadel of the encomenderos with his fiery lances and poisonous gases, pathological certainty, a sower of confusions, silly fantasies, it is impossible to conceive an egotism more childishly vainglorious, boastful tone, he possessed the natural art of covering up self-praise by assuming pious and altruistic attitudes, infantile blustering, a mania for argumentation, feeble intelligence, a complacent self-glorification, the fantastic pride of an imaginative child, an overweening self-importance, his impulsive misrepresentation of facts, his excessive moral tone, as blind to reality as a delirious person obsessed with chimerical projects, egocentric providentialism, his schemes, extravagent dreamer, impetuous, fixed ideas against encomenderos, his showy satisfaction, feverish delirium, super-arrogant arguments, unreasonable contradictions, insatiable egotism, backward Dominican, hot-headed inflexibility, total immersement in his own ideas, always away from the real world, always elated (*iluminado*), a fatal and unthinking self-praise, extravagant pretentiousness, choleric, never has there existed any man who admired himself as much.[84]

"Paranoiac"—of all the terms applied by Don Ramón in his characterization of Fray Bartolomé—is the one that has caused most repercussion. In the year 2066, Las Casas students concerned with the 500th commemoration of his death who look through the literature of 1966 will no doubt be puzzled by this term, as well as by the variety and nature of today's opinions on Las Casas. For they will also read the judgment on Las Casas by that remarkable French scholar Marcel Bataillon: "In this authentic apostle, even better than in Professor Francisco de Vitoria, is revealed the generous soul of colonial Spain."[85] And they will note that the German theologian, Cardinal Josef Höffner, in one of the most solid works of scholarship of our times on Spanish culture in the sixteenth century, has declared that "among all the Spaniards, it was the noble Las Casas who most profoundly understood the spirit of the Christian Gospel." The Cardinal was referring specifically to the question most at issue at Valladolid—whether force should be used by Christians in converting infidels—and he concluded that Las Casas had, "without doubt, interpreted ably the true sense of the gospels."[86]

Historians of Spanish law have devoted much attention to the treatises that were written because of the problems arising from the conquest of America. Moreover, works by theologians and jurists, such as Bartolomé Carranza, Melchor Cano, Diego Covarrubias, and Juan de la Peña, have recently been discovered, published, and analyzed. These historians, theologians, and jurists did not accept all of Las Casas's views—but none supported Sepúlveda's imperialism or his application of the doctrine of natural slavery to the Indians. Without exception, they "defended the doctrine that all men were equally free; on the basis of natural liberty they proclaimed their right to life, to culture, and to property."[87]

Students in 2066 will also see that Juan Pérez de Tudela Bueso, one of the outstanding Americanists in Spain today, concluded the excellent introduction to his five-volume edition of the writings of Las Casas thus: "He was a gigantic and indispensable protagonist in the construction of Hispanic America. . . . For those who do not assume that they know the truth, the Las Casas theme is one of the most valuable topics in history for meditation."[88]

Another Spaniard, the Dominican theologian Venancio Diego Carro, who more minutely than anyone else has examined the theological doctrines of Las Casas, has also rendered a very favorable general judgment. He concludes that Las Casas's ideas "coincide fundamentally with those of the great Spanish theologians and jurists" and that "he only applied Christian principles and the Christian concept."[89]

The present-day Mexican scholar Teresa Silva Tena admires the universal quality of Las Casas's views and points out that the latter's interpretation of Aztec human sacrifice reveals that he was the only one in his time who had the imagination to understand this much-discussed rite from the Indian point of view.[90] Still another Mexican, in his analysis of the information on Indian art in Las Casas's works, concluded that he exhibited a most "modern" attitude in his attempt to discern and understand what the Indian arts were trying to express.[91]

Thus Las Casas has become a more universal figure than ever before; indeed, Soviet Latin-Americanists, Japanese students, and others have participated in the 1966 commemoration.[92] But perhaps the most impressive proof of the present widespread interest in the life of Fray Bartolomé may be seen in the many editions of his writings and the extraordinary number and quality of studies about him in various languages.[93] (One of these studies, prepared by Father Lino Gómez Canedo, shows that many Franciscans were warm friends of Las Casas and shared his fundamental views on Indian problems.[94] This is not a new idea, but is well worth restating.)

One of the outstanding new editions is an impressive version of one of Las Casas's most significant works, the *Apologética Historia*, which not only contains the most complete and accurate text and a preliminary study by Edmundo O'Gorman that raises fundamental questions of interpretation, but also a most perceptive introductory essay by Miguel León-Portilla on the relevance of the *Apologética Historia* today to Spanish America and to the world at large.[95] León-Portilla considers the treatise the best possible reply to those who have accused Las Casas of *demencia* (probably a reference to Ramón Menéndez Pidal, though he does not say so), and emphasizes that his doctrines— along with the contributions of José de Acosta, Vasco de Quiroga, and Bernardino de Sahagún—have made possible a reconciliation between Spain and Spanish America. These sixteenth-century Spanish friars censured Spanish violence in the Conquest, but they also made possible, "on the level of human dignity, the birth of which is our mestizo culture." For the rest of the world, the ideas and attitudes in the *Apologética Historia* constitute a "valuable contribution to universal culture as well as the first and well-founded affirmation of that universal culture—often asserted but not always practiced—which constitutes a safeguard for human rights that cannot be postponed."[96]

Menéndez Pidal incorrectly asserted, incidentally, that Las Casas had no understanding of the role of *mestizaje* in America;[97] however, as Manuel Giménez Fernández has pointed out, mestizaje "is a key idea in all the plans of the Defender of the Indians." It was his great hope, as Las Casas explained in his April 1516 *Memorial de los Remedios* to Cisneros, that Spanish laborers and Indians "should be mixed by marrying the sons of one with the daughters of others." The result would be highly beneficial: "The land and the people would fruitfully multiply."[98]

Historians in 2066 may wonder whether anyone besides Don Ramón during the 400th commemoration of Las Casas's death, considered Las Casas to be a paranoiac, and they may find some who seemed to agree. Father Lino Gómez Canedo, in reviewing the biography, writes: "The central conclusion of the author, that Las Casas was a paranoiac, will appear excessive to many, but perhaps it might offer us one of the most plausible explanations of a personality which is certainly strange. What other [interpretation] is possible?"[99]

If we put ourselves in the place of the student in 2066, should we conclude that Gómez Canedo believed (with Menéndez Pidal) that Las Casas was in fact a paranoiac in the technical or medical sense of the term? In the same review he seems to support Don Ramón's general interpretation of Las Casas, for he refers to the "even temperament of Don Ramón" and says that the book is "written soberly in prose which is at once simple and beautiful." Don Ramón made "certain small errors of fact" and included "an excess of polemic commentaries and remarks," but "the author always dissents in measured language without adopting extremist positions."[100] May readers in 2066 not reasonably conclude, therefore, that Lino Canedo does not consider calling Las Casas a paranoiac an extreme statement, but a sober and truthful judgment?[101]

But now comes the real problem. Today some historians debate whether any sixteenth-century Spaniards ever meant to call Indians "animals" or "beasts" in the full anthropological or philosophical sense of these terms. How, then, can historians in the twenty-first century determine whether Menéndez Pidal and Lino Canedo really intended to classify Las Casas as a paranoiac in the full and rigorous scientific sense of this psychiatric term? Don Ramón did indeed consult certain medical specialists in Madrid before applying "paranoiac" to Las Casas, but he did not consider it necessary to accept their definitions. In an interview with an enthusiastic admirer of his interpretation, he maintained his position, and the interviewer quoted with approval Don Ramón's words in the biography:

Las Casas is a paranoiac, not demented or crazy. His ordinary lucidity makes his abnormality a difficult case to establish, as is the question of whether to confine some mentally ill persons to a hospital. . . . The only way to understand the Bishop is to assume that he is mentally ill.[102]

Don Ramón's view has been challenged by such writers as the late Benno M. Biermann, O. P., who, after discussing the subject with medical experts, sharply questioned Don Ramón's use of "paranoiac" as scientifically applicable.[103] We do not know whether Gómez Canedo consulted psychiatrists before writing his review of *El Padre Las Casas. Su doble personalidad,* in which he seems to follow Don Ramón's view that Las Casas was indeed a paranoiac and ends by asking "What other [interpretation] is possible?"

Perhaps enough has been said to indicate that, when passions ran high, Spaniards applied the words "brute animals," "beasts," "semi-beasts," "dogs," "incapable," "irrational," "pygmies," "natural slaves," and other pejorative terms to the Indians they met during the hectic early days of the conquest of America; but it does not satisfy the modern reader to dismiss all this by saying that of course they did not mean that the Indians were not men in the full anthropological or philosophical sense.

Would it not be more historically correct and meaningful to describe the doubts and disputes on Indian capacity, those expressed during the Conquest and especially in its first half century, as leading to a kind of polarization of Spanish reactions to the strange beings they found in the New World? Between an Oviedo, who declared that gunpowder used against Indians should be considered incense to the Lord, and a Las Casas, who believed passionately that all people could be civilized through education and Christianization, no compromise was possible. This polarization produced a wide spectrum of opinion, ranging from the "dirty dog" to the "noble savage" schools of thought, that never fully disappeared, though such simplistic generalizations began to have less force by the later years of the sixteenth century. The real question for many Spaniards in the sixteenth century was the capacity of the natives of the newly discovered lands for Christianity and for civilization, not whether they were "animals" or "beasts" in the philosophical or anthropological sense.

Today it is easy for scholars to show how different groups of Indians responded in different ways to the great missionary effort in America.[104] The enormous variety of people discovered by the Spaniards makes it impossible, however, to generalize about them. As Roberto Levillier asked a few years ago:

Which Indians of which regions were these jurists and theologians talking about in the sixteenth century?[105] Indians were the Tekestas and Tahinos of Duba, mild and hospitable; Indians, the cannibalistic Caribs; Indians, the primitive Otomí, who lived in caves; Indians, the savage Jívaros; Indians, the Uros, more fish than man, who lived in the waters of Lake Titicaca; Indians, the artistic Maya stone cutters and the Chibcha jewelry craftsmen and the wise Inca legislators and the delicate Yunga ceramic workers; and the Colla weavers; Indians, the heroic Aztecs, the cannibalistic Chiriguanaes, and the untamed Diaguitas and Araucanians; Indians, the timid Juri, the nomadic Iule, the sedentary Comechingon, the fierce Guaraní. Their intelligence, cruelty, and meekness varied as did the color of their skins, their languages, their rites, their theogonies, and the true owners were confused with those who subjected them to obedience. Neither in their juridical position, in their physical aspect, in their language, in their tastes, in their morality, nor in their creative capacities were they alike.[106]

Some present-day scholars have another reason for doubting the significance of the laws devised by Spain to protect the Indians, declaring them "paper laws" that were "largely unenforced."[107] They dismiss such arguments as the Valladolid disputation as similar to the fabled dispute between Tweedledum and Tweedledee. The widely read Chilean historian, the late Francisco Encina, was convinced that Las Casas and the supporters of his doctrine were in *"un estado delirante."*[108] At one time even Ramón Menéndez Pidal judged both disputants to be wrong:

> At the very moment when the ancient notion of European history-laden Empire was dying out, there arose the Spanish empire, without history, the first one of modern times not anchored to Roman and mediaeval law. Hence the opposition which existed between the humanitarian cleric Las Casas and the humanist scholar Ginés de Sepúlveda, both of them inhuman, for the former made all colonization impossible and the latter permitted it to flourish under tyranny.[109]

The bitter wrangle of Las Casas and Sepúlveda in 1550 and 1551 produced no clear decision, nor has agreement been reached by later generations on the true meaning of their confrontation.

NOTES

1. The first three or four pages of this chapter are based on Hanke (1970), pp. 74-75. The confrontation took place during one of Spain's most exciting and intellectually vigorous periods. For the general background, see Otis Green's rich presentations on "The Nature and Destiny of Man" and "Political Expansion: The Idea of Empire" (1963), II, 105-58, and III, 82-114.
2. See Friede's extensive bibliography in Hanke (1968), pp. 386-87. One historian considers that after 1550 Las Casas concentrated on affecting the consciences of Spaniards in the New World, as he had not been able to persuade the King to stop the conquests (Ramos [1967], pp. 10-12). He did influence encomenderos to provide in their wills for restitution to the Indians (Lohmann Villena [1966]), but he continued to strive mightily to affect the decisions of the King and the Pope until his death; and of course the post-Valladolid years were much devoted to completing such principal writings as the *Historia de las Indias,* the *Apologética Historia,* and the *Defense.*

3. For information on the circumstances of the publication of these treatises, see the prologues by Manuel Giménez Fernández and by Hanke in the latest edition of these works: Las Casas (1965), I, xi-lxxvii.

4. Ibid., p. lxxvii.

5. Las Casas (1951), III, 343. For an example of the way in which American problems continued to agitate Spanish legal circles during these years, see the work of Gregorio López. In 1543, when the Council of the Indies was busily engaged in charges and counter-charges on the treatment of Indians, López, as a trusted royal official, was sent to Seville to take evidence, which gave him much information on injustices against the Indians. The year after the Valladolid disputation he prepared a new edition of the *Siete Partidas*, which after publication in 1555 became the standard edition until 1800. For much detail on the work and views of his key official and jurist, see Martínez Cardos (1960) and García-Gallo (1972), p. 429-31.

6. Poole, *Defense*, p. 5. For Vega's activities during these years, see Bataillon (1965), pp. 259ff.

7. Hanke (1965a), p. 129.

8. This section is based on Hanke (1970), p. 78. Sepúlveda's correspondence contains much material on the aftermath of the Valladolid dispute; see Losada (1949), letters 40, 41, 42, 45, 46, 53, 60, 63. See also Losada (1966).

9. Losada (1966), p. 193.

10. Ibid., pp. 193-94.

11. For the text of the letters exchanged by Sepúlveda and Castro, see Hanke (1970), pp. 117-18. It is difficult for a non-theologian to understand this application of *correctio fraterna* to the waging of war against American Indians as a preliminary to their conversion, for it is defined as "une oeuvre de miséri-corde, accomplie sous l'impulsion de la charité et la direction de la prudence," in the *Dictionnaire de Théologie Catholique . . .*, III, Part 2 (Paris, 1938), 1907.

    It would seem that *correctio fraterna* is to be used only for the benefit of other Christians. Beginning with Christ, a number of important steps were set forth, in some detail, as the correct way to apply the doctrine. In certain cases, particularly when it has been ascertained that secret admonitions would do no good, direct action is permitted (ibid., pp. 1910-11). But how could anyone be certain that private, peaceful persuasion would not work with the Indians unless it had first been tried? And it would appear that the doctrine could not be used on the Indians, who had not previously known about Christianity, for the obligation to admonish one's neighbors "does not obtain, generally speaking, for the case of one who violates a law through invincible ignorance" (*The Catholic Encyclopedia* [New York, 1908], IV, 394).

12. Wagner (1967), pp. 226, 238.

13. Dr. Burrus has been revealing Alonso de la Vera Cruz's true dimensions to the world. See his edition of the writings of Vera Cruz (1968) and his own specialized studies, Burrus (1963, 1966). The Cervantes de Salazar description comes from his volume *Life in the Imperial and Loyal City of Mexico in New Spain, and the Royal and Pontifical University of Mexico*, as given in Hanke, ed. (1967), I, 296.

14. *Actas de cabildo de México*, VIII, 640.

15. Losada (1949), p. 105. The modern admirer is Teodoro Andrés Marcos, who commented thus on the gifts of the Mexico City council: "Pero ya hacía unos siete años que el *Democrates* andaba por el mundo. Y sobre esto, ¿le enviaron el presente? Lo recibió?" (Marcos [1947], p. 24).

16. Ricard (1966), p. 228.
17. Information on these and other treatise writers may be found in Hanke and Millares Carlo (1943).
18. This section is based on Hanke (1970), pp. 87-88.
19. As quoted in Hanke (1970), p. 87.
20. Esteve Barba (1964), p. 112.
21. Jiménez de la Espada (1889), p. 63. On the license for the publication of Jiménez de Quesada's "Los ratos de Suesca" is a note in the handwriting of Philip II: "Dígase al Cardenal que por decirse que trata de cosas de Indias, haga que se mire bien."
22. Padden (1956), pp. 352-54.
23. Phelan, in Pike, ed. (1969), p. 60.
24. Ibid., pp. 61-62.
25. As quoted from Mendieta's *Historia eclesiástica* by Boxer (1970).
26. As quoted by Luis González Cárdenas (1949), p. 336.
27. Huddleston (1967), p. 24. Fray Pedro de Gante also showed in a 1558 letter to Charles V that he had a low opinion of certain Indians: "Empero, la gente común estaba como animales sin razon, indomables, que no los podiámos traer al gremio y congregación de la Iglesia, ni a la doctrina, ni a sermón, sino que huían desto sobremanera" (García Icazbalceta [1858], II, 206).
28. For this figure, see Hanke and Millares Carlo (1943), pp. xix-xxiii. An abstract of the treatise is given on pp. 11-37. An eighteenth-century copy of the treatise is in the Bernardo Mendel Collection (Ms. 1572) of the Lilly Library, Indiana University. The Yugoslavian Dominican, Antonine Zaninovič of Dubrovnik, is preparing an edition of this treatise and a study of its author.
29. Hanke and Millares Carlo (1943), p. 13.
30. Ibid., pp. 25-26.
31. Ibid., p. 36.
32. *D.I.I.*, VII, 268.
33. Gómez Canedo (1955).
34. Goldwert (1955).
35. Santo Tomás (1951), p. xxiii. The grammar was originally published in 1560 in Valladolid. See also Cisneros (1953). For a recent analysis of the contributions of this outstanding Dominican, whose work has not yet been fully appreciated, see Mahn-Lot (1972).
36. Santo Tomás (1560), Preface.
37. Ibid.
38. D'Olwer (1957), p. 406.
39. Scholes and Roys (1948), pp. 619-20. See also the references in n. 41 in chapter I above.
40. Méndez Plancarte (1946); Ricard (1966), p. 275.
41. Poole (1965, 1966b). See also Poole (1961, 1963, 1966a).
42. Hanke and Millares Carlo (1943), pp. xxix-lxvi. See also Korth (1968).
43. Nichols (1944), p. 158.
44. Haring (1963), p. 126.
45. *D.I.I.*, XXIV, 152. Much the same opinion on the brutalizing effects of New World conditions was expressed about the same time by Pedro de Quiroga (1922), p. 49:
    "Cierto, esta tierra adelgaça los juicios, altera los animos, daña y corrompe las buenas costumbres, y engendra differentes condiciones, y hace en los

hombres otros effectos contrarios de los que primero tenían, y no solamente en los cuerpos humanos, pero aun en los animales y plantas causa esta tierra mutabilidad de bueno en malo, por que te torno a rogar me adviertas y avises de la vivienda desta tierra, que yo terne tu parescer por precepto de padre y amigo."

46. Serrano y Sanz (1930), p. 494.
47. My remarks are based on Crowder (1965). Landa (1941) translated and published chapter 20 of the López treatise, in which Indian idolatry and human sacrifices are discussed (p. 221-29).
48. Crowder (1965), p. 67, 77.
49. Real Academia de la Historia (Madrid), Muñoz Collection, vol. 42, fol. 267.
50. Crowder (1965), p. 74.
51. Ibid., p. 113.
52. For a comparison of López and Zorita, see ibid., p. 82-85.
53. My remarks on Zorita are based largely on the introduction by Benjamin Keen in Zorita (1963), pp. 3-77.
54. Ibid., p. 49.
55. Powell (1952), pp. 93-94.
56. Zorita (1963), pp. 69-70.
57. Ibid., p. 52.
58. Ibid., pp. 162-63, 169.
59. Ibid., p. 173.
60. Ibid., pp. 217-18.
61. Matienzo (1967), pp. 16-19.
62. Ibid., pp. 87, 135.
63. Egaña (1954), p. 300.
64. Baudot (1969), p. 81.
65. Albó (1966), p. 297.
66. Acosta (1954), pp. 394-96. For a succinct view of Acosta's attitudes toward the Indians, see Lopetegui (1942), pp. 371-78. It may be pertinent to observe that Jesuits in New France showed a similar split in their opinion of Indians. The Jesuit Pierre Biard (1567-1622) was inclined to condemn the Indians for their barbarism; another Jesuit, Paul Le Jeune (1591-1664), recognized and deplored their barbaric traits, but he did not consider that such a condition would endure. The Germans, Spanish, and English, he wrote, "were no more civilized before they became Christians" (Kennedy [1950], p. 99).
67. Acosta (1954), pp. 435-37.
68. Ibid., p. 477.
69. Ibid., p. 182.
70. Bernardo de Vargas Machuca, "Apologías y discursos de las Conquistas Occidentales," in Fabié (1879), II, 409-517, 429, 433.
71. Ibid., pp. 434, 435.
72. Ibid., p. 445.
73. Silva (1621), fol. 54v. I have used the copy in the British Museum. See also Zavala (1969b).
74. Dávalos y Figueroa (1602), p. 3.
75. For more information on this subject, see Hanke (1965b).
76. Moreno Toscano (1963b), p. 507. See also Moreno Toscano (1963a).
77. Zimdars (1965), p. 528.
78. Clavijero defended the Mexican Indians from charges made by the Scottish

historian William Robertson in his *History of America* (1777) in much the same way as Las Casas and other Indian supporters had done more than two centuries before:

"I protest . . . to all of Europe that the spiritual and mental qualities of the Mexican are in no way inferior to those of the Europeans; that they are capable of all learning, even the most abstract, and that if properly instructed from their earliest years and reared in school under good teachers, adequately protected and motivated by the hope of [fair] rewards, they could produce philosophers, mathematicians, and theologians . . . capable of competing with the most famous of Europe. But it is quite difficult, not to say impossible, to make progress in learning while living in slave-like misery and never-ending hardship. Without the evidence of their immortal works and the testimony of centuries, it would be difficult to convince a person today who pondered over the present state of Greece that there existed in that country at one time the outstanding men [of learning] with whom we are acquainted. Yet, the obstacles which present-day Greeks have to overcome to gain an education are in no way comparable to those which the aborigines have had and actually still have to surpass." Ronan (1960), p. 109.

79. The statement was made by Jorge Juan and Antonio de Ulloa, as given in Pike, ed. (1969), pp. 83-84.

80. Hernández Luna (1953).

81. León-Portilla (1958), p. 201. See also Eguiara y Eguren (1944).

82. Developments in Portuguese America merit consideration for comparative purposes. For example, Paulo da Silva Nunes, in 1724 representative of *moradores* of the Maranhão-Para, declared in a proposal to the Portuguese king that he agreed with those authorities who considered the Amerindians to be "not true human beings, but beasts of the forest incapable of understanding the Catholic faith." He further stigmatized them as "squalid savages, ferocious and most base, resembling wild animals in everything save human shape" (Boxer [1963], p. 96). For more on this fiery Portuguese colonist, see Alden (1968), pp. 35-37. For repercussions of the controversy in eighteenth-century Spanish America, see Córdova (1951), Fox (1941), Mörner (1965), and San José Muro (1798).

83. Menéndez Pidal (1963).

84. Hanke (1964), pp. 313-14. For those who wish to savor Menéndez Pidal's rich and varied vocabulary, here are his words (as cited in n. 83):

"Anticristiano, austero y vehemente exagerador, egotismo vanidoso, presuntuosa vanidad, vanagloria megalómana, le faltaba una mínima partecilla de la fuerza moral de un San Francisco de Asís o de un Savonarola, pueril vanidad, delirio de grandeza, inexactitudes tendenciosas, genialidades excéntricas, bullicioso, injuriador, delirio sistematizado, intemperamente vehemencia, hinchada truculencia, deleite descriptivo de bestialidades, lenguaje sañudo, chocante imprudencia de lenguaje, una irresistible propensión patológica, el vértigo de la enormización, exageración enormizante habitual irreprimible, maniática preocupación, una víctima inconciente de su delirio incriminatorio, prejuicio totalitario, canonista medieval, un rezagado, ataca con sus lanzallamas y con sus gases venenosos la ciudadela de los encomenderos, patológica certidumbre, confusionista, infantiles fantasías nobilarias, no es posible imaginar un egotismo más puerilmente vanidoso, tono jactancioso, tenía arte natural para paliar su autoelogio con actitudes piadosas y altruistas, infantil jactancia, manía protagonista, inteligencia débil, infatuación vanagloriosa, vanidad fantástica de un niño imaginativo, vanidosa altanería, su irrefrenable desfiguración de los hechos, ultrarigorismo moral, un ciego para la realidad como un delirante en planes quiméricos, su providencialismo egocéntrico, sus arbitrismos, ilusionista extravagante, impetuoso, sus obsesionantes ideas antiencomenderas, regocijo vanidoso, febril delirio, sobrearrogante alegato, contradicciones irrazonables, prurito egoista, dominico tardío, vehemente rigorismo, su total ensimismamiento, siempre extraído del mundo real, iluminado, alabancioso fatalmente irreflexivo, vanidoso engreimiento, iracundo, el hombre más admirado de sí mismo que ha existido."

In view of these high-powered words it is difficult to accept Father Gómez Canedo's interpretation of Don Ramón's attack on Las Casas: "Aunque el tono quizá sea excesivamente polemico—si bien esto resulta difícil de evitar en tema tan distorsionado—la crítica es lógica y en general equitativa, y el lenguaje siempre digno y sereno" (in *Handbook of Latin American Studies*, XXVI, 46).

"Paranoia" is defined as "Psychiatry. Mental disorder characterized by systemized delusions and the projection of personal conflicts, which are ascribed to the supposed hostility of others: the disorder often exists for years without any disturbance of consciousness" (*Random House Dictionary of the English Language*, 1967).

85. As quoted by Carro (1953).
86. Höffner (1957), pp. 517-18.
87. Pereña Vicente (1956), p. 309.
88. Las Casas (1957), I, clxxxiv-clxxxv.
89. Carro (1966), p. 245.
90. Silva Tena (1967), p. 355.
91. Manrique (1966), p. 14. See also Rodríguez Prampolini (1949).
92. Ortega y Medina (1967). The Akademiia Nauk in Moscow published a 228-page volume on Las Casas in 1966 in which a dozen or more writers discussed various aspects of his life and work. The Marxist review in Mexico, *Historia y Sociedad*, devoted its no. 5 (1966) issue to Las Casas, which had a number of articles by Russian writers, such as the article by Jorosháeva (1966). Other articles in this number were S. Sérov, "Bartolomé de Las Casas: su vida y su obra en los estudios de Lewis Hanke"; Juan Comas, "Los detractores del protector universal de indios y la realidad histórica"; I. Grigulévich, "Fray Bartolomé de Las Casas, enemigo de los conquistadores"; Y. Zubritski, "De la 'protección a los indios' del padre Las Casas al indigenismo contemporáneo." See also Enzensberger (1966), which was issued in Spanish in Havana (Enzensberger [1969]). For other signs of interest in Las Casas in Castro's Cuba, see Griñan Peralta (1962), and Le Riverend (1966). The latter, a mimeographed report, gives information on the papers presented 12, 13, 14, and 17 October 1966 in Havana to the Seminario sobre Problemas de Historia de Colonialismo en América, which was organized to commemorate the 400th anniversary of the death of Las Casas.
93. Professor Raymond Marcus of the Université de Paris (Bois de Vincennes) has in preparation a bibliography of these publications. A selective list by Professor Marcus appears in Friede and Keen (1971), pp. 603-16.
94. Gómez Canedo (1957). Father Gómez Canedo apparently wrote this article as a comment on a statement of mine in an article titled "¿Era Las Casas un erudito?" that analyzed an attack on Las Casas by a contemporary Franciscan. I concluded:
"Quizás la historia no se repita, pero es tentador creer que los historiadores

si se repiten, especialmente si son franciscanos que escriben sobre Las Casas. Pero esto no es completamente exacto, porque el respetado Juan de Torquemada, anticipando los juicios favorables de otros franciscanos, se refirió a Las Casas con estas palabras: 'Emulos hartos a tenido, por aver dicho claramente las Verdades.' Todavía más pertinente a la cuestión de la verdad de la denuncia de Las Casas de la acción española en América es el testimonio de tres franciscanos que habían tomado parte en la conquista de Chile—Juan de Torralba, Cristóbal de Rabaneda y Antonio de Carbajal—los cuales escribieron a Las Casas el seis de marzo de 1562 que en Chile se habían cometido crueldades aún más grandes que las que Las Casas había pintado en uno de sus tratados. Y en cuanto a la cuestión del número de indios matados por los españoles, el padre Motolinía, que no fue amigo de Las Casas, incluyó unos datos interesantes en su *Historia de los indios de Nueva España*. No se limitó al uso de cifras, sino afirmó que los aborígenes que murieron en las minas de oro 'no se pueden contar' y que el servicio en las minas de Oaxyecac era tan destructor que 'por media legua en torno y por gran parte del camino apenas se podia andar sino sobre cadáveres que casi ocultaban el sol.' " Hanke (1968), pp. 286-87.

Inasmuch as the reader of Father Gómez Canedo's article might conclude from his remarks that I thought all Franciscans have the same attitude toward Las Casas, I wish to make my real view clear. Father Gómez Canedo repeats his charge in a recent publication; see Gómez Canedo (1968). "A very strong part was played by the Franciscans," as a recent study has made clear (Poole [1961]). For additional evidence on Franciscan views on Indian questions, see Poole (1966a).

95. Las Casas (1967), I, vii-x.
96. Ibid., p. x.
97. Menéndez Pidal (1963), p. 56.
98. Giménez Fernández (1966), pp. 91-92.
99. Gómez Canedo (1964).
100. Ibid., pp. 209-11.
101. Carbonell Bassett (1963). For contrary views, see Bataillon (1965), Comas (1968), Giménez Fernández (1966), Carro (1963), and Konetzke (1964).
102. Carbonell Bassett (1963), p. 110.
103. Biermann (1964). See especially the professional psychiatric literature cited in this work.
104. Jiménez Moreno (1957).
105. Levillier (1935), I, 178.
106. As quoted in Hanke (1965a), p. 128.
107. Keen (1969), p. 704, n. 2.
108. Encina (1940), I, 389.
109. Menéndez Pidal (1950), p. 149.

A Summation

 NE of the positive results of the 1966 commemoration of the 400th anniversary of the death of Las Casas has been the publication of most of his writings in editions easily accessible to the public. Although predictions are dangerous in this field, it seems likely that no major treatise of his remains unpublished. Even if the second part of his argument at Valladolid turns up, the Spanish *apologia,* even if the dialogue of the interlocutors Senior and Juvenis on the title of Spain to the Indies is discovered in some library,[1] and even if the book he submitted to the Pope at the end of his long life is located in the archives in Rome,[2] it is reasonable to suppose that no startling new aspects of his doctrine will be revealed. And if Las Casas's tremendous collection of letters from correspondents throughout the Indies should somehow almost miraculously appear,[3] much new detail on his life and on Indian affairs would undoubtedly become available, but the principles that guided his actions for half a century are all to be found, in scattered and

repetitious fashion, in the works we now know: the treatises of 1552–1553, the *Historia de las Indias,* and *De Unico Vocationis Modo, De Thesauris,* and his *Defense* against the doctrine of Sepúlveda. Further analysis of these writings will doubtless yield valuable insights and facts, and his views on economic matters will perhaps be clarified as he was one of the first to notice and comment on the inflation caused by the influx of New World treasure into Europe.[4]

Las Casas might have become an archeologist, for he apparently divined some of the practices of this field of knowledge.[5] His observations of plants and animals in America has recently been characterized by Víctor Manuel Patiño as of "great scientific value, in many cases superior to that shown by the historian Oviedo." What is now needed, according to this Colombian scholar, is a careful scrutiny of Las Casas's writings for his competence in cultural and social anthropology: "Such an examination would demonstrate that Las Casas was not a confused crank, but one of the wisest and most faithful observers of American society."[6] Perhaps Miguel León-Portilla, director of the Instituto de Historia of the Universidad Nacional Autónoma de México, who has already made an important contribution by sponsoring a splendid edition of the text of the *Apologética Historia,* and Ignacio Bernal, director of the Instituto Nacional de Antropología e Historia, will undertake this task, which unfortunately the editor of this fundamental text did not undertake. Mexico, clearly, has already outstripped all other Latin American nations in the scientific study of anthropology, so that the preparation of a critical and professional analysis of Las Casas's contribution as an anthropologist—of the same high quality as Alfred M. Tozzer's edition of Diego de Landa—would manifest Mexico's scholarly competence and maturity in anthropology to the world just as the magnificent Museo Nacional de Antropología does in a more popular way.[7] It is regrettable, too, that the treatise Las Casas sent to Pope Pius V has not been located.[8]

The basic thoughts of Las Casas can nevertheless be obtained from several of his published works. One of his contemporaries, Bartolomé Frías de Albornoz, though not sympathetic to his doctrine, stated that one could get a good idea of his thought from reading any six *pliegos* of his writings.[9] Antonio María Fabié, the nineteenth-century editor who did so much to initiate Las Casas studies, had this to say: "It would be difficult to find a writer whose works are as uniform as those of the famous bishop of Chiapa." And the twentieth-century Dominican theologian, Diego Venancio Carro, who has studied his theories more intensively than anyone else, has remarked:

The contents of the works and writings of Las Casas are limited and determined by the arguments of his adversaries. They are books and writings of battle; he was not able nor did he need to concern himself with theoretical arguments or those invented by himself, as does a professor in the lecture hall. Las Casas writes and responds to the specific arguments that his adversaries repeat time and again. This explains why Las Casas also repeats himself frequently.[10]

Las Casas did alter his views somewhat from time to time, thus there are some differences to be noted. Silvio Zavala has commented on such a change after the failure of the New Laws, precisely in the years when Las Casas was working on his *Defense*:

He was more and more determined and energetic. His earlier view of considering the conquest and the encomienda system as abuses by individual Spaniards could not be continued when the Crown itself supported them. Then it was that Las Casas began to abandon his ancient regalism to give himself over to the defense of his thesis, even when it was contrary to legal decisions of the king, finding support for his views in the Thomistic theory of natural law. In an earlier letter Las Casas had recalled to Philip II that the prince could not make just by his laws what natural law held to be unjust. The regalism of Las Casas now seems to disappear entirely when he sees that the Crown has decided on a matter involving conscience in the light of its own material interests.[11]

Las Casas, who never doubted that God was always on his side, manifested confident independence even in the face of a Caribbean tempest. On his way to his bishopric in 1544, shortly after Christmas, his ship sailed into a storm that lasted many days. Her mast broke, waves higher than the poop deck broke upon her, and many passengers confessed in preparation for death. Las Casas, however, adopted a King Canute posture, according to Friar Tomás de la Torre, who kept a record of their trip from Salamanca to Chiapa: "The holy one ordered the sea in the name of Jesus Christ to calm itself, and at the same time his companions to be quiet and have no fear, for God was with them and . . . they would not perish."¹² And they did not perish! The friars were comforted and began to sing hymns; after a considerable time the tempest ceased, the friars began *Te Deum Laudamus,* and a great calm descended.

Kings, even Spanish kings as powerful as the Emperor Charles V, were to be obeyed, according to Las Casas, only insofar as they followed the proper Christian policies. At a time when royal officials often adopted a servile tone in addressing their monarchs, Las Casas wrote in his *Historia de las Indias* a chapter describing his first encounter with Charles V in Barcelona, which occurred in 1519 but was written down by Las Casas after his dispute with Sepúlveda:

> I am certain that I am rendering Your Majesty one of the greatest services that a vassal may make to his prince, and I do this not because I desire any kind of reward or prize, because I am not doing this to serve Your Majesty, since it is certain (speaking with all respect and reverence due such a great king and lord) that I would not move from this spot to another spot to serve Your Majesty, except for the fidelity I owe as a subject, unless I thought and believed that I was thereby making a great sacrifice to God.¹³

So Las Casas's movement away from *regalismo* need surprise no one.

It is somewhat more difficult to explain his apparent willingness to approve limited warfare against infidels who kill other innocent infidels so as to sacrifice them to their gods or to eat them, as he concedes in one of his last treatises, the *Tesoros del Perú.* Even here, however, he advised the kings of Spain to wage war *"moderadamente"* and only after they had tried "with all possible peaceful means to persuade [opponents] with kindly words and examples."¹⁴

These modulations and changes that have been noted in Las Casas's ideas over the years in no way changed his fundamental position, which is illustrated by his argument at Valladolid in 1550-1551. The *Defense* brings together all his principal contentions and illustrates how the various facets of his doctrine are in harmony with all the others. The following quotation is from the *De Unico Vocationis Modo,* but it contains the germs of his thoughts which were elaborated in greater detail—in certain respects—in the *Brevíssima Relación de la Destrucción de las Indias* and the *Apologética Historia:*

Worldly, ambitious men who sought wealth and pleasure placed their hope in obtaining gold and silver by the labor and sweat, even through very harsh slavery, oppression, and death, of not only innumerable people but of the greater part of humanity; they devised a means to hide their tyranny and injustices and to justify themselves in their own light.

This is the way they worked it out: to assert falsely that the Indians were so lacking in the reason common to all men that they were not able to govern themselves and thus needed tutors. And the insolence and madness of these men became so great that they did not hesitate to allege that the Indians were beasts or almost beasts, and publicly defamed them. Then they claimed that it was just to subject them to our rule by war, or to hunt them like beasts and then reduce them to slavery. Thus they could make use of the Indians at their pleasure.

But the truth is that very many of the Indians were able to govern themselves in monastic, economic, and political life. They could teach us and civilize us, however, and even more, would dominate us by natural reason as the Philosopher said speaking of Greeks and barbarians.[15]

The *Defense*, because it has so many of the essential parts of Las Casas's doctrine, will probably become the favorite treatise of those who wish to get a general appreciation of his theoretical labors. It was prepared as a part of his most solemn and bitter argumentation after an immensely long career marked by lively disputes. As background music, or noise, through all these disputes we hear the discussions on the nature of the Indians and their capacity for civilization, which have a direct relationship to *mestizo* capacity. As one Mexican writer has emphasized, "The problem of the incapacity of the Indian is not a merely academic interest. For Mexico it is a vital matter; to accept Indian incapacity is the same as admitting our social inferiority."[16] A Peruvian historian has suggested that Spaniards cultivated "a tremendous complex of inferiority" in the Indians that still influences the course of events.[17]

The universal element in Las Casas's thought gives his writings special relevance today: "No nation exists today, nor could exist, no matter how barbarous, fierce, or depraved its customs may be, which may not be attracted and converted to all political virtues and to all the humanity of domestic, political, and rational man."[18] Thus, Las Casas expressed the ancient Christian view: "He hath made of one blood all nations of men for to dwell on all the face of the earth."[19]

The same issues the Spaniards struggled over as they opened the New World face us today. One Spaniard links Pope Paul III's bull *Sublimis Deus* with the deliberations of the recent Vatican Council,[20] and another Spaniard has this to say:

Holy wars, wars for social and religious redemption, *Gott mit uns*, manifest destiny, and atomic bombs launched on behalf of human dignity, all these have an obscure, common background in the iniquity of the Indies.

Our time, a witness of the general failure of ethical values which has not yet received adequate attention, is peculiarly fitted to judge the deeds of those few daring persons who undertook the task of setting right the great injustice of the Indies. It is clear that it is not simply a question of arousing a sympathetic reaction, but of re-examining its spiritual basis—which for centuries has been conceived and discussed in simplistic terms—in order to ascend the difficult path by which man turns to evaluate himself critically. This great enterprise, which may lead us by various routes to achieve permanent results, may thus become one of the principal labors in the historic development of the spirit.[21]

One may add, too, that in certain American countries the depreciation of Indian character has inevitably led, as in the days of Sepúlveda, to their oppression. An anthropologist has this to report on the results of his researches in Ecuador:

In the universal dialectic of racism, the Indian is endowed with the very traits disesteemed by his white superiors. Even the kindliest among the latter tend to look upon the Indian as a child perpetually held at a developmental stage less than that of a full adult human being, or they regard him simply as a brute little better than any other animal capable of carrying a heavy load. Perhaps most insidious of all is the attitude of benevolent condescension that characterizes the patrón of classic mold and many would-be benefactors. The fact that some Indian groups in Ecuador are singled out for special comment or praise—the Otavaleños, for example, are said to be proud, clean, industrious, intelligent, etc.—is to commend them for having qualities that one is, in effect, surprised to find among Indians, and at the same time to damn other Indian groups with the implication that these are precisely the qualities they *don't* have. Thus, most Indians are generally regarded as being lazy, drunken, dirty, stupid, dishonest, or having other flaws of character. And so is fed the stereotype of the Indian that both keeps him at a distance and gives warrant to the ill treatment accorded him. . . .

It is widely believed in Ecuador that some if not all Indian groups are stigmatized by traits that mark them off as an inferior race. Such "folk genetic beliefs," although usually invidious, are often accepted by Indians themselves. Unhappily, many of these stigmata are all too evident; these populations are to a striking degree physically and functionally crippled. This fact serves to reinforce the image of the Indian as a less than human being, to justify the ill treatment accorded him and the low esteem in which he is held. A self-fulfilling prophecy, it operates in short to perpetuate the very circumstances that make him what he is. And so is the vicious circle closed.[22]

The period of the Renaissance and the Reformation, in which Las Casas lived, has usually been considered an age in which the horizons of men were widened: "New vistas of the world were being opened up by the voyagers; new types of men, of modes of life, of societies and states, were being discovered and described . . . and new questions, which were nevertheless as old as the hills, made eddies and rapids in the swift current of thought, and cried out for an answer."[23] Today, despite the voyages to the moon, we live in an "age of diminished man," according to the poet Archibald MacLeish in his speech at the Charter Day ceremonies at the University of California in May 1969. However we may explain the "paradoxical diminishment in our own eyes at the moment of our greatest technological triumphs," Macleish maintained that a "belief in man—a return to a belief in man—is the reality on which a new age can be built."[24] Was not Las Casas addressing himself essentially to this same question at Valladolid?

Did he really expect to win the argument? From his earliest years as Defender of the Indians he had been a resourceful and determined political strategist in the world of the Emperor Charles V. Yet at Valladolid, with many years of struggle in Spain and America behind him, he formally proposed that all conquests be stopped. Did he really believe that at that late date, more than half a century after Columbus, the clock could be turned back—that the whole machinery of empire, from which so many politically powerful Spaniards (both lay and ecclesiastical) profited, could be dismantled? Perhaps he did. Like the Liberator, Simón Bolívar, he rarely vacillated when he believed he was right.

Whatever may be the correct answers to these questions, the historian, looking back on the conflict over the nature of the American Indians, can see why the late Jóse Almoina characterized it as "perhaps the most transcendental controversy that took place at the threshold of the Modern Age."[25] This controversy raised permanent problems for the modern age. As Carmelo Viñas y Mey observed almost half a century ago:

The discovery of America initiated unsuspected problems which were to change the direction of the modern age. The question of how to treat the natives of America posed the problem of human personality, the system devised to profit from their labor but at the same time preserving their personal freedom led to consideration of the fundamental aspects of the social problem. Both questions were involved in the fundamental colonial problem: the relation between civilized peoples and inferior races, and the responsibility of one group toward the other.[26]

Now we may see that Las Casas stood in the forefront of those Renaissance theologians who labored to understand what a modern Catholic scholar has termed "the theological significance of America." The tendency among these post-Council of Trent theologians was "to admit for the infidels the type of faith that Thomas Aquinas allowed to those who lived before the promulgation of the Gospel, and to insist that God will employ extraordinary means to bring the conscientious pagan to justification, according to the axiom, *Facienti quod in se est, Deus non denegat gratiam* (God does not refuse grace to one who does his best)."[27]

Las Casas went even further. He recognized the relevance of ancient and medieval concepts to sixteenth-century problems, but he never accepted the proposition that Indians were an inferior race—in comparison with Spaniards or anyone else. It is certainly clear today that inasmuch as his argumentation against Sepúlveda focused on one of the overriding themes of the modern world—the relations between peoples of different customs, capability, color, religion, and values— the *Defense* stands out starkly as one of the fundamental positions on the bitter and continuing conflicts that divide mankind. If this be true, will not both the American reality of the sixteenth century as it affected the clashing ideas of Las Casas and Sepúlveda be of unquestioned meaning to our troubled age, and can we not see in the Valladolid dispute yet another illustration of the fact that some of past history is also contemporary history? Can anyone doubt that the comment of Bishop Antonio Augustin in April 1550, on the eve of the

Valladolid disputation, is just as valid today as when he declared that the problem is "a question worthy of being considered in the theater of all mankind"?[28]

NOTES

1. *Documentos inéditos para la historia de España*, VIII, 558.
2. Las Casas (1958), V, 541.
3. Referred to in his will, in ibid., p. 540.
4. Las Casas (1822), I, 302. Other references on economic matters have been collected by Márquez Miranda (1953). After I completed this section, a valuable study by a young French scholar reached me, which promises to be a fundamental contribution on this subject; see Milhou (1973).
5. Huddleston (1967), p. 24.
6. Patiño (1966).
7. Landa (1941). León-Portilla is an excellent scholar who could provide both the scientific evaluation of Las Casas as an anthropologist and the *"enfoque humanista e integral,"* if we may judge from his remarks on Sahagún (León-Portilla [1958]). Professor Raymond Marcus has already made a valuable analysis of Las Casas's Peruvian material (Marcus [1966]). For a comparative work on Torquemada, see Cline (1969).
8. Las Casas (1957), V, 541. This "Petición a Su Santidad Pio V" was undated, and has been given the title "Qué cosas son necesarias para la justificada forma de promulgar el Evangelio y hacer lícita y justa guerra." In 1933 a Vatican librarian searched on my behalf for the *Libro* sent by Las Casas but could not find it.
9. Fabié (1879), I, 356.
10. Carro (1966), p. 241. Manuel Giménez Fernández (1966) has this to say: "Admiramos y amamos a Las Casas por ese su monoideismo fundamental; porque, como ha dicho de manera insuperable Alberto Mario Salas: 'Esas pocas y tan bien puestas ideas eran nada menos que los corolarios de una fe ortodoxa y pura: la igualdad del hombre, la convicción de su perfectibilidad, la negación de toda violencia y su repudio a la crueldad; su afirmación, en fin, frente a la conquista marcial, de que el único modo posible de atraer a los pueblos a la fe de Cristo era la observancia de una conducta cristiana' " (p. 129).
11. Zavala (1935), pp. 190, 200.
12. Torre (n.d.), p. 113.
13. Hanke (1968), p. 195.
14. Las Casas (1958), p. 385.
15. Las Casas (1942), pp. 363-64.
16. López-Portilla (1944), p. 150.
17. Málaga Medina (1965), p. 169.
18. Hanke (1965a), p. 125.
19. Acts, XVII, 26 (King James version).
20. Seco Carro (1967).
21. Las Casas (1957), I, xxiii-xxiv.

22. Casagrande *A*, p. 2, and Casagrande *B*, p. 5.
23. Myres (1910), p. 591.
24. Macleish (1969), p. 69.
25. Almoina (1962), p. 78.
26. Viñas y Mey (n.d.).
27. See the pithy "Theological Significance of America" in *A Catholic Dictionary of Theology* (London: Nelson, 1962), I, 69-70.
28. After I wrote this conclusion the veteran scholar Silvio Zavala sent me a copy of his reflections on the basic issues discussed in these pages. All students of this subject will want to ponder his concise presentation of the theoretical discussions of the Spaniards and their significance for the modern world; see Zavala (1970). Today, some educational specialists in the United States hold that Whites are more intelligent than Negroes, which reminds us of the sixteenth-century discussions among Spaniards on the capacity of the Indians. See the *Saturday Review*, 17 May 1969. The final phrase comes from the foreword by Bishop Antonio Augustín in the Rome edition of Sepúlveda's treatise *Apologia pro libro de justis belli causis* (1550).

Appendices

Appendix 1

Statement by Dr. Richard Konetzke

These remarks by Dr. Konetzke, made during the Conference on the Evangelization of America, are reproduced with his permission and that of the Academy of American Franciscan History.

Creo que no debe confundirse la reconquista en la Peninsula ibérica, la guerra del moro, con una cruzada para expulsar a los infieles o convertirlos a la fe verdadera. La reconquista de España que terminó precisamente en el año del descubrimiento de América, no era una empresa misional. Se garantizó a la población mora sometida el libre ejercicio de su creencia mahometana. Todavía en la capitulación de Granada los Reyes Católicos aseguraban a los vencidos que podían permanecer en el país con su religión, sus bienes y sus costumbres. Es verdad que la iglesia española ya comenzó en el siglo XIII la época de las misiones, que se debió preponderantemente a las grandes órdenes mendicantes entonces fundadas. Se iniciaron las misiones exteriores en el norte de Africa y Asia y también había misiones de los frailes en las Canarias y moros y judiós. No se ocurrió a las instituciones eclesiásticas que ocupaban tantos millares de moros en las tareas de campo y en los oficios mecánicos, convertir estos infieles a la fe cristiana. Por ejemplo, al comienzo del siglo XV la Abadesa de las Huelgas, cerca de Burgos, ocupaba muchos moros en el cultivo del campo y un día el cabildo de Burgos prohibió a estos moros que acudiesen a la Mezquita de Burgos, aduciendo que no pagaban el tributo y la Abadesa vino para que sus gentes, sus moros, pudiese ejercer su culto en la Mezquita de Córdoba. También debo referirme a la guerra del moro en el siglo XV. En esta guerra del moro había de todo, pero no existía una preocupación de salvar a las almas y de convertir a estos moros al cristianismo. Los hechos importantes son este cambio que se verificó a fines del siglo XV. El primer hecho es la expulsión de los judíos en el año 1492. Se aplicaba la idea conversión o expulsión y la misma idea es aplicada en el año 1500 a los moros del reino de Granada, a quienes se había garantizado el libre ejercicio de sus creencias, y creo es necesario estudiar los motivos de ese cambio. Quiero solamente indicar una cosa: la actitud del Estado español para la nueva monarquía hispánica de los Reyes Católicos, el afan misional de las órdenes mendicantes presentó un importante aspecto político; la oposición en el mismo territorio del Estado español, las tres religiones—cristianos, mahometanos y judíos—las cuales se distinguen entre sí en culto, en el traje y las costumbres y se odiaban como extranjeros; esto daba lugar a constantes disturbios de la paz pública. Así, el establecimiento de la unidad religiosa por medio de la mision católica, tenía que aparecer en estas circunstancias como una medida para la unificación política de España.

Appendix 2

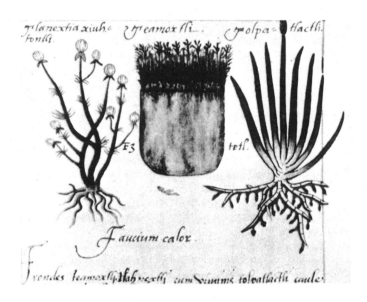

Comments by Dr. Harold B. Johnson, Jr., on Dr. Konetzke's Statement in Appendix 1

To indicate how complicated and relatively little studied are the fundamental questions raised by Dr. Konetzke in appendix 1, I reproduce, with deep gratitude, the comments that Professor Harold B. Johnson, Jr., of the University of Virginia was kind enough to prepare at my request:

The problem of crusade, reconquest, and conversion, both in Iberia as well as later in America, is an intricate subject, further complicated by ramifications, both legal and political, as well as religious and economic. As yet so little of it all has been properly untangled that I certainly cannot hope to do so in this short note to you; but I will say that most of the general treatments I have read seem to me to err greatly in trying to schematize something that is highly resistant to simplification.

First we have in medieval Iberia contacts limited essentially to Moors and Jews, who although they were treated similarly in some ways, were regarded quite differently in many more. Then, later, there is Castile's brief experience with the Guanches of the Canaries who fitted into neither of these two previous categories; and finally the American Indians who presented problems different from any of the foregoing.

One of the first distinctions that has to be made, it seems to me, is that in medieval Iberia the Christian authorities were dealing with a *reconquest* situation in which the problem of religious beliefs and cultural differences was essentially *secondary*. That is to say, Christian rulers saw themselves as engaged in recovering territory that they considered to be rightfully theirs. Thus they had no doubts as to their claims. The problem never arose as to whether the reconquest was "just" or not. It was accepted as given. The fact that they incorporated dissident communities in the process was almost incidental; and their solution here was purely practical. Due to the relative weakness of the state and to the ingrained Ibero-Muslim tradition of tolerance, these groups were simply accepted, without much thought of conversion. Why should the Christian rulers have done otherwise? These minorities didn't threaten the state; they could be taxed heavily; and their existence was useful, rather than noxious, to the royal purpose. Thus they were, in fact, protected by the kings as a kind of special ward. Sporadic attempts at conversion—mainly the work of ecclesiastical entrepreneurs—were made, but they had small significance.

This situation, however, begins to change at the end of the fourteenth century, due mainly, I think, to social turmoil and economic depression. And from this point on, it is popular pressure and animosity against the Jews that first brings intolerance as an organized force to medieval Iberia. Conversion in this situation was a protective reflex action on the part of the Jews (Moors generally did not bear the brunt of this popular hostility), although in reality there was little popular desire to integrate these people into Christian society. The majority would certainly have preferred to see them despoiled and expelled. And for about a century afterward, royal authority—which was none too strong during this period—risked its general popularity in order to protect these dissident minorities, a traditional policy that was increasingly out-of-date.

By the end of the century, however, we have an about-face on the part of the Crown. Now, Ferdinand and Isabella demand conversion or expulsion. Why? I can think of several reasons. First, a desire to win popular support for their "New Monarchy" and moves against Jews and Moors were popular. Secondly, the conversions of the fifteenth century had the effect of creating new Christians who increasingly infiltrated themselves (possibly as a protective device) into the royal and ecclesiastical bureaucracy, and expulsion would tend to reduce this flow. Thirdly, with royal revenues on the increase for various reasons, the class of Jewish money-lenders that had played so large a role in royal finance during the Middle Ages was of less use to the Crown, and it could scuttle its unpopular policy of protection. But this ultimate acceptance of popular intolerance was essentially a matter of Castilian internal politics, hardly the same thing as, or even closely related to (though superficially it may seem to be), the problem faced by the Castilian Crown in the Indies. And it would be a serious mistake in my opinion to try to subsume them under the same generalizations, or to see them as closely related phenomena.

In the Indies conditions were radically different from those prevailing in Iberia during the reconquest. For one thing, the Indians had an indisputable prior claim to the land—thus the theoretical agonies of the royal advisers over "just" wars. Further, although the Indians were not Christians, yet neither were they Moors or Jews; they had never rejected Christianity; they were not enemies of the faith. *Ergo*, how could a Castilian conquest, or even a Castilian presence, be justified?

Here Castile had little applicable experience to go on. Only in the Canaries had Castile met with an even remotely comparable situation. But the Canary denouement was one over which the Castilian Crown had very little control until the end. It had been undertaken by private entrepreneurs for the most part; and they had simply raided and enslaved the natives at will. When the Crown did manage to get hold of the situation, it prohibited such activities, but its intervention came too late since most of the natives had already perished.

But why in any case was the Crown interested in protecting the Guanches? Well, because it wanted, so it said, to convert them and enslavement was not a good beginning for that. But why did it wish to convert them? It had not been especially eager to convert Jews and Moors until the late fifteenth century, and then only for reasons of Castilian internal politics. Here we come, I think, to the crux of the matter; for the Canaries experience does provide a kind of abortive model for the Indies. The charge to convert that was laid upon Columbus and thereafter incessantly repeated in royal instructions regarding new territories was the best claim to title that could be established for lands that were not properly subject to "reconquest." It was recognized by the Papacy, and was the prime condition for papal approval of conquest; it also did much to establish the 'justness' of the wars which conquest often required. This is why Columbus' instructions regarding the treatment to be given to people on the islands found en route (these, like the Guanches, were to be converted), and [those] that [were] to be followed in the populous kingdoms of the East expected at the end of the voyage were so different. In the latter case, only treaties of friendship were envisioned and nothing else. In one case there was an attempt to lay the groundwork for title; in the other no such aim was contemplated.

But when vast kingdoms were found in America, nothing the Castilian rulers had experienced before was entirely applicable. And thus the vast amount of conflict and discussion. Once, of course, the intent to convert had been proclaimed and established as policy, then ecclesiastical and royal interest flowed into the situation and institutionalized the whole process. But I think the important thing is that there was nothing coherently elaborated either in medieval Iberia nor at the time of Columbus that was *directly* applicable to the Indies. The elements for a synthesis were there, but the elaborated synthesis had not yet been given shape.

I doubt I have done much to illuminate the "missionary spirit" you asked about. But, in any case, I think Konetzke is far too general in his formulations and I would object to seeing the Indies situation as any extension or continuation of the Reconquest patterns with regard to conversion. The more one delves into the background, the more one finds, I think, that superficial verbal carryovers from Iberia to America often mask very different structures and functions. That at least is what I have tried to suggest in the foregoing.

For more information on the complicated Iberian background, see Harold B. Johnson, Jr., ed. *From Reconquest to Empire. The Iberian Background to Latin American History.* New York: Knopf, 1970.

Appendix 3

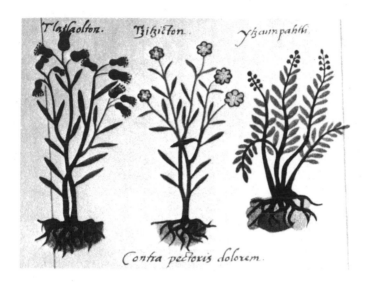

Tlatlaolton.   Tzitzicton.   yhauinpahtli

Contra pectoris dolorem.

The Retraction of Domingo de Betanzos, O. P., Dated 13 September 1549

En la muy noble villa de Valladolid a treze dias del mes de setienbre del año del Señor de mill e quinientos e quarenta e nueve años, ante mi Antonio de Canseco, escribano de sus magestades, estando en el monesterio de señor San Pablo, desta dicha villa, de la horden de señor Santo Domingo de los predicadores y en un aposento de la dicha cassa e monesterio donde estaba un hombre viejo rapada la barba e corona y hechado en la cama y a lo que pareçe enfermo pero en su buen seso que se dixo e llamó fray Domingo de Betanços e dió e entregó a mi el dicho escribano un priego de papel que él me dijo del estar escripto e declarado çiertas cosas que tocaban a su concençia e descargo que señaladamente tocaban en cosas de Indias, el qual dicho escripto e declar-ación que ansí me dió y entregó, estaba firmado de una firma que dezía: fray Domingo de Betanços e de otras quatro firmas que dizen: fri [sic] Didacus Ruiz, prior, fray Petrus de Ulloa, fray Antonino de la Madalena, fray Biçente de las Casas, commo por él pareze su tenor del qual es este que se sigue:

Digo yo fray Domingo de Betanços, frayle de Santo Domingo, que por que yo muchas vezes he hablado en cosas que tocaban a los indios diziendo algunos defetos dellos y dexé en el Consejo de las Indias de su magestad e firmado de mi nonbre, un memorial el qual trata de los dichos defetos, diziendo que heran bestias e que tenían pecados y que Dios los avía sentençiado y que todos perezerían, de donde podía aver resultado grandes escándalos e aver tomado ocasión los españoles a hazer más males e agravios y muertes a los dichos indios que por ventura hizieran no escándalo, puesto que mi yntençión no fúe tal qual ellos o algunos pensaron o publicaron, sino avisar al Consejo para que pusiesen buena governaçión e los remedios / que conbenían y por bentura muchos abían hecho a los dichos indios grandes destruiciones e muertes por sus cudicias y se abían querido escusar e abtoriçallas con muchas cosas que me an lebantado que yo dixe e porque yo estoy enfermo e podrá ser que Nuestro Señor sea servydo llevarme desta enfermedad y quiero satisfacer lo que al presente puedo por descargo de mi conçiençia por ende por esta firmada de mi nonbre, digo y suplico al dicho Consejo real de las Indias e ruego a todos los questa vieren o oyeren en las Indias o en España o en otra qualquier parte que ésta vieren [sic] que ningún crédito den a cosa que yo por dicho ni por escripto aya hablado e dicho contra los indios en su perjuizio porque no me acuerdo aver hecho tal, pero si se hallare, digo que soy honbre e pude herrar e ansí creo que herré por no haber sabydo su lengua pero por otra ygnorancia las quales segund el juizio de Dios y de otros honbres más sabios y entendidos que yo son juzgadas por dañosas e dignas de retrataçión e ansí las retrato y digo el contrario de todas ellas e no afirmo ni quiero afirmar cosa que segund el juizio de Dios no conbenga, especialmente siendo en perjuizio o estorbo de la pedricaçión de la fee e contra la hutilidad de la salud de aquellas ánimas e cuerpos ni contra qualquier cosa que sea de buenas costumbres por manera que todo lo que en esta materia o en otra qualquiera he dicho e dixere hasta el artículo de la muerte y ansí le someto a la correçión de la santa madre iglesia en la fee e determinaçión de la qual protesto sienpre bibir e morir / y digo que quisiera tener salud e me pessa por no poder haser esta retrataçión delante todos los Consejos de Indias y delante todo el mundo que fuera neçesario e reboco e doy por ningunas todas ellas prepusiciones que en el parezer que dexé en el Consejo hecho e firmado de mi nombre en poder del secretario Sámano, del Consejo de Indias muy herróneas, escandalosas, mal sonantes y todo lo que en perjuizio de los dichos indios dixe afirmé en aquel memorial o fuera del contra la salud de aquellas ánimas e cuerpos lo reboco e por ques verdad lo firmo de mi nombre fecha en San Pablo de Valladolid, biernes treze de setienbre de 1549.

FRAY DOMINGO DE BETANÇOS

Fr. Bartolomé de las Casas. *Tratado de Indias y el Doctor Sepúlveda* (pp. 184-86). Caracas: Biblioteca de la Academia Nacional de la Historia, 1962. Reproduced by permission of the Academia.

Appendix 4

A Note on Dr. Edmundo O'Gorman's Views on the *Apologética Historia* of Las Casas

Dr. Edmundo O'Gorman and the Institute of History of the University of Mexico have made a great contribution to Las Casas studies by publishing the third edition of the *Apologética Historia* (1967). At considerable length, Dr. O'Gorman's "Estudio Preliminar" (in Las Casas, [1967], I, xv-1xxix) developed his hypotheses that the *Apologética Historia* was written after 1552 and had little or nothing to do with Las Casas's argument at Valladolid against Sepúlveda. Without attempting to give a detailed opinion, I have set down my present thoughts on these two statements as follows:

The Date of Composition

Dr. O'Gorman is probably correct in saying that the text of the manuscript, as it is now known was composed largely after 1552. However, the text of the third edition contains two puzzling statements by Las Casas:

1. At the end of chapter 24 in Book II Las Casas writes *"Desta materia más largo hablaremos en nuestro libro en latín escripto, cuyo título es:* De unico vocationis modo omnium gentium ad veram religionem" (Las Casas [1967], I, 125). Inasmuch as this latter treatise was composed in the early 1530s, Las Casas's reference to it would suggest that the *Apologética Historia* manuscript, at least up to the point of this reference, had been written long before 1552, or perhaps even as early as 1527, when he began his *Historia de las Indias.* The decade after his entrance, in 1522, into the Dominican Order may very well have been spent studying the theoretical problems that he developed in both the *Apologética Historia* and the *De Unico Vocationis Modo.*

2. Las Casas comments in chapter 68 of Book III on certain areas of the New World he had known: *"Que yo cognosci de cuarenta y tantos años a esta parte"* (Las Casas [1967], I, 355), which would seem to indicate that he was writing in the early 1540s.

The two puzzles are solved, however, when the original manuscript in the Real Academia de la Historia is examined, as Dr. Juan Pérez de Tudela was kind enough to do on my behalf. This manuscript reads *"hablamos,"* not *"hablaremos,"* and *"cincuenta y tantos años,"* not *"cuarenta y tantos años."* All three printed versions of the *Apologética Historia* contain these errors—these variations from the original manuscript.

The Relation of the Apologética Historia *to the Valladolid Dispute*

If Las Casas prepared most of the only known manuscript of the *Apologética Historia* after 1552, as seems likely, this does not alter the fact, in my opinion, that the argument Las Casas presented against Sepúlveda was directly related to all of the former's principal beliefs, including those in the *Apologética Historia.* Besides referring to the analysis of the *Defense* given above (chap. IV), one may point out that the last four chapters of the *Apologética Historia* on the various kinds of barbarians have a definite relationship to the argument at Valladolid. Las Casas concluded the manuscript (Las Casas [1967], II, 633) with a denunciation of those who depreciated the Indians because of the Indians' "defects" and rude customs. Then he added four more chapters on the nature of the term "barbarian," which readers of the *Defense* are familiar with. He applied this term only to those who *"son muy alejados de razón, no viviendo ni pudiendo vivir según las reglas della, o por falta de entendimiento, o por sobra de su malicia y costumbres depravadas."* This is how Aristotle used the term, Las Casas said, and he noted that he had already proved this usage (Las Casas |1967|, II, 653).

Disputes over Las Casas have an astonishingly perennial quality, but historians sometimes change their opinions of this controversial friar. Dr. O'Gorman in 1951, for example, described Las Casas in these terms: "His head was confused, his learning as diffuse as it was undigested, his passion great, his intention good, his style extremely digressive. . . . Las Casas proceeded through life illuminated by an ideal, a curious and difficult mixture of heroic piety and systematic rationalism . . . the most credulous person that ever lived . . . to expect a bit of coherence from him is to ask an elm tree to produce pears" (O'Gorman [1951], pp. 131, 141, 132, 141). Now, however, Dr. O'Gorman praises the *Apologética Historia,* and refers to its *"índole científico— teórico y su intención de pureza doctrinal"* (in Las Casas [1967], I, xvii, n. 8, and lix, n. 80), but still considers it—and perhaps the *De unico vocationis modo* as well—an exception. The rest of Las Casas's works are *"tan teñida y afeada de pasión, incongruencias y exageraciones"* (ibid., p. lix, n. 80). For the latest statement by Dr. O'Gorman on these controversial topics, see his critical review of the anthology prepared by Marcel Bataillon and André St. Lu (O'Gorman [1971]).

Discussion on these questions has been going on for some years between Dr. O'Gorman and myself. His article "Sobre la naturaleza bestial del indio americano" (1941) was followed by my *La lucha por justicia en la conquista española de América* (1949). Then appeared my "¿Bartolomé de Las Casas, existencialista?" (1953), to which Dr. O'Gorman made a brief reply in his "El método histórico de Lewis Hanke. Réplica a una sorpresa" (1953), which reveals more about his methods than about mine, which are illustrated in my *Estudios sobre*

Fray Bartolomé de Las Casas y sobre la lucha por la justicia en la conquista española de América (1968).

Readers who wish to reach their own conclusions about the controversial figure of Las Casas and about the complicated reality of Spanish-Indian relationships in sixteenth-century America should read the treatises of Las Casas and Sepúlveda.

BIBLIOGRAPHY

Acosta, José de. *Obras del P. José de Acosta,* edited by Francisco Mateos, S. J. Vol. LXXV. Madrid: Biblioteca de Autores Españoles, 1954.

Actas del Cabildo de la Ciudad de México. 12 vols. Mexico: 1889-1900.

Adib, Víctor. "Los indios en la Historia de Motolinía," *Ábside* (Mexico) XIII, no. 1 (1949): 89-97.

Albó, Xavier, S. J. "Jesuítas y culturas indígenas," *América Indígena,* primera parte, XXVI, no. 3 (1966): 249-308; segunda parte, XXVI, no. 4 (1966): 395-445.

Alden, Dauril. "Economic Aspects of the Expulsion of the Jesuits from Brazil: A Preliminary Report," in *Conflict and Continuity in Brazilian Society,* edited by Henry H. Keith and S. F. Edwards. Columbia, S.C.: University of South Carolina Press, 1968.

———. "Black Robes versus White Settlers: The Struggle for 'Freedom of the Indians' in Colonial Brazil," in *Attitudes of Colonial Powers toward the American Indian,* edited by Howard Peckham and Charles Gibson (pp. 19-46). Salt Lake City: University of Utah Press, 1969.

Almoina, José. "La primera 'Doctrina' para indios," *Revista de Historia de América* (Mexico), nos. 53 and 54 (1962): 75-98.

Altamira, Rafael. "Contribution to the History of Colonial Ideas in Spain: Unpublished Documents," in *Hispanic American Essays: A Memorial to James Alexander Robertson,* edited by A. Curtis Wilgus (pp. 31-38). Chapel Hill: University of North Carolina Press, 1942.

Atiya, Aziz A. *The Crusade in the Later Middle Ages.* London: Methuen, 1938.

———. *Crusade, Commerce, and Culture.* Bloomington: Indiana University Press, 1962.

Azcona, Tarsicio de, O. F. M. Cap. *Isabel la Católica. Estudio crítico de su vida y su reinado.* Madrid: Biblioteca de Autores Cristianos, 1964.

Azevedo, J. Lúcio de. *Os jesuitas no Grão-Pará. Suas missões e a colonização.* 2d ed. Coimbra: Imprensa da Universidale, 1930.

Bataillon, Marcel. "Evangélisme et millénarisme au Nouveau Monde," in *Courants Religieux et Humanisme à la fin du XVe et au début du XVIe Siècle (Colloque de Strasbourg 1957)* (pp. 25-36). Paris: Presses Universitaires de France, 1959.

———. *Études sur Bartolomé de Las Casas. Réunies avec la collaboration de Raymond Marcus.* Paris: Centre de Recherches de l'Institut d'Études Hispaniques, 1965.

———. *Erasmo y España. Estudios sobre la historia espiritual del siglo XVI.* 2d ed. Mexico and Buenos Aires: Fondo de Cultura Económica, 1966.

Batres Jaúregui, Antonio. *Los indios.* Guatemala: 1894.

Baudet, Henri. *Paradise on Earth: Some Thoughts on European Images of Non-*

European Man. New Haven and London: Yale University Press, 1965.

Baudot, Georges. "La biblioteca de los evangelizadores de México: un documento sobre Fray Juan de Gaona," *Historia Mexicana,* no. 68 (1968): 610-617.

———. "Fray Rodrigo de Sequera, avocat du diable pour une Histoire interdite," *Cahiers du Monde Hispanique et Luso-Brésilien (Caravelle)* (Toulouse), no. 12 (1969): 47-82.

Bayle, Constantino, S. J. "España y el clero indígena en América," *Razón y Fe* (Madrid) XCIV (1931): 213-225, 521-535.

———. *España y la educación popular en América.* Madrid: Instituto Pedagógico F.A.E., 1934.

———. *España en Indias.* 3d ed. Madrid: Editora Nacional, 1942.

———. "La comunión entre los indios americanos," *Revista de Indias* (Madrid), año IV, no. 12 (1943): 197-254.

Beckmann, J. "China im Blichfeld der Mexikanische Bettelorden des 16. Jahrhunderts," *Neue Zeitschrift für Missionswissenschaft* (Beckenried, Switzerland) XIX and XX (1963): 81-82, 195-214, and 27-41.

Beinert, Berthold. "La idea de Cruzada y los intereses de los príncipes cristianos en el siglo XV," *Cuadernos de Historia. Anexos de la revista Hispania* (Madrid) (1967).

Belmonte y Clemente, Fernando. "Colección de documentos históricos, noticias y extractos." 5 vols. 1886. Manuscript in the Archivo General de Indias Library, Seville.

Beltrán de Heredia, Vicente, O. P. "El Maestro Domingo de Soto en la controversia de Las Casas con Sepúlveda," *La Ciencia Tomista* XLV (1932): 35-49, 177-193.

———. *El Maestro Juan de la Peña, O. P.* Salamanca: Calatrava, 1935.

———. *Las corrientes de espiritualidad entre los dominicos de Castilla durante la primera mitad del siglo XVI.* Salamanca: 1941.

———. "Nuevos datos acerca del padre Bernardino de Minaya y del licenciado Calvo de Padilla, compañeros de Las Casas," *Simancas. Anuario de Historia Moderna* (Valladolid), no. 1 (1943).

Bennassar, Bartolomé. *Valladolid au siècle d'or. Une ville de Castille et sa campagne au XVI⁰ siècle.* Paris: Mouton et Cie, 1967.

Biermann, Benno M., O.P. "Las Casas—Ein Geisteskranker?" *Zeitschrift für Missionswissenschaft und Religionswissenschaft* XLVIII (1964): 176-191.

———. "Don Vasco de Quiroga und seine Schrift de Debellandis Indis," *Neue Zeitschrift für Missionswissenschaft* XXII (1966): 189-200.

———. *Las Casas und seine Sendung. Das Evangelium und die Recht des Menschen.* Mainz: 1968.

———. "Don Vasco de Quiroga y su tratado de Debellandis Indis (II)," *Historia Mexicana* XVIII (1969): 615-622.

Bishko, Charles Julian. "The Iberian Background of Latin American History: Recent Progress and Continuing Problems," *Hispanic American Historical Review* XXXVI (1956): 50-80.

Blau, Joseph L. "An Unpublished English Translation of Justinian's Life of Columbus," *Columbia Library Columns*, XIII: 3 (1964).

Borges, Pedro, O.F.M. "El sentido transcendente del descubrimiento y conversión de Indias," *Missionalia Hispánica* XIII (1956): 141-177.

———. *Métodos misionales en la cristianización de América. Siglo XVI*. Madrid: Consejo Superior de Investigaciones Científicas, 1960.

Boxer, Charles R. *The Golden Century in Brazil*. Berkeley and Los Angeles: University of California Press, 1962.

———. *Race Relations in the Portuguese Colonial Empire 1415-1825*. Oxford: Clarendon Press, 1963.

———. "The Problem of the Native Clergy in the Portuguese and Spanish Empires from the Sixteenth to the Eighteenth Centuries," in *The Mission of the Church and the Propagation of the Faith*, edited by G. J. Cuming (pp. 85-106). Cambridge: The University Press, 1970.

Buarque de Holanda, Sérgio. *Visão do Paraíso. Os motivos edênicos no descobrimento e colonização do Brasil*. 2d ed. São Paulo: Companhia Editora Nacional, Editora da Universidade de São Paulo, 1969.

Burns, Robert Ignatius, S. J. "Journey from Islam, Incipient Cultural Transition in the Conquered Kingdom of Valencia (1240-1280)," *Speculum* XXXV (1960): 337-356.

———. "Social Riots on the Christian-Moslem Frontier, Thirteenth-Century Valencia," *American Historical Review* LXVI (1961): 378-400.

Burrus, Ernest J., S. J. "Cristóbal Cabrera on the Missionary Methods of Vasco de Quiroga," *Manuscripta* (St. Louis) V, no. 1 (1961): 17-27.

———. "Alonso de la Vera Cruz's Defence of the American Indians (1553-1554)," *The Heythrop Journal* (Oxford), no. 3 (1963): 224-253.

———. "Las Casas and Vera Cruz: Their Defence of the American Indians Compared," *Neue Zeitschrift für Missionswissenschaft* (Beckenreid, Switzerland) XXII (1966): 201-212.

Campos, Leopoldo, O.F.M. "Métodos misionales y rasgos biográficos de Don Vasco de Quiroga según Cristóbal Cabrera," in his *Don Vasco de Quiroga y arzobispado de Morelia* (pp. 107-158). Mexico: Editorial Jus, 1965.

Carbonell Basset, Delfín. "En torno al P. Las Casas con Don Ramón Menéndez Pidal," *Duquesne Hispanic Review* (Pittsburgh), año II, no. 2 (1963): 107-113.

Carreño, Alberto María. *Fray Domingo de Betanzos, fundador en la Nueva España de la venerable orden dominicana*. Mexico: Imprenta Victoria, 1924-1934.

———. "La irracionalidad de los indios," *Divulgación Histórica* (Mexico) I (1940): 272-282, 328-339, 374-385.

Carro, Diego Venancio, O. P. *Bartolomé de Las Casas y las controversias teológico-jurídicas de Indias*. Madrid: Maestre, 1953.

———. *España en Indias, sin leyendas*. Madrid: Librería Ope, 1963.

———. "Los postulados teológico-jurídicos de Bartolomé de Las Casas. Sus aciertos, sus olvidos y sus fallos, ante los maestros Francisco de Vitoria y Domingo de Soto," in *Estudios Lascasianos. IV Centenario de la muerte de Fray Bartolomé de Las Casas (1566-1966)* (pp. 105-246). Seville: Facultad de Filosofía y Letras de la Universidad de Sevilla, Escuela de Estudios Hispano-americanos, 1966.

Cartas de Indias. Mexico: 1877.

Casagrande, Joseph B. "Strategies for Survival: The Indians of Highland Ecuador." Unpublished manuscript.

———. "Closing Vicious Circles: An Ecological Model for Understanding Population Biology in Indian Communities of Highland Ecuador." Unpublished manuscript.

Castañeda Delgado, Paulino. *La teocracia pontifical y la conquista de América.* Vitoria: Editorial Eset 1968.

Castillero R., Ernesto. "Fernández de Oviedo, veedor de Tierra Firme," *Revista de Indias,* año XVII, nos. 69-70 (1957).

Chamberlain, Robert S. *Castilian Backgrounds of the Repartimiento-Encomienda.* Carnegie Institution Publ. No. 509, pp. 15-66. Washington, D.C.: Carnegie Institution, 1939.

Chinchilla Aguilar, Ernesto. "Algunos aspectos de la obra de Oviedo," *Revista de Historia de America* (Mexico), no. 28 (1949): 303-330.

Chipman, Donald. "Nuño de Guzman and the Black Legend." Unpublished manuscript.

Choy, E. "De Santiago matamoros a Santiago mataindios," *Revista del Museo Nacional* (Lima) XXVII (1958): 195-271.

Cisneros, Luis Jaime. "La primera gramática de la lengua general de la lengua del Perú," *Boletín del Instituto Riva-Agüero 1951-1952* (Lima) I (1953): 197-264.

Cline, Howard F. "A Note on Torquemada's Sources and Historiographical Methods," *The Americas* XXV (1969): 372-386.

Coles, Paul. *The Ottoman Impact in Europe.* New York: Thames and Hudson, 1968.

Concha, Jaime. "Las Relaciones sobre los indios de Francisco de Vitoria," *Atenea* (Santiago de Chile), año XLIII, tomo 163, no. 413 (1966): 101-120.

Córdova, Matías de. "El problema del indio (1797)," *Ateneo* (Tuxtla Gutiérrez, Chiapas), no. 2 (1951): 13-30.

Cortés, Hernán. *Letters from Mexico,* edited and translated by A. R. Pagden. New York: Grossman, 1971.

Crowder, Constance Ann. "Tomás López Medel: Oidor, Treatise Writer and Critic of Spain in America." M. A. thesis, Columbia University, 1965.

Cuevas, Mariano, S. J. *Documentos inéditos del siglo XVI para la historia de México.* Mexico: Museo Nacional de Arqueología, Historia y Etnología, 1914.

———. *Historia de la iglesia en México.* 5 vols. Mexico: Asilo "Patricio Sanz," 1922.

D. I. España. *Colección de documentos inéditos para la historia de España.* Edited by Martín Fernández de Navarrete. 112 vols. Madrid, 1842-1895.

D. I. I. *Colección de documentos inéditos relativos al descubrimiento, conquista y organ-*

ización de las antiguas posesiones españolas de América y Oceanía. Edited by Joaquín F. Pacheco, Francisco de Cárdenas and Luis de Mendoza. 42 vols. Madrid: 1864-1884.

D. I. *Ultramar. Colección de documentos inéditos relativos al descubrimiento, conquista y organización de las antiguas posesiones de ultramar.* Segunda serie. 25 vols. Madrid: 1885-1928.

Dávalos y Figueroa, Diego. *Miscelánea austral.* Lima: 1602.

Degler, Carl N. *Neither Black nor White: Slavery and Race Relations in Brazil and the United States.* New York: Macmillan, 1971.

Díaz del Castillo, Bernal. *The True History of the Conquest of New Spain,* edited by Alfred Percival Maudsley. 5 vols. London: Hakluyt Society, 1908.

———. *The Discovery and Conquest of Mexico,* edited by Irving A. Leonard. New York: Grove Press, 1958.

D'Olwer, L. Nicolau. "Comments on the Evangelization of the New World," *The Americas* XIV (1957): 399-410.

Egaña, Antonio, S. J. "La visión humanística del indio americano en los primeros jesuítas peruanos (1568-1576)," *Studi sulla Chiesa Antica e sull Llmanesimo, Analecta Gregoriana* (Rome) LXX, (1954): 291-306.

Eguiara y Eguren, Juan José. *Prólogos a la Biblioteca Mexicana,* edited by Agustín Millares Carlo. Mexico: Fondo de Cultura Económica, 1944.

Elliott, John H. *Imperial Spain 1469-1716.* London: Edward Arnold, 1963.

———. *The Old World and the New 1492-1650.* Cambridge: Cambridge University Press, 1970.

———. "The Discovery of America and the Discovery of Man," *Proceedings of the British Academy* (London) LVIII (1972): 3-27.

Encina, Francisco. *Historia de Chile.* 20 vols. Santiago: Nascimento, 1940-1952.

Ennis, Arthur, O.S.A. "Fray Alonso de la Vera Cruz, O.A.A. (1507-1548): A Study of His Life and His Contribution to the Religious and Intellectual Affairs of Early America," *Augustiniana* V-VII (1955-1957). Offprint. Louvain: 1957.

Enzensberger, Hans Magnus. "Las Casas oder ein Ruckblick in die Zukunst," in his *Bartolomé de Las Casas Kurzgefasster Bericht von der Verwüstung der Westindischen Länder* (pp. 131-165). Frankfort am Main: Insel Verlag, 1966.

———. *Las Casas y Trujillo.* Havana: Cuadernos de la revista Casa de las Américas, No. 8, 1969.

Epstein, Lewis, trans. "Juan Ginés de Sepulveda: Apology for the Book on the Just Causes of War." Honors paper for the Department of Classics, Bowdoin College, 1973.

Esteve Barba, Francisco. *Historiografía indiana.* Madrid: Editorial Gredos, 1964.

Fabíe, Antonio M. *Vida y escritos de Don Fray Bartolomé de Las Casas.* 2 vols. Madrid: 1879.

Fernández de Encisco, Martín. *Suma de geografía.* Seville: 1519.

Fernández de Oviedo y Valdés, Gonzalo. *Historia general y natural de las Indias,* edited by Natalicio González. 14 vols. Asunción: 1944-1945.

———. *Sumario de la natural historia de las Indias,* edited by José Miranda. Mexico: Fondo de Cultura Económica, 1950.

———. "Homenaje Fernández de Oviedo," *Revista de Indias,* año XVII (1957): 391-705; año XVIII (1958): 9-126.

———. *Historia general y natural de las Indias,* edited by Juan Pérez de Tudela y Bueso. 5 vols. Madrid: Biblioteca de Autores Españoles, 1959.

———. *Natural History of the West Indies,* edited and translated by Sterling A. Stoudemire. University of North Carolina Studies in the Romance Languages and Literature, No. 32. Chapel Hill: University of North Carolina Press, 1959.

Figuera, Guillermo. *La formación del clero indígena en la historia eclesiástica de América.* Caracas: Archivo General de la Nación, 1965.

———. *Documentos para la historia de la iglesia colonial en Venezuela. Estudio preliminar de Guillermo Figuera.* 2 vols. Caracas: Academia Nacional de la Historia, 1965.

Fox, John S. "Antonio de San José Muro: Political Economist of New Spain," *Hispanic American Historical Review* XXI (1941): 410-416.

Frías de Albornoz, Bartolomé. *Arte de los contratos.* Valencia: 1573.

Friede, Juan. "Las Casas y el movimiento indigenista en España y América en la primera mitad del siglo XVI," *Revista de Historia de América* (Mexico), no. 34 (1952): 339-411.

———, and Benjamin Keen, eds. *Bartolomé de Las Casas in History: Toward an Understanding of the Man and His Work.* DeKalb: Northern Illinois University Press, 1971. (All the articles in this volume contain valuable information, but Ángel Losada's "The Controversy between Sepúlveda and Las Casas in Valladolid" [pp. 279-308] is of special interest.)

García-Gallo, Alfonso. "Las Indias en el reinado de Felipe II. La solución del problema de los justos titulos." in his *Estudios de historia del derecho indiano* (pp. 425-471). Madrid: Instituto Nac. de Estudios Jurídicos.

Garcia Icazbalceta, Joanquin. *Coleccion de documentos para la historia de Mexico.* 2 vols. Mexico: 1858-1866.

———. *Nueva colección de documentos para la historia de México.* Mexico: 1886-1892.

———. *Obras de D. Joaquín García Icazbalceta.* 10 vols. Mexico: 1896-1899.

García Oro, José, O.F.M. *La reforma de los religiosos españoles en tiempo de los Reyes Católicos.* Valladolid: Instituto de Historia Eclesiástica, Consejo Superior de Investigaciones Científicas, 1969.

García Villoslada, Ricardo, S.J., and Bernardino Llorca, S.J. *Historia de la iglesia católica.* 4 vols. 2d ed. Madrid: Biblioteca de Autores Cristianos, 1967.

Getino, Luis Alonso, O. P. *Influencia de los dominicos en las Leyes Nuevas.* Seville: Escuela de Estudios Hispanoamericanos, 1945.

Gibson, Charles. "The Spanish Conquest as Reality and Symbol." Paper prepared for the First Newberry Library Conference on Hispanic American Studies, 2 April 1955, in Chicago. Mimeographed.

———. *The Aztecs under Spanish Rule.* Stanford: Stanford University Press, 1964.

———. *The Spanish Tradition in America.* New York: Harcourt Brace Jovanovich, 1968.

———. *The Black Legend: Anti-Spanish Attitudes in the Old World and the New.* New York: Knopf, 1971.

Giménez Fernández, Manuel. *Bartolomé de Las Casas.* 2 vols. Seville: Publicaciones de la Escuela de Estudios Hispano-Americanos de Sevilla, 1953-1960.

———. "Últimos días de Bartolomé de Las Casas," *Miscellanea Paul Rivet octogenario dicta* (Mexico) II (1958): 702-715.

———. "Sobre Bartolomé de Las Casas," *Actas y Memorias. XXXVI Congreso Internacional de Americanistas 1966* (Buenos Aires) IV (1968): 71-129.

Goldwert, Marvin. "La lucha por la perpetuidad de encomiendas en el Perú, 1550-1600," *Revista Histórica* (Lima) XXII (1955): 336-360.

Gómez Canedo, Lino, O.F.M. "Un intento de evangelizar a los indios Araucas en 1553," *Revista de Historia de América* (Mexico), no. 40 (1955): 575-593.

———. "Bartolomé de Las Casas y sus amigos franciscanos," *Libro jubilar de Emeterio S. Santovenia en su cincuentario de escritor* (Havana) (1957): 75-84.

———. "Review of Ramón Menéndez Pidal, *El Padre Las Casas*," *The Americas* XXI, no. 2 (1964): 209-211.

———. "La cuestión de la racionalidad de los indios en el siglo XVI (nuevo examen crítico)," *Actas y Memorias. XXXVI Congreso Internacional de Americanistas 1966* (Buenos Aires) IV (1968).

———. "Conventuales, observantes y reformados (política espiritual de los primeros franciscanos de Indias)," *Anuario de estudios americanos* (Seville) XIII (1966): 611-622.

———. "¿Hombres o Bestias? (Nuevo examen crítico de un viejo tópico)," *Estudios de Historia Novohispana* (Mexico) I (1967): 29-51.

———. "Différentes attitudes face à l'indien: Les franciscains," in *Le Decouverte de l'Amérique* (po. 195-210). Paris: De Petrarque a Descartes, 1968.

———. "Toribio Motolinía and His Historical Writings," *The Americas* XXIX, no. 3 (1973): 277-307.

González, Luis. "Fray Jerónimo de Mendieta," *Revista de Historia de América* (Mexico), no. 28 (1949): 331-376.

Green, Otis. *Spain and the Western Tradition: The Castilian Mind in Literature from El Cid to Calderón.* 4 vols. Madison: University of Wisconsin Press, 1963.

Greenleaf, Richard E. *Zumárraga and the Mexican Inquisition.* Washington, D. C.: Academy of American Franciscan History, 1961.

Griñan Peralta, Leonardo. "Bartolomé de Las Casas como propagandista," *Revista de la Universidad de Oriente* (Santiago de Cuba) I (1962): 3-39.

Hanke, Lewis. *La teorías políticas de Bartolomé de Las Casas.* Buenos Aires: Publicaciones del Instituto de Investigaciones Históricas, no. 67, Universidad de Buenos Aires, 1935a.

———. *The First Social Experiments in America: A Study in the Development of Spanish Indian Policy in the Sixteenth Century.* Cambridge: Harvard University Press, 1935b.

———. *Cuerpo de documentos del siglo XVI sobre los derechos de España en las Indias y las Filipinas,* edited by Agustín Millares Carlo and Lewis Hanke. Mexico: Fondo de Cultura Económica, 1943.

———. *La lucha por la justicia en la conquista de América.* Buenos Aires: Editorial Sudamericana, 1949.

———. "¿Bartolomé de Las Casas, existencialista? Ensayo de hagiografía y de historiografía," *Cuadernos Americanos,* año XII, no. 2 (1953): 176-193.

———. "More Heat and Some Light on the Spanish Struggle for Justice in the Conquest of America," *Hispanic American Historical Review* XLIV (1964), 293-340.

———. *The Spanish Struggle for Justice in the Conquest of America.* Boston: Little, Brown, 1965a.

———. *Bartolomé Arzáns de Orsúa y Vela's History of Potosí.* Providence, R. I.: Brown University Press, 1965b.

———. ed. *History of Latin American Civilization: Sources and Interpretations.* 2 vols. Boston: Little, Brown, 1967.

———. *Estudios sobre Fray Bartolomé de Las Casas y sobre la lucha por la justicia en la conquista española de América.* Caracas: Universidad Central de Venezuela, 1968.

———. *Aristotle and the American Indians.* Chicago: Henry Regnery Company, 1959; paperback, Bloomington: Indiana University Press, 1970.

Haring, C. H. *The Spanish Empire in America.* New York: Harcourt Brace Jovanovich, 1963.

Haubert, Maxime. "Indiens et Jésuites au Paraguay. Rencontre de deux messianismes," *Archives de Sociologie des Religions,* no. 27 (1969): 119-133.

Heath, Shirley Brice. *Telling Tongues. Language Policy in Mexico, Colony to Nation.* New York: Teachers College Press, 1972.

Hera, Alberto de la. "El derecho de los indios a la libertad y a la fe. La bula 'Sublimis Deus' y los problemas indianos que la motivaron," *Anuario de Historia del Derecho Español* (Madrid) XXVI (1956): 89-181.

Hernández, Pablo. *Organización social de las doctrinas guaraníes de la Compañía de Jesús.* 2 vols. Barcelona: 1913.

Hernández Luna, Juan. "El iniciador de la historia de las ideas en México," *Filosofía y Letras* (Mexico) XXVI (1953): 65-80.

Höffner, Josef. *La ética colonial española del siglo de oro.* Madrid: Ediciones Cultura Hispánica, 1957.

Huddleston, Lee Eldridge. *Origins of the American Indians: European Concepts, 1492-1729.* Austin: University of Texas Press, 1967.

Iglesia, Ramón. *Cronistas e historiadores de la conquista de México.* Mexico: Colegio de México, 1942.

———. *Columbus, Cortes, and Other Essays,* translated by Lesley B. Simpson. Berkeley and Los Angeles: University of California Press, 1969.

Instrucciones que los virreyes de la Nueva España dejaron a sus sucesores. Mexico: 1867.

Jacobs, Wilbur R. *Dispossessing the American Indian: Indians and Whites on the Colonial Frontier.* New York: Scribner's, 1972.

Jiménez de la Espada, Marcos. *Juan de Castellanos y su Historia del Nuevo Reino de Granada.* Madrid: 1889.

Jiménez Moreno, Wigberto. "The Indians of America and Christianity," *The Americas* XIV (1957): 411-431.

Johnson, Harold B., Jr., ed. *From Reconquest to Empire. The Iberian Background to Latin American History.* New York: Knopf, 1970.

Jorosháeva, I. "Bartolomé de Las Casas y Motolinía," *Historia y Sociedad* (Mexico), no. 5 (1966): 85-95.

Keen, Benjamin. "The Black Legend Revisited. Assumptions and Realities," *Hispanic American Historical Review* XLIX (1969): 703-719.

———. *The Aztec Image in Western Thought.* New Brunswick: Rutgers University Press, 1971.

Kennedy, John H. *Jesuit and Savage in New France.* New Haven: Yale University Press, 1950.

Kobayashi, José María F. Kazuhiro. "La educación como conquista. Empresa franciscana." Ph.D. dissertation, Colegio de México, 1972.

Konetzke, Richard. "Islam und christliches Spanien im Mittelalter," *Historisches Zeitschrift,* Bd. 184 (1957): 573-591.

———. "Points of Departure for the History of Missions on Hispanic America," *The Americas* XIV (1958): 517-523.

———. "Probleme der Beziehungen zwischen Islam und Christentum im spanischen Mittelalter," in *Antike und Orient im Mittelalter.* Vörtrage der Kölner Mediaevistentagungen 1956-1959. Hrsg. v. Paul Wilbert. Miscellanea Mediaevalia. Veroffentlichungen des Thomas-Institutes an der Universität Köln. Hrsg. v. Paul Wilbert. Bd. 10, pp. 219-238. Berlin: Walter de Gruyter and Co., 1962.

———. "Ramón Menéndez Pidal und der Streit um Las Casas," *Romanische Forschungen* LXXVI (1964): 447-453.

Korth, Eugene H., S. J. *Spanish Policy in Colonial Chile: The Struggle for Social Justice, 1535-1700.* Stanford: Stanford University Press, 1968.

Kubler, George. *Mexican Architecture of the Sixteenth Century.* 2 vols. New Haven: Yale University Press, 1948.

Lamb, Ursula. *Frey Nicolás de Ovando. Gobernador de las Indias (1501-1509).* Comentarios preliminares por Miguel Muñoz de San Pedro. Madrid: Consejo Superior de Investigaciones Científicas, 1956.

Landa, Diego de. *Landa's Relación de las cosas de Yucatán,* edited by Alfred M. Tozzer. Papers of The Peabody Museum of American Archaeology and

Ethnology, XVIII. Cambridge, Mass.: Harvard University, 1941.

Langnas, I.A. "Democracy and Dictatorship," *Dissent* (1962).

Las Casas, Bartolomé de. *Colección de las obras del Obispo de Chiapa, Don Barto-lomé de Las Casas,* edited by Juan Antonio Llorente. 2 vols. Paris: 1822.

―――. *Del único modo de atraer a todos los pueblos a la verdadera religión,* edited by Agustín Millares Carlo and Lewis Hanke. Mexico: Fondo de Cultura Económica, 1942.

―――. *Historia de las Indias,* edicion de Agustín Millares Carlo; estudio preliminar de Lewis Hanke. 3 vols. Buenos Aires and Mexico: Fondo de Cultura Económica, 1951.

―――. *Obras escogidas de Fray Bartolomé de Las Casas,* edited by Juan Pérez de Tudela Bueso. 5 vols. Madrid: Biblioteca de Autores Españoles, 1957.

―――. *Los tesoros del Perú,* edited by Ángel Losada García. Madrid: Consejo Superior de Investigaciones Científicas, 1958.

―――. *Tratado de Indias y el Doctor Sepúlveda. Estudio preliminar de Manuel Jiménez [sic] Fernández.* Vol. 56. Caracas: Biblioteca de la Academia Nacional de la Historia, 1962.

―――. *Tratados,* prólogos de Lewis Hanke y Manuel Giménez Fernández; transcripción de Juan Pérez de Tudela y Bueso y traducciones de Agustín Millares Carlo y Rafael Moreno. 2 vols. Mexico: Fondo de Cultura Económica, 1966.

―――. *Apologética Historia Sumaria,* edición preparada por Edmundo O'Gorman, con un estudio preliminar, apéndices y un índice de materias. 2 vols. Mexico: Universidad Autónoma Nacional de México, 1967.

―――. *De regia potestate, o derecho de autodeterminación,* edición crítica bilingüe por Luciano Pereña, J. M. Pérez-Prendes, Vidal Abril y Joaquín Azcárraga. Corpus Hispanorum de Pace. Vol. VIII. Madrid: Consejo Superior de Investigaciones Científicas, 1969.

―――. *In Defense of the Indians,* translated and edited by Stafford Poole, C. M. DeKalb: Northern Illinois University Press, 1974.

Leite, Serafim, S. J., ed. *Dialogo sobre a conversao do gentio pelo P. Manuel da Nóbrega.* Vol. 1. Lisbon: IV Centenário da Fundação de São Paulo, 1954.

―――. "A vida sacramental e os seus reflexos sociais no Brasil do tempo de Nóbrega (1549-1570)," *Broteria* (Lisbon) LXXV (1962): 28-47.

Lejarza, Fidel de, and Ángel Uribe, O.F.M. "¿Cuando y dónde comenzó Villacreces su Reforma?" *Archivo Ibero-Americano* (Madrid), año XX, no. 77 (1960): 79-94.

León-Portilla, Miguel. "Sahagún y su investigación integral de la Cultura Náhuatl, *Siete ensayos sobre Cultura Náhuatl* (pp. 11-29). Mexico: Universidad Nacional Autónoma de México, 1958.

Le Riverend, Julio. "Conclusiones. Seminario sobre problemas de historia del colonialismo en América." Havana, 1966. Mimeographed.

Lery, Jean de. *Indiens de la Renaissance. Histoire d'un voyage fait en la terre du Brésil, 1557.* Présentation par Anne-Marie Chartier. Paris: Epi Editeurs, 1972.

Levillier, Roberto. *Don Francisco de Toledo, supremo organizador del Perú: su obra (1515-1582).* 3 vols. Madrid: Espasa-Calpe 1935-1942.

Llaguno, José A., S. J. *La personalidad jurídica del indio y el III Concilio Provincial Mexicano.* Mexico: Editorial Porrúa, 1963.

Lohmann Villena, Guillermo. "La restitución por conquistadores y encomenderos: Un aspecto de la incidencia lascasiana en el Perú," in *Estudios lascasianos. IV Centenario de la muerte de Fray Bartolomé de Las Casas (1566-1966)* (pp. 21-89). Seville: Facultad de Filosofía y Letras de la Universidad de Sevilla, Escuela de Estudios Hispanoamericanos, 1966.

————. "El licenciado Francisco Falcón (1521-1587). Vida, escritos y actuación en el Perú de un procurador de los indios," *Anuario de Estudios Americanos* (Seville) XXVII (1970): 131-194.

Lopetegui, León, S. J. *El Padre José de Acosta y las misiones.* Madrid: 1942.

López, Atanasio, O.F.M. "Los doce primeros apóstoles de Méjico," *Bibliotheca Hispana Missionum* II (1930): 203-266.

López-Portillo, José. "La incapacidad del indio," *Cuadernos americanos* XIII, no. 1 (1944): 150-162.

Losada, Ángel. "Juan Ginés de Sepúlveda," *Revista Bibliográfica y Documental* (Madrid) I, nos. 3 and 4 (1947): 315-393.

————. "Hernán Cortés en la obra del cronista Sepúlveda," *Revista de Indias*, nos. 31 and 32 (1948): 127-169.

————. *Juan Ginés de Sepúlveda a través de su "epistolario" y nuevos documentos.* Madrid: Consejo Superior de Investigaciones Científicas, 1949.

————. *·Epistolario de Juan Ginés de Sepúlveda.* Madrid: Ediciones Cultura Hispánica, 1966.

————. "La 'Apologia' obra inédita de Fray Bartolomé de Las Casas: actualidad de su contenido," *Boletín de la Real Academia de la Historia* CLXII, no. 2 (1968): 201-248.

————. *Fray Bartolomé de Las Casas a la luz de la moderna crítica histórica.* Madrid: Editorial Tecnos, 1970.

Lourie, Elena. "A Society Organized for War: Medieval Spain," *Past and Present* (London), no. 35 (1966): 54-76.

MacLeish, Archibald. "The Age of Diminished Man," *Saturday Review*, 7 June 1969.

Mahn-Lot, Marianne, *Barthélemy de Las Casas: l'Évangile et la force.* Paris: Les Éditions du Cerf, 1964.

————. "Transculturation et Évangélisation dans le Pérou du XVIᵉ siècle. Notes sur Domingo de Santo Tomás, disciple de Las Casas," in *Méthodologie de l'Histoire et des sciences humaines. Mélanges en l'Honneur de Fernand Braudel* (pp. 353-365). Paris: Privat, Editeur, 1972.

Málaga Medina, Alejandro. "Los obrajes en la Colonia (Centros de manufactura textil)," *Revista de la Facultad de Letras* (Arequipa), no. 3 (1965): 85-173.

Manrique, Jorge Alberto. "Las Casas y el arte indígena," *Revista de la Universidad de México* XX, no. 11 (11 June 1966): 11-14.

Maravall, José Antonio. "La utopia político-religiosa de los franciscanos en Nueva España," *Estudios Americanos* (Seville), no. 3 (1949): 199-227.

Marcos, Teodoro Andrés. *Los imperialismos de Juan Ginés de Sepúlveda.* Madrid: Instituto de Estudios Políticos, 1947.

Marcus, Raymond. "Las Casas pérouaniste," *Caravelle* (Toulouse), no. 7 (1966): 25-44.

Márquez Miranda, Fernando. "El P. Las Casas y su Historia de las Indias," *Revista Chilena de Historia y Geografía,* nos. 122 and 123 (1953): 5-63 and 27-82.

Martín, Melquíades Andrés. "Evangelismo, humanismo, reforma y observancias en España (1450-1525)," *Missionalia Hispánica,* año XXII, no. 67 (1966): 5-24.

Martínez, Manuel María, O.P. "Notas críticas: Réplica a la conferencia de dón Ramón Menéndez Pidal sobre el P. Las Casas," *La ciencia tomista,* no. 286 (1963): 236-318.

Martínez Cardos, José. "Gregorio López, consejero de Indias, glosador de las Partidas (1496-1560)," *Revista de Indias* (Madrid) (1960): 65-176.

Mateos, Francisco, S. J. "Ecos de América en Trento," *Revista de Indias* (Madrid), no. 22 (1945): 559-606.

Matienzo, Juan de. *Gobierno del Perú (1567),* edited by Guillermo Lohmann Villena. Paris and Lima: Travaux de l'Institut Francais d'Études Andines, XI: 1967.

Maza, Francisco de la. "Fray Diego Valadés, escritor y grabador," *Anales del Instituto de Investigaciones Estéticas* (Mexico), no. 3 (1945): 15-44.

Méndez Plancarte, Gabriel. "Fray Diego Valadés, humanista franciscano del siglo XVI," *Ábside* (Mexico) X (1946): 265-282.

Mendieta, Jerónimo de. *Historia eclesiástica indiana,* edited by Joaquín García Icazbalceta. Mexico: 1870.

Menendez Pidal, Ramón. *The Spaniards in Their History,* edited by Walter Starkie. New York: W. W. Norton, 1950.

———. *El Padre Las Casas. Su doble personalidad.* Madrid: Espasa-Calpe, 1963.

Meseguer Fernández, Juan, O.F.M. "Contenido misionológico de la 'Obediencia' e 'Instruccion' de fray Francisco de los Ángeles a los Doce Apóstoles de México," *The Americas* XI (1955): 473-500.

Milhou, Alain. "Las Casas et la Richesse," in *Études d'Histoire et de Littérature ibéro-amérocaines* (pp. 111-154). Centre de Recherches Ibéro-Americaines de Rouen. Paris: Presses Universitaires de France, 1973.

Millares Carlo, Agustín. *Investigaciones biobibliográficas iberoamericanas.* Mexico: Universidad Nacional Autónoma de México, 1950.

Miranda, José. "La fraternidad cristiana y la labor social de la primitiva iglesia mexicana," *Cuadernos Americanos* CXLI, no. 4 (1965): 148-158.

Montero, Mariano A. "La etnología en México," *Cuadernos Americanos,* año II, vol. 9, no. 3 (1943).

Moreno Toscano, Alejandra. *Fray Juan de Torquemada y su Monarquía Indiana.* Xalapa: Universidad Veracruzana, 1963.

————. "Vindicación de Torquemada," *Historia Mexicana* XII (1963): 497-515.

Mörner, Magnus. "¿Separación o integración? En torno al debate dieciochesco sobre los principios de la política indigenista en Hispano-América," *Journal de la Société des Américanistes* (Paris) LIV, no. 1 (1965): 31-45.

Muro Orejón, Antonio. "Ordenanzas reales sobre los indios (las leyes de 1512-1513)," *Anuario de Estudios Americanos* (Seville) XIII (1956): 417-471.

Myres, John L. "The Influence of Anthropology on the Course of Political Science," *Report of the British Association for the Advancement of Science 1909* (London), 1910, pp. 591-594.

Nichols, Madaline W. "An Old Questionnaire for Modern Use: A Commentary on *Relaciones geográficas de Indias*," *Agricultural History* XVIII (1944): 156-160.

O'Gorman, Edmundo. "Sobre la naturaleza bestial del indio americano," *Filosofía y Letras* (Universidad Nacional Autónoma de México), nos. 1 and 2 (1941): 141-158 and 305-315.

————. "El método historico de Lewis Hanke. Réplica a una sorpresa," *Cuadernos Americanos,* no. 3 (May-June 1953).

————. "La idea antropológica del Padre Las Casas: edad media y modernidad," *Historia Mexicana* XIV (1967): 309-319.

————. *La idea del descubrimiento de América.* (Ediciones del IV Centenario de Universidad del Mexico, 5), Mexico: Universidad Nacional Autónoma de México, Centro de Estudios Filosóficas, 1951.

————. "Comentarios a un nuevo libro sobre el padre Las Casas," *Estudios de Historia Novohispana* (Mexico) VI (1971): 163-168.

Ojer, Pablo, S.J. "La política indiana de Rodrigo de Navarrete, escribano de Margarita e informador de Las Casas," in *Estudios lascasianos. IV Centenario de la muerte de Fray Bartolomé de Las Casas (1566-1966)* (pp. 305-327). Seville: Facultad de Filosofía y Letras de la Universidad de Sevilla, Escuela de Estudios Hispanoamericanos, 1966.

Olaechea Labayen, Juan B. "Opinión de los teólogos españoles sobre dar estudios mayores a indios," *Anuario de Estudios Americanos* (Seville) XV (1958): 113-200.

————. "Experiencias cristianos con el indio antillano," *Anuario de Estudios Americanos* (Seville) XXVI (1969), 65-114.

————. "Obispos indios en la América hispana," *Boletín de la Real Academia de la Historia* (Madrid) CLXVIII (1971): 421-439.

————. "Como abordaron la cuestión del clero indígena los primeros misioneros de México," *Missionalia Hispánica,* año XXV, no. 73 (1968): 95-124.

Olivart, Marqués de, ed. *Bartolomé de Las Casas. Disputa o controversia con Ginés de Sepúlveda conteniendo acerca de la licitud de las conquistas de las Indias.* Madrid: 1908.

Olmedo, Daniel, S. J. "La primera evangelización de América (1492-1504)," *Ábside* (Mexico) XVII (1953): 35-67.

Ortega, Ángel. "Las primeras maestras y sus colegios-escuelas de niñas en Méjico (1530-1535)," *Archivo Iberoamericano* (Madrid) XXXI (1929): 259-387.

Ortega y Medina, Juan A. "Bartolomé de Las Casas y la historiografía soviética," *Historia Mexicana* XIV (1967): 320-340.

Padden, Robert C. "The Ordenanza del Patronazgo, 1574: An Interpretative Essay," *The Americas* XII (1956): 333-354.

———. *The Hummingbird and the Hawk*. Columbus: Ohio State University Press, 1967.

Paso y Troncoso, Francisco, ed. *Epistolario de Nueva España, 1505-1818*. 16 vols. Mexico: Antigua Librería Robredo, 1939-1942.

Patiño, Víctor Manuel. "La historia natural en la obra de Bartolomé de Las Casas," *Revista de Historia de América* (Mexico), nos. 61 and 62 (1966): 167-186.

Peña y Cámara, Isabel de. "Índice onomástico de la Historia general y natural de las Indias de Fernández de Oviedo," *Revista Histórica* (Lima) XXIX (1966): 1-59.

Peña y Cámara, José de la. "Contribuciones documentales y críticas para una biografía de Gonzalo Fernández de Oviedo y Valdés," *Revista de Indias* (Madrid), año XVIII, nos. 69 and 70 (1957): 603-705.

Pereña Vicente, Luciano. *Diego de Covarrubias y Leyva. Maestro de derecho internacional*. Madrid: Asociación Francisco de Vitoria, 1947.

———. *Misión de España en América, 1540-1560*. Madrid: Instituto Francisco de Vitoria, Consejo Superior de Investigaciones Científicas, 1956.

Pérez de Tudela, Juan. *Las armadas de Indias y los orígines de la política de colonización (1492-1502)*. Madrid: Instituto Gonzalo Fernández de Oviedo, 1956.

Phelan, John Leddy. "Some Ideological Aspects of the Conquest of the Philippines," *The Americas* XIII (1957): 221-239.

———. *The Kingdom of Quito in the Seventeenth Century: Bureaucratic Politics in the Spanish Empire*. Madison: University of Wisconsin Press, 1969.

———. *The Millennial Kingdom of the Franciscans of the New World*, rev. ed. Berkeley: University of California Press, 1970.

Pike, Fredrick B., ed. *Latin American History: Select Problems*. New York: Harcourt Brace Jovanovich, 1969.

Poole, Stafford, C. M. "The Indian Problem in the Third Provincial Council of Mexico (1585)." Ph.D. dissertation, University of St. Louis, 1961.

———. "The Church and the Repartimientos in the Light of the Third Mexican Council, 1585," *The Americas* XX (1963): 3-36.

———. "War by Fire and Blood: The Church and the Chichemecas, 1585," *The Americas* XXII (1965): 115-137.

———. "The Franciscan Attack on the Repartimiento System (1585)," in *Indian Labor in the Spanish Indies*, edited by John Francis Bannon, S. J. (pp. 66-75). Boston: Heath, 1966.

————. "Successors to Las Casas," *Revista de Historia de América,* nos. 61 and 62 (1966): 89-114.

Pou y Martí, José María. "El libro perdido de las pláticas o coloquios de los doce primeros misioneros de México," *Miscellanea Francesco Ehrle* (Rome) III (1924): 281-333.

Powell, Philip W. *Soldiers, Indians, and Silver: The Northward Advance of New Spain.* Berkeley: University of California Press, 1952.

Quirk, Robert E. "Some Notes on a Controversial Controversy: Juan Ginés de Sepúlveda and Natural Servitude," *Hispanic American Historical Review* XXXIV (1954): 356-364.

Quiroga, Pedro de. *Libro intitulado "Coloquios de la Verdad."* Seville: 1922.

Ramos, Demetrio. "Las ideas de Fernández de Oviedo sobre la técnica de colonización en América," *Cuadernos Hispanoamericanos* (Madrid), no. 96 (1957): 279-289.

————. "El P. Córdoba y Las Casas en el plan de conquista pacífica de Tierra Firme," *Boletín Americanista* (Barcelona), no. 3 (1959): 175-210.

————. "La etapa lascasiana de la presión de conciencias," *Anuario de estudios americanos* (Seville) XXIII (1968): 861-954.

————. "Fernández de Oviedo y el 'enigma' de la edición de 1547 de su Historia General," *Historia* (Santiago), no. 18 (1969): 443-461.

————. *Ximénez de Quesada en su relación con los cronistas y el Epítome de Conquista del Nuevo Reino de Granada.* Seville: Escuela de Estudios Hispano-Americanos, 1972.

Ricard, Robert. *La "Conquête Spirituelle" du Mexique. Essai sur l'apostolat et les méthodes missionaires des ordres mendiants en Nouvelle-Espagne de 1523 à 1572.* Vol. XX. Paris: Travaux et Mémoires de l'Institut d'Ethnologie, 1933.

————. *The Spiritual Conquest of Mexico: An Essay on the Apostolate and the Evangelizing Methods of the Mendicant Orders in New Spain, 1523-1572,* translated by Lesley Byrd Simpson. Berkeley and Los Angeles: University of California Press, 1966.

————. " 'La Conquête Spirituelle de Mexique.' Revue après trente ans," in *La Decouverte de l'Amérique* (pp. 229-239). Paris: De Pétrarque a Descartes, 1968.

Rodríguez Prampolini, Ida. "El arte indígena y los cronistas de Nueva España," *Anales del Instituto de Investigaciones Estéticas* (Mexico), no. 17 (1949): 5-16.

Ronan, Charles E., S. J. "Francisco Javier Clavigero, Historian," Ph.D. dissertation, University of Texas, 1960.

Rumeu de Armas, Antonio. "Los problemas derivados del contacto de razas en los albores del Renacimiento," in *El tránsito de la Edad Media al Renacimiento* (pp. 61-103). Anexos de la revista Hispania I. Madrid: Cuadernos de Historia, 1967.

Saint-Lu, André. *La Vera Paz. Esprit Évangélique et Colonisation.* Paris: Centre de Recherches Hispaniques, Institut d'Études Hispaniques, 1968.

Sala Balust, Luis. "La espiritualidad en la primera mitad del siglo XVI," in *El tránsito de la Edad Media al Renacimiento* (pp. 169-187). Anexos de la revista *Hispania* I. Madrid: Cuadernos de Historia, 1967.

Salas, Alberto Marío. "Pedro Martir y Oviedo ante el hombre y las culturas americanas," *Imago Mundi* (Buenos Aires) I, no. 2 (1953): 16-33.

———. "Fernández de Oviedo crítico de la conquista y de los conquistadores," *Cuadernos Americanos* LXXIV, no. 2 (1954): 160-170.

———. *Tres cronistas de Indias.* Mexico: Fondo de Cultura Económica, 1959.

San José Muro, Fray Antonio de, et al. *Utilidades y medios de que los indios y ladinos vistan y calzan a la espanola.* Guatemala: 1798.

Santiago Vela, Gregorio de, O.S.A. *Ensayo de una biblioteca ibero-americana de la Orden de San Agustín.* 8 vols. El Escorial: 1913-1931.

Santisteban Ochoa, Julián. "Fray Vicente Valverde, protector de los indios, y su obra," *Revista de Letras* (Cuzco), año I, no. 2, segundo semestre (1960-1961): 117-182.

Santo Tomás, Domingo de. *Grámatica, o arte de la lengua general de los indios del Perú.* Valladolid, 1560.

———. *Gramática o arte de la lengua general de los indios de los reynos del Perú,* edited by Raúl Porras Barrenechea. Lima: 1951.

Sariola, Sakari. *Power and Resistance: The Colonial Heritage in Latin America.* Ithaca, N.Y.: Cornell University Press, 1972.

Scholes, France V. "Fray Diego de Landa and the Problem of Idolatry in Yucatán," in *Cooperation in Research* (pp. 585-620). Carnegie Institution Publ. No. 501. Washington, D.C.: Carnegie Institution, 1938.

———. "Freedom for the Historian," in *The New World Looks at Its History: Proceedings of the Second International Congress of Historians of the United States and Mexico,* edited by Archibald R. Lewis and Thomas F. McGann. Austin: University of Texas Institute of Latin American Studies, 1963.

———, and Ralph L. Roys. *The Maya Chontal Indians of Acalan-Tixchel: A Contribution to the History and Ethnography of the Yucatan Peninsula.* Washington, D.C.: Carnegie Institution of Washington, 1948.

Seco Caro, Carlos. "De la bula 'Sublimis Deus' de Paulo III (1-VI-1537) a la constitución 'Guadium et Spes' del Concilio Vaticano II (7-XII-1965)," *Anuario de Estudios Americanos* (Seville) XXIII (1967): 1821-1841.

Sepúlveda, Juan Ginés de. "Apología del libro de las justas causas de la guerra." Unpublished Spanish translation by Ángel Losada of the book printed in Rome in 1550. *See also* Epstein (1973).

———. *Opera quae reperiri potuerunt omnia.* Cologne: 1602. (A copy of this rare edition is in the William Clements Library, Ann Arbor, Michigan.)

———. *Demócrates segundo o de las justas causas de la guerra contra los indios,* edited by Ángel Losada. Madrid: Consejo Superior de Investigaciones Científicas, Instituto Francisco de Vitoria, 1951.

———. *Tratados politicos de Juan Ginés de Sepúlveda,* translated and edited by Ángel Losada. Madrid: Instituto de Estudios Politicos, 1963.

Serrano y Sanz, M. "Un discípulo de Fr. Bartolomé de Las Casas: Don Pedro Mexía de Ovando (siglo XVII)," *Archivo de Investigaciones Históricas* (Madrid), año 1, no. 2 (1911): 165-212.

————. "Algunos escritos acerca de las Indias de Tomás López Medel," *Erudicica Ibero-Americana* (Madrid) I (1930): 487-497.

Silva, A. da. *Trent's Impact on the Portuguese Patronage Missions.* Lisbon: Centro de Estudos Históricos Ultramarinos, 1969.

Silva, Juan de. *Advertencias importantes acerca del buen govierno y administracion de las Indias assi en lo espiritual como en lo temporal.* 1621.

Silva Tena, María Teresa. "El sacrificio humano en la *Âpologética Historia,*" *Historia Mexicana* XIV (1967): 341-357.

Stevenson, Robert. *Music in Aztec and Inca Territory.* Berkeley and Los Angeles: University of California Press, 1966.

Suárez Fernández, Luis. *La España de los Reyes Católicos, 1474-1516.* 2 vols. Madrid: Instituto de Historia, Universidad Nacional Major de San Marcos, 1969.

Tellechea Idígoras, J. Ignacio. "Bartolomé de Las Casas y Bartolomé Carranza. Una página amistosa olvidada," *Scriptorium Victoriense* VI (1959): 7-34. (For a fuller statement, see this author's *El arzobispo Carranza y su tiempo* [Madrid: Ed. Guadarrama, 1968], II, 15-62).

————. "Perfil americanista de Fray Bartolomé Carranza, O.P.," *XXXVI Congreso Internacional de Americanistas—España 1964* (Seville) IV (1966): 691-699.

Torre, Tomás de la. *Desde Salamanca, España, hasta Ciudad Real, Chiapas. Diario del viaje, 1544-1545,* prologue and notes by Franz Blom. Mexico: n.d.

Torre Villar, Ernesto de la. "Los presentes de Moctezuma, Durero y otros testimonios," *Revista de Historia Americana y Argentina* (Mendoza), nos. 1 and 2 (1957): 55-84.

Tozzer, Alfred M., ed. *Landa's Relación de las cosas de Yucatan. A Translation* Papers of the Peabody Museum of American Archaeology and Ethnology XVIII, Cambridge: 1941.

Turner, E. Daymond. "Biblioteca Ovetense: A Speculative Reconstruction of the Library of the First Chronicler of the Indies," *Papers of the Bibliographical Society of America* LVII (1963): 157-183.

————. *Gonzalo Fernández de Oviedo y Valdés: An Annotated Bibliography.* Chapel Hill: University of North Carolina Press, 1966.

————. "Los libros del alcaide: La biblioteca de Gonzalo Fernández de Oviedo y Valdés," *Revista de Indias,* nos. 125 and 126 (1971): 139-198.

Valadés, Diego, O.F.M. *Rhetorica Christiana.* Perouse: 1579.

Vargas Ugarte, Rubén, S. J. *Manuscritos peruanos en las bibliotecas del extranjero.* Vol. I: *Biblioteca peruana.* Lima: Empresa periodística, 1935.

Vázquez Vera, Josefina Zoraida. *El indio americano y su circunstancia en la obra de Oviedo.* Mexico: Universidad Nacional Autónoma de México, 1956.

————. "El indio americano y su circunstancia en la obra de Fernández de Oviedo," *Revista de Indias* (Madrid), año XVII, nos. 69 and 70 (1957): 469-510.

————. *La imagen del indio en el español del siglo XVI.* Xalapa: Universidad Veracruzana, 1962.

Velasco, B., O. Carm. "El alma cristiana del conquistador de América,"

Missionalia Hispánica, año XXI, no. 63 (1964): 257-288; año XXII, no. 66 (1965): 257-287; año XXIV, no. 7 (1967): 129-166.

Vera Cruz, Alonso de la. *The Writings of Alonso de la Vera Cruz,* edited by Ernest J. Burrus, S. J. Vols. III-V. Sources and Studies for the History of the Americas. Rome and St. Louis: Jesuit Historical Institute and St. Louis University, 1968.

Vial Correa, Gonzalo. "Teoría y práctica de la igualdad en Indias," *Revista Historia* (Universidad Católica de Chile), no. 3 (1964): 87-163.

Vicens Vives, Jaime. *Approaches to the History of Spain,* translated by Joan Connelly Ullman. Berkeley: University of California Press, 1967.

Villoro, Luis. *Los grandes momentos del indigenismo en México.* Mexico: El Colegio de México, 1950.

Viñas y Mey, Carmelo. *España y los orígenes de la política social (Las leyes de Indias).* Madrid: 1922[?].

———. "El espíritu castellano de aventura y empresa y la España de los Reyes Católicos," *Archivo de Derecho público* (Granada) V (1952): 13-83.

Wagner, Henry R., with Helen Rand Parish. *The Life and Writings of Bartolomé de Las Casas.* Albuquerque: University of New Mexico Press, 1967.

Wölfel, Dominik J. "La curia romana y la corona de España en la defensa de los aborígenes canarios," *Anthropos* XXV (1930): 1011-1083.

Ybot León, Antonio. *La iglesia y los eclesiásticos españoles en la empresa de Indias.* 2 vols. Barcelona: Salvat, 1954-1963.

Zavala, Silvio. *La encomienda indiana.* Madrid: Centro de Estudios Históricos, 1935.

———. *Ideario de Vasco de Quiroga.* Mexico: El Colegio de México, 1941.

———. *Servidumbre natural y libertad cristiana, según los tratadistas españoles de los siglos XVI y XVII.* Publicaciones de Instituto de Investigaciones No. 87. Buenos Aires: Instituto de Investigaciones Históricas, 1944.

———. *Recuerdo de Vasco de Quiroga.* Mexico: Porrúa, 1965.

———. *Recuerdo de Bartolomé de Las Casas.* Guadalajara: Librería Font, 1966.

———. "Las Casas ante la encomienda," *Revista de la Universidad de México* XX, no. 11 (11 June 1966): 8-10.

———. "En busca del tratado de Vasco de Quiroga, *De Debellandis Indis,*" *Historia Mexicana* XVII (1968): 485-515.

———. "En busca del tratado *De Debellandis Indis* de Vasco de Quiroga," *Historia Mexicana* XVIII (1969a): 623-626.

———. "La evangelización y la conquista de las Indias, según Fray Juan de Silva, O.F.M.," *Cahiers de Monde Hispanique et Luso-Brésilien (Caravelle)* (1969b): 83-96.

———. "Los títulos de posesión a las Indias Occidentales," *Memoria de El Colegio Nacional* (Mexico) VI (1970): 135-220.

———. *Las instituciones jurídicas en la conquista de América.* 2d ed. Mexico: Porrúa, 1971.

Zimdars, Benjamin F. "A Study in Seventeenth-Century Peruvian Historiography: The Monastic Chronicles of Antonio de la Calancha, Diego de

Córdoba Salinas, and the *Compendio y Descripción* of Antonio Vázquez de Espinosa." Ph.D. dissertation, University of Texas, 1965.

Zorita, Alonso de. *Life and Labor in Ancient Mexico: The Brief and Summary Relations of the Lords of New Spain,* edited by Benjamin Keen. New Brunswick: Rutgers University Press, 1963.

Zubillaga, Félix, S. J. "Intento de clero indígena en Nueva España en el siglo XVI y los jesuitas," *Anuario de Estudios Americanos* (Seville) XXVI (1969): 426-469.

Index